HUMAN RIGHTS AND DRUG CONTROL

It has become almost accepted knowledge within international policy circles that efforts against drug trafficking and drug abuse violate human rights, and that the entire international drug control regime needs to be changed (or even discarded altogether) to adopt a more 'rights respecting' approach. Though this view has been promoted by many prominent figures and organisations, the author of this book uses his expertise in both human rights and drug control to show that the arguments advanced in this area do not stand close scrutiny. The arguments are in fact based on selective and questionable interpretations of international human rights standards, and on a general notion—more and more clearly stated—that there is a human right to take drugs, and that any effort to combat drug abuse by definition violates this right. There is no such right in international law, and the author objects to the misuse of human rights language as a marketing tool to bring about a 'back door' legalisation of drugs. Human rights issues must be addressed, but that in no way means that the international drug control regime must be discarded, or that efforts against drugs must be stopped.

Volume 59 in the series Studies in International Law

Studies in International Law

Recent titles in this series

Democratic Statehood in International Law: The Emergence of New States in Post-Cold War Practice
Jure Vidmar

International Law and the Construction of the Liberal Peace
Russell Buchan

The OIC, the UN, and Counter-Terrorism Law-Making: Conflicting or Cooperative Legal Orders?
Katja Samuel

Statelessness: The Enigma of the International Community
William E Conklin

The Reception of Asylum Seekers under International Law: Between Sovereignty and Equality
Lieneke Slingenberg

International Law and Child Soldiers
Gus Waschefort

The Contractual Nature of the Optional Clause
Gunnar Törber

Non-State Actors in International Law
Edited by Math Noortmann, August Reinisch and Cedric Ryngaert

The Rule of Law at the National and International Levels: Contestations and Deference
Edited by Machiko Kanetake and André Nollkaemper

Human Rights Obligations of Non-State Armed Groups
Daragh Murray

Security and International Law
Edited by Mary E Footer, Julia Schmidt and Nigel D White

For the complete list of titles in this series, see 'Studies in International Law' link at www.hartpub.co.uk/books/series.asp

Human Rights and Drug Control

The False Dichotomy

Saul Takahashi

•HART•

OXFORD • LONDON • NEW YORK • NEW DELHI • SYDNEY

HART PUBLISHING
Bloomsbury Publishing Plc
Kemp House, Chawley Park, Cumnor Hill, Oxford, OX2 9PH, UK

HART PUBLISHING, the Hart/Stag logo, BLOOMSBURY and the Diana logo are trademarks of Bloomsbury Publishing Plc
First published in Great Britain 2016

First published in hardback, 2016
Paperback edition, 2019

A catalogue record for this book is available from the British Library.

Library of Congress Cataloging-in-Publication Data

Names: Takahashi, Saul, author.

Title: Human rights and drug control : the false dichotomy / Saul Takahashi.

Description: Oxford ; Portland, Oregon : Hart Publishing, an imprint of Bloomsbury Publishing Plc, 2016. | Series: Studies in international law ; v. 59 | Includes bibliographical references and index.

Identifiers: LCCN 2016015256 (print) | LCCN 2016015645 (ebook) | ISBN 9781849467063 (hardback : alk. paper) | ISBN 9781509901135 (Epub)

Subjects: LCSH: Drugs of abuse—Law and legislation. | Drug abusers—Civil rights. | Drug legalization.

Classification: LCC K5282 .T357 2016 (print) | LCC K5282 (ebook) | DDC 345/.0277—dc23

LC record available at https://lccn.loc.gov/2016015256

ISBN: HB: 978-1-84946-706-3
PB: 978-1-50992-643-5
ePDF: 978-1-50990-112-8
ePub: 978-1-50990-113-5

Series: Studies in International Law volume 59

Typeset by Compuscript Ltd, Shannon

To find out more about our authors and books visit www.hartpublishing.co.uk. Here you will find extracts, author information, details of forthcoming events and the option to sign up for our newsletters.

Table of Contents

1

Introduction

UNTIL 20 YEARS or so ago, human rights was not part of the debate on drug control. Drug control was viewed as a completely separate issue from human rights; the two were rarely, if ever, discussed as connected or in any way related. Outside of circles of the drug legalisation movement in some countries, the notion that drug control violated human rights would have been viewed as extremely odd, if not downright laughable.

That is not to say that there was no debate regarding drug control issues: there was, and it has always tended to be polarised and acrimonious. The emotive nature of the debate is hardly unique to drug control, but it is arguably somewhat surprising, given that, in theory at least, the two sides would appear to share many common assumptions. Both sides agree that what are now classified as illicit drugs have the potential of causing serious health risks—an obvious fact, but something which bears repeating. This common assumption leads to the clear conclusion that persons should be discouraged from consuming these substances, a conclusion which, again, most (though not all) people on both sides would agree. Finally, both sides also generally agree that it is a desirable goal to exclude criminal elements, which have so far profited from huge wealth and power through the illicit drug trade.

There is (or at least should be), therefore, much agreement at the point of departure. It is how to tackle those questions where the disagreements start, and the acrimony begins. There is of course a wide spectrum of views on this topic, but at the core the debate is between those who believe that criminal justice has a large role to play in deterring people from abusing illicit drugs on the one hand, and, on the other hand, those who believe that the approach based on criminal justice has been a failure, and that removing drugs from the criminal justice system is the best way forward. The former camp is rife with scare stories of 'gateway' drugs and immediate and irrevocable addiction that have no basis in reality, and which often result in discrediting the movement itself. The opposing side, for its part, presents an overly rosy picture of the potential benefits of legalisation, and often bandies around the term 'evidence based' to describe the policies it proposes. In fact, the 'evidence' it cites is often scant, arbitrarily selected, and often not applicable to broader contexts.

The reality, it is submitted, is that the position of many people on this issue is based largely on ideology. That is not in and of itself something to be criticised—the word 'ideology' has a bad reputation, but using one's ethical and political principles as a compass to guide one's actions and beliefs is not necessarily undesirable. It is when ideology blinds people to the reality on the ground that it can become part of the problem, and this has often been the case with drug control.

It was against the backdrop of this highly polarised landscape that the language of human rights appeared, around the early 2000s, and this has changed the situation dramatically. The idea that efforts to combat illicit drugs violate human rights has gained increased momentum in mainstream policy fora, both at the international level and in several countries. This idea is propagated by some influential human rights non-governmental organisations (NGOs) and prominent academics in the field of human rights, and has appeared in the positions adopted by international agencies, some of which have made comments suggesting they also believe that drug control as such violates human rights. Important figures such as former high-ranking officials of the United Nations (UN) and even former heads of state have also joined in. At first glance, it would appear that these ideas are passing into the mainstream of international policy, and that a momentous sea change in the international approach towards illicit drugs is imminent.

The international drug control regime, consisting of the three international drug control conventions and international institutions created to promote these conventions, remains alive and well, and, though many of the actors cited in this study may hope otherwise, the prospects for immediate dismantling of this regime seem slim. Nevertheless, the injection of human rights into the debate has arguably brought about a convergence around the view that human rights obligations dictate a radical change in, if not even a complete termination of, drug control. In this way, the advent of human rights in this policy debate has brought about a significant change in perspective, and the way that drug control issues are being viewed. As an (American) Professor at Oxford once said to this author, human rights is like motherhood—it is difficult to argue outright against it. Human rights has proved an extremely effective tool, therefore, for those people who argue against drug control, and for the legalisation of drugs.

The starting point for the human rights arguments is generally the same: that the 'war on drugs' has been not only a miserable failure, but has resulted in a litany of human rights abuses throughout the globe. The human rights of persons abusing drugs are subject to widespread violations through overzealous enforcement, arbitrary imprisonment, use of the death penalty, and other abuses. Indeed, persons unrelated to drug abuse have also been victims—the militarisation of drug law enforcement in many countries has resulted in the excessive use of force by officials across the board, as well as violations of human rights through arbitrary monitoring and other excesses. The point is clear: the 'war on drugs' is synonymous with human rights violations.

The international drug control regime is said to be at the heart of these abuses. The three international drug control conventions are 'punitive' and 'oppressive', so the argument goes, and demand that governments adopt an uncompromising and unforgiving stance towards drugs and the 'immoral' persons who dare to use them. The international institutions responsible for monitoring application by states of these conventions are equally tyrannical, and condemn states that do not tow the line. In essence, the regime promotes, requires, and self-propagates the 'war on drugs', and the violations that stem from it. The human rights abuses noted above, therefore, are not unintended or accidental consequences, but a necessary result of the current international drug control regime.

Therefore, so the argument goes, there is no way the current international drug control regime can be reconciled with human rights. The only way that states can live up to their human rights obligations is to revise the drug control regime fundamentally, or discard it altogether. The expression 'human rights approach to drug control', often used by persons making these arguments, is in fact misleading—since to the persons using the term, human rights in fact requires doing away with drug control altogether.

One body that has had a large impact has been the Global Commission on Drug Policy (GCDP), a group of prominent individuals including Kofi Annan (former UN Secretary General), Louise Arbour (former UN High Commissioner for Human Rights), George Schultz (former US Secretary of State), four former heads of state of Latin American countries, and others. Human rights features prominently in the arguments of the GCDP that the international drug control regime must be overhauled. They argue:

> Drug policies must be based on human rights and public health principles. We should end the stigmatization and marginalization of people who use certain drugs and those involved in the lower levels of cultivation, production and distribution … Of particular relevance to drug policy are the rights to life, to health, to due process and a fair trial, to be free from torture or cruel, inhuman or degrading treatment, from slavery, and from discrimination.[1]

In another, paper, the GCDP asserts that:

> A new and improved global drug control regime is needed that better protects the health and safety of individuals and communities around the world. Harsh

[1] GCDP, 'War on Drugs' (Rio de Janeiro, 2011) 5.

> measures grounded in repressive ideologies must be replaced by more humane and effective policies shaped by scientific evidence, public health principles and human rights standards … [G]lobal drug policy continues to treat all drug use as if it constitutes a grave threat to society. Drug policy remains narrowly framed in terms of 'combating' the 'evil' of drug addiction. It is from this initial, flawed, generalization of all drug use as an 'evil' to be tackled with repressive criminal justice-based measures, that so many irrational and ineffective policy responses have flowed, and so many dysfunctional institutions emerged. … Punitive approaches to drug policy are severely undermining human rights in every region of the world. They lead to the erosion of civil liberties and fair trial standards, the stigmatization of individuals and groups—particularly women, young people, and ethnic minorities—and the imposition of abusive and inhumane punishments.[2]

Though they stop short of arguing for an immediate termination of the prohibition of illicit drugs, GCDP advocates for eventual legalisation, stating that governments should:

> Allow and encourage diverse experiments in legally regulating markets in currently illicit drugs, beginning with but not limited to cannabis, coca leaf and certain novel psychoactive substances. Much can be learned from successes and failures in regulating alcohol, tobacco, pharmaceutical drugs and other products and activities that pose health and other risks to individuals and societies … Ultimately the most effective way to reduce the extensive harms of the global drug prohibition regime and advance the goals of public health and safety is to get drugs under control through responsible legal regulation.[3]

Numerous NGOs also now use human rights language to frame arguments against drug control. There have of course always been NGOs advocating for the welfare of persons abusing drugs, but what has changed is the use by these organisations of the human rights framework in their advocacy, and the expansion of this advocacy to the international arena such as the UN, in particular the human rights bodies of that organisation. Prominent international human rights NGOs are included in this movement, in particular Human Rights Watch (HRW), which has conducted sustained research on issues related to human rights and the treatment of persons abusing drugs. Second only to Amnesty International in its international reach and influence, the work of HRW has been pivotal in promoting the relation between human rights and drug control.

Various UN human rights bodies have also expressed sentiments similar to that of the above NGOs, in particular, as shall be examined, UN Special Rapporteurs on the Right to Health and on Torture, and to a lesser extent, the High Commissioner for Human Rights have all, in some

[2] GCDP, 'Taking Control: Pathways to Drug Policies that Work' (Rio de Janeiro, 2014) 6, 11, 12.

[3] GCDP, 'Taking Control' (n 2) 6, 11, 12, 31.

form or another, taken positions focusing on the rights of persons who abuse drugs, expressing concern about how efforts for drug control have negatively affected these rights. This is neither a coincidence, nor is it an unusual phenomenon—it is a well established pattern in human rights that NGOs lobby UN bodies to take up their concerns, since it is perceived (rightly or wrongly) that the voice of the UN is more weighty than that of a non-governmental entity. Naturally, such lobbying requires a certain level of expertise, and once again the fact that the aforementioned organisations have been able to retain such expertise—and the funding for it—has been key in pushing this forward.

Attention given to this issue within academic circles has also increased. The International Centre on Human Rights and Drug Policy (ICHRDP), which publishes a number of regular journals and runs seminars and courses, was created in 2009. The centre was first housed by the National University of Ireland Galway but later moved to the University of Essex (this author's alma matter) where it is now located. Both Galway and Essex are traditionally two of the top universities in Europe, indeed in the world, for research into human rights issues, and the housing of this centre by such prestigious institutions lends it respectability. Besides this centre, there is also the International Centre for Science in Drug Policy (ICSDP), located in St Michael's Hospital in Toronto, and an ongoing research project focusing on these issues at the London School of Economics.

However, the academic rigour of these research centres and projects is open to question. A cursory examination of their publications would suggest that they exist less as fora for a free exchange of ideas, but rather to promote the view that drug control cannot be reconciled with human rights obligations. Mainly they serve as platforms for likeminded persons to publish their views as to why the drug control regime violates human rights. Indeed, the mission statement of the ICHRDP states clearly that it exists to '[h]ighlight the obligations of all governments and international organisations to respect, protect and fulfill human rights in the context of drug policy; [and to p]romote a human rights-based approach to drug policy'.[4] ICSDP conducts 'campaigns' on particular policy issues, and the LSE project starts with the foregone conclusion that the international drug control regime is flawed, its stated objective being 'a deep strategic re-evaluation of the international drug control system'.[5]

[4] International Centre on Human Rights and Drug Policy, 'Mission Statement', at www.hr-dp.org/mission-statement.

[5] London School of Economics, 'LSE Ideas International Drug Policy Project', at www.lse.ac.uk/IDEAS/Projects/IDPP/International-Drug-Policy-Project.aspx.

Of course, this would hardly be the first case of purported academic institutions having an ideological slant—indeed, there is at least one journal focusing on drug policy that has been accused of highlighting only the opposing views.[6] The point is that the mere conferring of an academic sounding title does not necessarily indicate objectivity or quality.

The same can be said of the NGOs involved in this network—there is an underlying premise to their work in this area that means their work inevitably results in the same conclusion, namely that international drug control violates human rights. For example, most NGOs argue that persons who abuse drugs are particularly 'vulnerable to abuse' at the hands of law enforcement officials. Though there is some justification for this claim, in most cases, practically all persons who come into contact with law enforcement in the countries they highlight are subject to similar violations. And yet, the NGOs put the spotlight only on persons who abuse drugs, as if they are the only ones who suffer. NGO condemnation of the death penalty for drug-related offenders is another good example. Though much is made of this issue by these NGOs, they are silent on the widespread executions of persons found guilty of other offences. The rights of persons who abuse drugs are, therefore, highlighted as if they were a 'particularly vulnerable group'—a recurring theme throughout the arguments of these NGOs—when in fact that is not the case. NGO arguments that there is a 'human right to harm reduction' are equally spurious, and essentially have been created to promote the agenda of harm reduction and decriminalisation. These issues shall be examined more closely in this study.

The above is, of course, not to say that violations do not take place, nor that they are not worthy of condemnation by NGOs and the international community. The point is that the objectivity of these arguments is questionable. The research presented generally has a foregone conclusion, namely that the international drug control regime should be discarded. This conclusion frames and dictates the research, which in turn is conducted and presented in a manner that suits it.

The above organisations and individuals are many, but they share common goals, and are loosely connected in practice. Many of them are frequent contributors to each other's publications, individuals move between positions in different organisations within the network, and research reports cite heavily from one another. The result is a constant circle of self-reference, with each component producing material that cites material produced by other components, increasing the critical mass of research, reports, and statements.

[6] *Journal of Global Drug Policy and Practice*, which is funded by the United States Department of Justice, has been accused by critics of having a political agenda slanted towards law enforcement approaches in drug control. See eg Roger Collier, 'Medical journal or marketing device?' (2009) 5 *Canadian Medical Association Journal* E83.

There is nothing necessarily untoward about this—it is natural for like-minded individuals and organisations to co-operate. Nevertheless, it is worth noting that while the bulk of the material produced by this movement may at first glance seem impressive, much of it does little more than regurgitate what has been said previously by others in the network (or by the same person in a different capacity). That does not necessarily mean that the argument is wrong, but it does suggest that perspective is called for. When one is faced with over a dozen papers from various sources calling for similar policy revisions, it is easy to overestimate the size of the movement. In fact, in the case of human rights and drug control, those dozen papers may have been written by only a handful of persons, citing work by each other.

Minor differences in tone aside, the above organisations and individuals advance essentially the same arguments. For the sake of convenience, this author will use the expression, 'advocates of drug liberalisation', to describe them in this study.

Another point worthy of note is that of funding. The sudden proliferation of these advocates of drug liberalisation, and the equally sudden appearance of these issues on the agenda of international policy, is startling. Human rights organisations are known for being perennially strapped for cash—there is no global level research on this topic of which this author is aware, but certainly nobody with experience in this field would argue against the proposition that human rights NGOs as a rule are doomed to constantly be in a search for funds to perform their activities. The same can be said of academic institutions—research grants in human rights are few and far between, and competition is fierce. In human rights, as in all fields, money talks—and one cannot help but note that, in the space of a few years, these same cash-strapped organisations suddenly have had copious funds to hire highly qualified staff and to expand their research and advocacy base in this field. The above academic institutions appear to be equally well endowed, with the capacity to organise many international conferences and seminars with prominent speakers. All of this requires money, and quite a bit of it.

Anecdotal evidence suggests that many of these initiatives are funded by a small number of sources, one of them being the Open Society Foundations (OSF). OSF operates the Global Drug Policy Program, which states on its website that 'Current drug policies are failing. Worse, they're causing enormous harm to individuals, communities, and entire nations. Around the world, poorly designed drug laws that seek to punish production ... ion, use, and even dependence have fuelled violence, ... n rights violations, and health crises.'[7] The program

... rug Policy Program', at www.opensocietyfoundations.org/about/ ... g-policy-program.

seeks to remedy the situation, 'through grant making and programmatic efforts … that promote security, social justice, human rights, and public health',[8] and OSF lists an expenditure for 2014 of USD 5,295,000 under the program.[9] Though relatively small within the broad scheme of OSF, this is a hefty sum in most human rights circles, and while there is no breakdown readily available, OSF is listed as a donor for many of the projects and organisations touched upon in this study. The GCDP lists OSF as a 'partner' on its website, and OSF is listed as having provided support for the GCDP's report in 2011.[10] The LSE International Drug Policy Project is funded by OSF and the British Council.[11] OSF funds other prominent organisations in the network of advocates of drug liberalisation: just as an example, the International Harm Reduction Association lists OSF at the top of its donors,[12] and the International Drug Policy Consortium also lists OSF as a donor.[13]

One news report states that OSF has donated approximately USD 200 million to drug reform from 1994 to 2014, including USD 5 million annually to the Drug Policy Alliance,[14] an organisation that states in its mission statement that it:

> envisions a just society in which the use and regulation of drugs are grounded in science, compassion, health and human rights, in which people are no longer punished for what they put into their own bodies … Our mission is to advance those policies and attitudes that best reduce the harms of both drug use and drug prohibition, and to promote the sovereignty of individuals over their minds and bodies.[15]

As is well known, OSF was created by George Soros, a multi billionaire who supports the legalisation of drugs.[16] This is not to suggest that there is a sinister or secretive conspiracy at play—Soros is as free as any individual to donate his money to whatever cause he wishes, and in any case he himself surely is not involved in each and every grant decision. Nor is it to insinuate that human rights NGOs are up for sale—surely the individuals in the organisations working on these issues honestly believe that efforts to control drugs lead to human rights abuses. However, it is worth pointing to the fact that when one overwhelmingly large donor enters the picture, the playing field can be distorted. Richard Branson, the founder of the

[8] Ibid.
[9] OSF, 'Open Society Foundations 2014 Expenditures', New York, 2015.
[10] GCDP (n 1) 20, and GCDP, 'Partners', at www.globalcommissionondrugs.org/partners/.
[11] London School of Economics (n 5).
[12] International Harm Reduction, 'Donors', www.ihra.net/donors.
[13] International Drug Policy Consortium, 'About', idpc.net/about.
[14] 'An Inside Look At The Biggest Drug Reformer In The Country: George Soros', *Forbes*, 2 October 2014.
[15] Drug Policy Alliance, 'Mission Statement', at www.drugpolicy.org/mission-and-vision
[16] *Forbes* (n 14).

Virgin Group, is also listed as a donor by many organisations advocating drug liberalisation.[17]

In any case, the organisations advancing these arguments have been successful in putting forward their message, and in many ways the advent of human rights has been a game changer. The success of the organisations advancing these arguments is of course related in large part to the well-funded nature of their activities, but arguably they would not have made such inroads if it were not for their framing of the issue in human rights terms. Presenting drug control as a human rights issue makes the arguments much easier to accept, for both governments and the general public.

Nevertheless, the idea that efforts to control drugs by definition violate human rights, and that human rights obligations require the dismantling of the drug control regime, requires closer scrutiny. Ultimately, this notion can only be sustained if we accept that there is a human right to abuse drugs; notwithstanding the creative reading of international legal standards by some commentators, it will be argued that such a right does not exist.

This study will first examine the legal standards of both human rights and drug control. There are provisions that are highly relevant in both regimes, some of which are (so it would seem) wilfully ignored by those making the aforementioned arguments.

The study will then explore the arguments advanced by these advocates for drug liberalisation, and refute them one by one. First, the issue of abuses caused in the course of drug control law enforcement, which form the bulk of arguments that drug control violates human rights. Issues of excessive use of force by police officers and the harassment of persons who abuse drugs will be examined, as will the question of the application by some countries of the death penalty for drug-related offences. In fact, as will be shown, none of these arguments are truly about drug control, but are standard issues of human rights in criminal justice matters. It goes without saying that human rights must be protected in the administration of criminal justice, and in any policy implementation. The abuses mentioned obviously must be stopped—however, the issue is hardly unique to drug control.

Connected with these arguments is the notion that persons who abuse drugs are a 'vulnerable group' in human rights terms, whose special situation requires special attention and protection. While the precarious health situation of many drug addicts clearly leaves them in need of some form of support, to argue that they warrant special protection against human rights abuse in the same way as ethnic minorities or refugees strains credibility, and must be rejected.

[17] See eg GCDP (n 1) 20.

The question of harm reduction shall also be examined, as it is a key concept in these debates. Though somewhat ill-defined, many of the policy approaches usually classified as harm reduction certainly have a part to play in any kind of comprehensive approach by governments—a truism recognised by all players in the debate, including the much maligned International Narcotics Control Board (INCB), the monitoring body charged with overseeing application of the international drug control conventions. However, many advocates for drug liberalisation argue that human rights obligations (in particular the right to the highest attainable standard of health) dictate that harm reduction should be the overarching, indeed the only, goal of drug policy, not just an integral part. As shall be examined, there is little justification for this argument.

Finally, this book will explore briefly the concept of the right to abuse drugs. Most (though not all) of the organisations mentioned in this book have been reticent of calling openly for a 'human right to abuse drugs', perhaps because of a recognition that the idea would be politically too controversial. However, the logic of most of their arguments inevitably leads to this conclusion, and the issue will be examined.

As shall be shown throughout this study, the human rights arguments against drug control are generally without justification. They are based on misreadings of the legal standards, or widely expansionary interpretations of these standards, made to fit the foregone conclusion that drug control violates human rights. Indeed, the logic of the advocates of drug liberalisation can only be accepted if we accept their underlying premise, namely that there is a right to abuse drugs. Excessively creative reading of international legal standards by some advocates for drug liberalisation notwithstanding, there is no such right in international law, and the notion that such a right does exist is arguably based on a culturally specific, near-libertarian view of natural rights. It is submitted that in fact, to the advocates of drug liberalisation, human rights is a mere marketing tool, a gimmick to sell the idea of legalisation through the backdoor. It is this that this author finds the most objectionable—if people wish to argue for legalisation, they should do so openly, and not present the issue as if it were a human rights concern.

I. SOME TERMINOLOGY ISSUES—LEGALISATION, DECRIMINALISATION, AND DEPENALISATION

It is worthwhile examining briefly the terminology most often used to describe various drug control regimes.[18] Many of the terms are used in

[18] See eg Jonathan P Caulkins, Angela Hawken, Beau Kilmer and Mark AR Kleiman, *Marijuana Legalization: What Everyone Needs to Know* (New York, Oxford University Press, 2012) Kindle edition 2140.

a jumbled or even interchangeable manner by both 'sides' of the debate, causing confusion—something that, at times, may arguably be intentional. There are no universally accepted definitions, but an outline of what the general understanding is (or should be) on the basis of the normal usage of the terms can be attempted.

The current international drug control regime is often described by advocates of drug liberalisation as 'punitive', 'repressive', or even 'oppressive'. Colourful as these terms may be, taken on their own, they offer little in terms of concrete explanation. Nevertheless, to most well-intended readers and concerned citizens, they convey a negative image, and it is submitted that using these terms has been effective in painting the international drug control regime in a negative light. The same may be said for the term 'war on drugs', which is not internationally defined and which has now served advocates of drug liberalisation as a 'catch-all' phrase describing an oppressive drug control regime gone amok.[19]

The international drug control regime is also often described as 'prohibitive' or 'based on prohibition', once again with negative implications. This description is not entirely accurate, since one of the main aims of international drug control law is to ensure that there is an adequate amount of drugs available for licit, mainly medical purposes. Nevertheless, any use of drugs outside of these narrowly defined purposes is banned, and in this regard there is indeed a prohibitory element to drug control. Under the current regime, it is required that states make such illicit use in all its forms (eg cultivation and production, transport, selling, and consuming) a criminal offence—though, as we shall see, there is considerable leeway under the international drug control conventions for states to interpret this requirement in a manner which suits their national context.

Several 'alternatives' to the current regime have been proposed by advocates of drug liberalisation and other actors, in particular depenalisation and decriminalisation. Though these two terms are often used interchangeably, they are not synonymous. Depenalisation describes a regime where the illicit use of drugs would remain a criminal offence, but not subject to heavy sanctions such as imprisonment. What is usually envisioned under this regime is not that all illicit uses of drugs would be depenalised, but only consumption, ie the abuse of illicit drugs. Therefore, illicit cultivation and selling would remain subject to criminal penalties. It is worthy to note that depenalisation in practice is in fact very common. Many countries already operate a regime of this kind, where persons

[19] The term 'war on drugs' was in fact first used by US President Nixon in describing the measures he would take against illicit drugs. See eg Drug Policy Alliance, 'A brief history of the drug war', at www.drugpolicy.org/new-solutions-drug-policy/brief-history-drug-war. However, there is no definition for this term internationally, or even within the US.

possessing small amounts of illicit drugs (particularly cannabis) for their own consumption are sanctioned under the criminal justice regime, but are only subject to light penalties that do not involve incarceration. There are of course notable exceptions, such as the United States and Russia, where possession of even small amounts of drugs can result in heavy penalties, including imprisonment.

Decriminalisation is similar to depenalisation, but goes one step further in that the consumption of drugs is no longer a criminal offence, but an administrative one—proponents often describe the penalties as akin to that of a minor traffic violation. Actions such as illicit manufacture and selling generally remain criminal offences under this regime. Decriminalisation, either de jure or de facto, is more rare, with most examples limited once again to cannabis (eg the Dutch system of 'coffee shops', whereby cannabis remains illegal but there is a formal, openly-stated commitment on the part of the government not to prosecute offences inside licensed 'coffee shops'). Portugal is an example of a country that has decriminalised the consumption of all illicit substances, though persons are still subject to procedures with specialised commissions that attempt to persuade the individual to undergo treatment. The practical implications for the jurisdiction concerned have generally not been overly negative (or negative at all).

In arguing for decriminalisation, some advocates of drug liberalisation state specifically that the abuse of drugs could be dealt with by states as an administrative offence. Other advocates for drug liberalisation remain silent on this, and it is unclear whether they envision that removing drugs from the criminal justice would mean that there would be no penalty for drug abuse (which would in essence make this regime essentially the same as legalisation, below).

Another issue which is often unclear is the treatment under the above two systems of drug traffickers, as opposed to persons who abuse drugs. It is generally implied that both depenalisation and decriminalisation are foreseen only for persons who abuse illicit drugs, whereas drug traffickers would remain subject to criminal penalties. Nevertheless, this is by no means a given, and it is submitted that the general lack of clarity on this point on the part of advocates of drug liberalisation contributes to the perception amongst many in the general public that both depenalisation and decriminalisation are just steps towards eventual legalisation (and, therefore, should be resisted).

Legalisation implies a broader, more radical reform. It is generally understood to mean that what are now illicit substances would cease to be illicit, and their consumption, production, and sale would be legitimate, legal activities. It is usually suggested that the drug market would be regulated in a similar fashion to that of alcohol, with 'common sense' restrictions, eg to protect minors. Legalisation remains condemned by international bodies such as the INCB and the UN.

Some advocates of drug liberalisation argue for a regime whereby the state would play a heavy role in controlling the production and distribution of drugs. Others are less clear on this, and appear to be satisfied with the state getting out of drug control altogether, perhaps with only a minor role in ensuring the quality of drugs on the market.

Only a very small number of jurisidictions have legalised illicit drugs, and only for cannabis. Several states in the United States have recently legalised the production and consumption of that drug, and Uruguay is the first country to adopt national legislation to that effect. At the time of writing, a recent judgment of the Supreme Court in Mexico seems to point towards the legalisation of cannabis in that country, though how exactly this judgment will be implemented remains to be seen.

It is crucial to keep in mind the distinction between decriminalisation and legalisation, since as shown above, the two are very different. Nevertheless, the two in particular are often mixed by both sides of the debate. Advocates of drug liberalisation often use the 'decriminalisation' terminology when they are in fact describing legalisation. This would appear, at least in some cases, to be intentional, since 'decriminalisation' sounds far less threatening and radical. Opponents of drug liberalisation, on the other hand, tend to use 'legalisation' in describing any kind of liberalisation of drug policies, perhaps in an effort to scare the audience into believing that there would be enormous and disastrous consequences for any policy change in that direction.

Recently, some advocates of drug liberalisation have attempted to introduce 'regulation' as a term to replace 'legalisation'. For example, in their report in September 2014, the GCDP put as one of its pillar recommendations to '[r]egulate drug markets to put governments in control.'[20] Stating that '"[l]egalization" is merely a process—of making something illegal, legal. What most reform advocates understand by the term is more usefully described as "regulation", "legal regulation" or "legally regulated markets". These terms refer to the end point of the legalization process—the system of rules that govern the production, supply and use of drugs',[21] they argue that:

> Drug regulation is not as radical as many believe. Such a move does not require a fundamental rethink of established policy principles. The regulation and management of risky products and behaviors is a key function of all government authorities around the world, and is the norm in almost all other areas of policy and law. Governments regulate everything from alcohol and cigarette consumption to medicines, seatbelts, the use of fireworks, powertools and high-risk sports. If the potential risks of drugs are to be contained and minimized,

[20] GCDP (n 2) 26.
[21] GCDP (n 2) 29.

> governments must apply the same regulatory logic to the development of effective drug policies.[22]

The substance of this message is generally the same as those put forward by other advocates of legalisation, and the picture painted is an overly optimistic one, of governments retaking control of what are now illicit drug markets, and injecting order into what is now a chaotic situation:

> Drug markets that are subject to strict legal regulation are not 'free markets'. Nor does exploring alternatives to prohibition imply a drug market 'free for all', where access to drugs is unrestricted and availability is dramatically increased. Regulation is about taking control, so that governments, not criminals, make decisions on the availability and non-availability of different substances, in different environments. Inevitably, while some drugs will be accessible with appropriate controls and some only available via medical prescription, other more harmful drugs will necessarily remain prohibited. Unlike in criminal drug markets, legal regulation enables governments to control and regulate most aspects of the market.[23]

The above notwithstanding, the arguments of the GCDP—and of advocates of drug liberalisation in general—are replete with sweeping and unclear terminology, such as the 'war on drugs' and a 'punitive' or 'repressive' approach. The overall approach appears to be to use emotive and ill-defined terms to describe the international drug control regime, while using measured and rational words to advance the legalisation agenda. It is difficult to see the new 'regulation' narrative as anything other than yet another marketing tool, to make the prospect of wholesale drug legalisation less threatening to policy makers.

II. USE/ABUSE/CONSUMPTION

Equally unclear, and perhaps even more contentious, is the terminology surrounding the use / abuse / consumption of drugs.

Actors representing the international drug control regime, such as INCB or the UN Office on Drugs and Crime (UNODC), tend to differentiate between 'use' and 'abuse', though the differentiation appears to be much more loose in the case of UNODC. The differentiation is logical: since nearly all internationally controlled substances have legitimate uses, persons who avail themselves of licit methods would be 'using' drugs, whereas persons outside of these channels would be 'abusing' them. Thus, a person who had been prescribed amphetamine by a doctor, and using the drug strictly in the prescribed manner, would be using the

[22] GCDP (n 2) 26.
[23] GCDP (n 2) 29.

drug. A person who purchased amphetamine on the street for recreational purposes, on the other hand, is abusing the substance. On the other hand, the 10th International Classification of Diseases adopted by the World Health Assembly does not use the term 'abuse'. According to the World Health Organisation (WHO), 'the term "abuse" is sometimes used disapprovingly to refer to any use at all, particularly of illicit drugs. Because of its ambiguity, the term is not used … harmful use and hazardous use are the equivalent terms in WHO usage, although they usually relate only to effects on health and not to social consequences.'[24]

Advocates of drug liberalisation shun the term 'abuse', presumably because they believe the word has negative and judgmental connotations. To them, individuals only 'use' drugs, including for recreational purposes. Using the terminology in this manner has the effect of normalising recreational drug use, which arguably is the desired effect.

Advocates of drug liberalisation also use the term 'consume', eg 'drug consumer', which has a similar effect as the word 'use' in this context—it has a non-judgmental ring to it, and normalises drug use. Many countries, in particular in Western Europe, have also adopted this terminology, at least in describing their harm reduction approaches. For example, the European Monitoring Centre for Drugs and Drug Addiction (EMCDDA) refers to 'drug consumption rooms' to refer to state run facilities where persons can abuse illicit drugs openly, whereas INCB calls such facilities 'injection rooms' (lest the 'consumption' term result in a normalisation of illicit drug abuse).

Confusingly, the term 'consumption' is also used within the international drug control regime, usually to refer to the traditional (and no longer applicable) distinction between 'drug producing countries' (the developing countries that were long the source of many illicit drugs) and 'drug consumer nations' (the developed countries that were the destination of drug trafficking).

Throughout this study, this author will abide by the use/abuse distinction, and use the term 'persons who abuse drugs'. This is not intended to be a moral pronouncement on those persons, or to insinuate that they are in any way ethically deficient. Rather, it is a simple statement of fact—despite what advocates of drug liberalisation might wish the case to be, international law currently distinguishes between licit and illicit use, and this terminology reflects that distinction.

[24] WHO, 'Lexicon of alcohol and drug terms published by the World Health Organisation', www.who.int/substance_abuse/terminology/who_lexicon/en/.

2

Legal Standards and Regimes

ANY EXPLORATION OF the issue of human rights and drug control, in particular whether drug control efforts violate human rights, must necessarily start with an examination of the applicable legal regimes, ie the international legal standards of drug control on the one hand, and of human rights on the other. The international law of drug control outlines what the goals and objectives of international drug control are, and, in very broad terms, what actions states are expected to take in this regard. The international law of human rights, on the other hand, stipulates the 'red lines' which states must not cross, in addition to outlining some positive goals for which states must strive (though these efforts can be progressive in some cases, ie states need not necessarily achieve the goals immediately). It is these two legal frameworks which advocates of drug liberalisation allege conflict, definitely in practice but also, according to some, in principle.

As with all international law, there are different levels of obligation in accordance with the type of legal standard. Often referred to as 'hard law', treaties or conventions are binding legal standards, and create legal obligations for states that become party to them. The ever present difficulty for advocates is that states have to first take the positive action of becoming party to a particular convention for it to have legal effect within the jurisdiction of that country—so, for example, a human rights advocate will (at least legally speaking) not be able to denounce a country for violating a particular human rights convention if that country has not first become state party.[1] This presents complications for the human rights movement, but it is not really an issue in the case of the issues explored in this book: the international drug control conventions have near universal ratification, meaning that nearly all countries in the world are state party, and most of the countries examined here are state party to the relevant international human rights conventions as well.

[1] The issue of customary international law is of limited relevance for the discussion in this study, and will, therefore, not be examined.

Lower in the hierarchy is 'soft law', which includes declarations or resolutions adopted by international bodies such as the UN General Assembly or the UN Commission on Narcotic Drugs. These are not binding in and of themselves, but, given that the bodies that adopt them are made up of state representatives, they do represent a certain measure of international consensus and, therefore, should be (though not always are) treated by states with a certain measure of deference. Most of the legal standards relevant to the discussion in this book are of the treaty, 'hard law' variety, though some declarations and resolutions will come into play.

Many international conventions, including those in both fields explored in this study, have committees that monitor the application of the treaty provisions and provide authoritative interpretations of how the provisions should be applied by states. There are different models for these kinds of bodies, with varying degrees of political independence from state parties,[2] but interestingly enough, as shall be shown, both human rights and drug control operate on the basis of an almost identical model—a quasi-judicial body—made of experts in the field elected through a political process but who sit on the committee in an independent capacity (ie not as representatives of their respective, or of any, state). There is little indication as to why these very differing bodies of law ended up with an identical model of treaty monitoring, which appears to simply have been the favoured model of that era. Nevertheless, the structural similarities between the International Narcotics Control Board (INCB)—the drug control monitoring committee—and the human rights 'treaty bodies'—the usual term used to indicate the numerous monitoring committees in human rights—may have made it somewhat easier for advocates of drug liberalisation to launch criticisms of the INCB's functioning and working methods, which they see as lacking in comparison with human rights treaty bodies. This topic shall be explored in this chapter.

In relation to both drug control and human rights, the views adopted by these monitoring committees are considered to be 'soft law', ie they are not binding on states, even state parties to that particular convention. Being the opinion of bodies of experts officially mandated to pronounce themselves on the provisions of the convention in question, the views are recognised as authoritative, and should not be simply dismissed out of hand by state parties. Nevertheless, they remain non binding, and the fact remains that, faced with the lack of a true enforcement mechanism (in this area, and in most of international law in general), state parties, for whatever reason, quite often do not implement the recommendations of

[2] For example, the UN Convention against Transnational Organised Crime of 2000 establishes, in Article 32, a 'Conference of the Parties to the Convention to promote and review implementation of this Convention'.

these committees. The views issued by these committees, however, are important tools for national and international advocates, who use them to pressure governments to comply with their obligations.[3]

Advocates of drug liberalisation argue that the two bodies of law—drug control on the one hand and human rights on the other—have evolved in isolation from one another. The suggestion is that this has resulted in the international drug control regime evolving without any regard for human rights, and that this major problem needs speedy rectification. Typical is the statement by Barrett and Nowak that the two have evolved in a 'parallel universe'.[4] They state that: '[t]he international drug control conventions ... were developed and have been interpreted in a vacuum from human rights law[5] ... Despite their impacts, the drug conventions are all but silent on the question of human rights.'[6] They go on to assert that:

> All too often, the drug control conventions are considered in an artificial legal vacuum. From these conventions have developed the twin pillars of international drug policy—supply and demand reduction, with little or no regard for the requirements of human rights law. Within this limited and restrictive policy structure, it is extremely difficult to incorporate harm reduction/HIV prevention, access to medicines, development, environmental protection, conflict resolution, cultural heritage and indigenous people's rights, and other core concerns relating to drugs.[7]

Whether the two bodies of law could benefit from more synchronisation is an open question. As shall be shown, some standards were in fact developed on the basis of consultation. However, the implication, that somehow the law of drug control is the odd man out that was never properly co-ordinated with human rights whereas all other bodies of international law were, is misleading. Some international conventions, such as those pertaining to international criminal justice developed in the 2000s, do include specific provisions pertaining to human rights.[8] Nevertheless, the reality is that the vast majority of bodies of international law are

[3] See eg Philip Alston and James Crawford (eds), *The Future of UN Human Rights Treaty Monitoring* (Cambridge, Cambridge University Press, 2000) for a general discussion.

[4] Damon Barrett and Manfred Nowak, 'The United Nations and Drug Policy: Towards a Human Rights-Based Approach', in Aristotle Constantinides and Nikos Zaikos (eds), *The Diversity of International Law: Essays in Honour of Professor Kalliopi K. Koufa* (Leiden, Brill/Martinus Nijhoff, 2009) 455.

[5] Barrett and Nowak, 'The United Nations and Drug Policy' (n 5) 449.

[6] Barrett and Nowak (n 5) 456.

[7] Barrett and Nowak (n 5) 457.

[8] See eg the Protocol to Prevent, Suppress and Punish Trafficking in Persons, Especially Women and Children, supplementing the United Nations Convention against Transnational Organised Crime, which states in Article 14: 'Nothing in this Protocol shall affect the rights, obligations and responsibilities of States and individuals under international law, including international humanitarian law and international human rights law'.

developed generically, in near total if not total isolation from one another. Whether this is desirable is debatable—probably it is not—but it is a common result of the silo-like functions of national and international bureaucracies, and of the narrow-minded viewpoints of most specialist groups. To suggest that it is somehow a negative point only of drug control law is disingenuous.

Some advocates of drug liberalisation have developed a somewhat strained argument, noting that human rights is one of the fundamental principles of the UN Charter, and that this means that, when the bodies of law conflict, human rights must 'trump' drug control. For example, the International Drug Policy Consortium (IDPC) argues that:

> Drug control bodies and national governments are also bound by the overarching obligations created under articles 55 and 56 of the 1945 UN Charter, which promote universal respect for, and observance of, human rights and fundamental freedoms … According to article 103 of the UN Charter, the obligations contained in the Charter prevail upon every international agreement, including the three drug conventions.[9]

Naturally, this argument is based on the assumption that the two bodies of law do conflict, an assumption which, as shall be shown, has little basis in fact. In any case, the need for cognisance of human rights in examining drug control, and any other issue, would seem to be obvious, so there seems to be little need to cite the UN Charter in this area.

I. THE INTERNATIONAL DRUG CONTROL REGIME

The effort against illicit drug trafficking and abuse is one of the oldest forms of international co-operation, and predates not only the UN but also the League of Nations. This is not to argue that it is somehow more important than human rights, but merely to state the fact: since the beginning of the 20th century, states have recognised the need to eradicate the illicit drug trade and to pool efforts in this regard.

The beginning of the international drug control regime is usually held to be the 1909 Shanghai Conference, where nine European colonial powers (Great Britain, the US, France, Netherlands, Portugal, Germany, Austria-Hungary, Italy, and Russia), Japan, China, Persia, and Siam gathered to discuss the problem of increasing opium abuse, in particular in China. In its official history of the conference, UNODC notes that:

> As news of the devastating impact large scale opium addiction was having on China, religious and ethically-minded groups within the UK and other western

[9] IDPC, 'Drug Policy Guide second edition' (London, 2012) 5 and endnote 2.

> countries (notably the USA) began calling for withdrawal from direct involvement in the trade. Christian churches protested on moral grounds … Groups involved in temperance movements (who opposed substance abuse in general), anti-slavery and human rights activists already organised and experienced in protest, lent their voice to the pressure on governments and commerce to withdraw from what they saw as a parasitic, immoral and greedy trade.[10]

Comprehensive data on cultivation, production, and consumption of opium was presented at the conference, together with data regarding government revenue from the opium trade, which, in the case of many governments, was significant—for example, opium revenue amounted to over 17 percent of total French revenue in Indochina, and almost 16 percent of revenue in Siam.[11] Nevertheless, the conference moved to restrict the opium trade, finding that 'the use of Opium in any form otherwise than for medical purposes is held by almost every participating country to be a matter for prohibition or for careful regulation' and that:

> … the unrestricted manufacture, sale and distribution of Morphine already constitute a grave danger, and that the Morphine habit shows signs of spreading: the International Opium Commission, therefore, desires to urge strongly on all Governments that it is highly important that drastic measures should be taken by each Government in its own territories and possessions to control the manufacture, sale and distribution of this drug, and also of such other derivatives of Opium as may appear on scientific enquiry to be liable to similar abuse.[12]

Some advocates of drug liberalisation have criticised the Shanghai Conference, even portraying it as a farcical event dominated by one ambitious American official. Oft cited is the role of Anslinger, the Commissioner of the US Federal Bureau of Narcotics, who played a key part in moving the process forward. Davenport-Hines describes Anslinger as:

> … egotistical, authoritarian, energetic, brutal and unscrupulous. Wily rather than intelligent, he was suspicious of conspicuous intelligence in others. He was the first American to be dubbed a drug 'czar': the word is inapt, for it promises an absolutist's solution to a problem that is in fact chronic … Anslinger's despotic influence was not only enduring but had global ramifications. Since 1909 American drug prohibition has impinged on underdeveloped countries as well as on the industrialised world.[13]

McAllister also has a similar, negative view of Anslinger, and states that he had a prominent role in the formulation of the international drug control regime.

[10] UNODC, *A Century of International Drug Control* (Vienna, 2010) 31.

[11] UNODC, *A Century of International Drug Control* (n 10) 43.

[12] International Opium Commission, 'Report of the International Opium Commission' (1909) paras 3, 5.

[13] Richard Davenport-Hines, *The Pursuit of Oblivion: a Social History of Drugs* (Phoenix, WW Norton, 2004) Kindle version 6651/13059.

> [Anslinger] exerted a profound influence on the shape and operation of the global regime. Yet it is often underappreciated that his principal focus was frequently on how to protect his domestic position. Beset by near-constant threats of the reorganisation or elimination of his Bureau, Anslinger frequently used international proceedings as a way to shore up support at home.[14]

Courtwright points to the role of the pharmaceutical industry in the setting up of controls on what he terms as 'some drugs but not others', ie controls on opiates and cocaine on the one hand, and a lack of regulation of alcohol on the other. He notes:

> In contrast to alcohol, Western governments had less of a financial stake in the narcotic traffic … While viticulture, brewing, and distilling [of alcohol] were concentrated in Western Europe and North America, most opium and coca crops came from poorer and less influential regions. Manufacturing was another story. Western drug companies did a brisk business in cocaine and morphine, and the powerful German pharmaceutical industry was reluctant to go along with the international controls … Defeat in World War I, however, forced Germany (and its opium-growing ally, Turkey) to accept export controls, supervised by the new League of Nations.[15]

Less cynical perhaps, McAllister also points to other factors at play, in stating that:

> … what is often misunderstood …was that its early framers were interested in balance. They did not want to limit supplies of necessary medicinals to an extent that would drive up the price, especially since the rules were solidified just as the world slipped into the Great Depression, and pharmaceutical sales represented one of the few potential bright spots in the global economy … [A] conundrum is built in the [current international] system; the goal is to manufacture enough useful substances to supply medical need at a reasonable price, while preventing the excess capacity necessary to hold the price down from being diverted into illicit traffic.[16]

These accounts have value as an examination of the history of the international drug regime, but in truth, they point to little more than the obvious, namely that international law is created by political actors (mainly states, but also individuals and institutions within states) that have their own independent political objectives, often which are not directly related to the ostensible goal of the legal negotiations themselves. A wide array of political factors come into play in any international negotiations.

[14] William B McAllister, 'Reflections on a Century of International Drug Control', in LSE Ideas (ed), *Governing the Global Drug Wars* (London, London School of Economics, 2012) Kindle version 293/2572.

[15] David T Courtwright, 'A Short History of Drug Policy or Why We Make War on Some Drugs but not on Others', in LSE (ed) *Governing the Global Drug Wars* (London, London School of Economics, 2012) Kindle version 636/2572.

[16] McAllister (n 14) 401/2572.

Some advocates of drug liberalisation appear to use such contextual information (including anecdotes about particular individuals such as Anslinger) in an attempt at somehow arguing that the stated goals of the international drug control regime (ie the control of drugs) are somehow tainted by a less than angelic drafting history. This is hardly meaningful, in particular a century later. The reality is that, taking the situation at face value, there was an international consensus against drug abuse and trafficking. The drafting history of human rights is also bereft with political factors and constraints.

On the other hand, advocates of drug liberalisation are correct in pointing out that the situation surrounding the introduction of cannabis into international control can only be described as bizarre, bringing into question the entire legitimacy of the endeavour. Cannabis was first put under control in the 1925 Geneva Opium Convention, after a memorandum was submitted by the Egyptian government that 70 percent of persons in mental health facilities in the country were abusers of cannabis. The memorandum was clearly more fiction than fact, but Mills notes that:

> … the Egyptian delegation took the initiative to include cannabis into the agenda that had initially been designed simply to deal with opium, opiates and cocaine. Few other delegations had much information to hand about cannabis, and some impressively forceful rhetoric on the part of the Egyptian representatives seems to have been enough to convince most of the case against the drug.[17]

Mills notes that the memorandum in question was the product of a sole British doctor stationed in the mental health system in Egypt:

> Despite Warnock's frank admissions that he had very little idea of what was going on upon his arrival in Egypt—and indeed had no reliable means of remedying this situation beyond hazarding a few guesses of his own and trying to interpret the lunatic translations of his delusional clerk—it seems he was happy to jump to conclusions about the cause of illness among a large proportion of his patients.[18]

In any case, the recommendations of the Shanghai Conference led to the first international drug control treaty, the 1912 International Opium Convention. Numerous different treaties were adopted and then replaced throughout the years, resulting finally in the three current international drug control conventions that form the core of the international drug control regime: the 1961 Single Convention on Narcotic Substances (1961 Convention), the 1971 Convention on Psychotropic Substance (1971 Convention), and the 1988 UN Convention against Illicit Traffic in Narcotic Drugs and Psychotropic Substances (1988 Convention).

[17] James Mill, 'Science, Diplomacy and Cannabis: the Evidence Base and the International Drugs Regulatory System, 1924–1961', in LSE Ideas (ed) (n 14) Kindle version 759/2572.

[18] Mill, 'Science, Diplomacy and Cannabis' (n 17) 820/2572.

The 1961 Convention, as the name 'Single Convention' suggests, supersedes and consolidates all preceding treaties on the subject, and, being the first of the three conventions, forms the general model for the international regime that exists today. The preamble of the convention states the goals of the convention succinctly, stating that state parties are:

> … [c]oncerned with the health and welfare of mankind, [r]ecognizing that the medical use of narcotic drugs continues to be indispensable for the relief of pain and suffering and that adequate provision must be made to ensure the availability of narcotic drugs for such purposes, [r]ecognizing that addiction to narcotic drugs constitutes a serious evil for the individual and is fraught with social and economic danger to mankind, [and c]onscious of their duty to prevent and combat this evil.

The preamble to the 1971 Convention has similar language, stating that state parties are:

> concerned with the health and welfare of mankind, [n]oting with concern the public health and social problems resulting from the abuse of certain psychotropic substances, [d]etermined to prevent and combat abuse of such substances and the illicit traffic to which it gives rise, … [r]ecognizing that the use of psychotropic substances for medical and scientific purposes is indispensable and that their availability for such purposes should not be unduly restricted.

There is, therefore, a two-pronged objective of the 1961 Convention, and of the international drug control regime as a whole, namely to combat illicit drug trafficking and abuse, while at the same time ensuring that there is an adequate supply of controlled substances (ie drugs) for legitimate, licit purposes—mainly medical and scientific ones. The potential for conflict in practice between these two objectives is of course not negligible, but it is worth stressing that the international drug control regime exists not only as a law enforcement regime aimed at prohibition, but also to ensure that those in need are supplied with drugs for medical and scientific purposes. As shall be examined later, some criticism has been leveled at the international drug control regime for not fulfilling the objective of ensuring an adequate supply of medicines—criticism that is generally misplaced.

The subject matter of the 1961 Convention is narcotic drugs, ie psychoactive substances that are generally plant based, such as cannabis, heroin, and cocaine. The convention divides these substances into four control schedules, and requires differing levels of control from states, according to the international control schedule it is included in. Schedule 4 is the strictest control schedule, containing substances with 'particularly dangerous properties' which state parties may, if they so wish, ban completely, save for scientific or medical use under direct governmental supervision. Cannabis is included in Schedule 4, as is heroin. There is a procedure for state parties to reschedule substances, on the basis of a recommendation by the World Health Organisation (WHO). This procedure is relatively straightforward and has been used on several occasions for various substances,[19] though the political hurdles in attempting to reschedule cannabis are currently significant.

The 1971 Convention followed closely after the 1961 Convention, with recognition of the growing abuse problem of psychotropic substances, which were at the time freely available in most countries. Heavy lobbying by the pharmaceutical industry ensued,[20] but ultimately the 1971 Convention was drafted and adopted. The 1971 Convention is based largely on the 1961 Convention and contains many similar, and even identical, provisions. Nevertheless, the control system established by it is weaker in many respects—yet another example of how political factors can affect international negotiations. In 1972, a Protocol amending the 1961 Convention was adopted, fine-tuning the 1961 Convention somewhat, mainly to add some focus on illicitly cultivated drugs.

Both the 1961 and 1971 Conventions are very technical, containing, for example, requirements on the specific types of data to be submitted by state parties on drug requirement and imports. This is mainly because the conventions were meant to provide a technical framework for governments in operating a complex system of estimates and quotas for drugs. Under the 1961 Convention, Governments produce regular estimates as to how much of each drug they require for licit purposes. The total of these estimates are tallied with the total production of the few countries that engage in international export of these controlled substances, and consumption by countries is also checked regularly against their initial estimates. The overarching goal of this system is to regulate and control the licit production and flow of narcotic drugs, to ensure that there is no diversion of controlled substances into the illicit market. A similar system exists for substances controlled under the 1971 Convention, under which states provide not 'estimates' but 'assessments' of psychotropic substances.

The INCB is the body established by the 1961 Convention to administer this system of estimates, and which was later charged with administering the system of assessments for the 1971 Convention. The INCB is made up of thirteen members, each of whom serve five years and are to be 'persons who, by their competence, impartiality and disinterestedness, will command general confidence.'[21] Three of these members are selected from a list of at least five nominees prepared by the World Health Organisation (WHO), each of whom has 'medical, pharmacological or pharmaceutical experience.'[22] INCB sits three times a year in Vienna, and

[19] See eg UNODC, 'Changes in the scope of control of substances—Note by the Secretariat' (Vienna, UN index E/CN.7/2015/7, 16 December 2014).

[20] UNODC, *A Century of International Drug Control* (Vienna, 2010) 64.

[21] 1961 Convention, Article 9(2).

[22] 1961 Convention, Article 9(1).

is provided secretariat services by the UN Secretary General, specifically by the UN Office on Drugs and Crime (UNODC), an organisation of the UN Secretariat.

Besides the many technical articles on administration of the estimates system, the 1961 Convention also contains broader, policy-oriented articles on issues such as illicit drug trafficking,[23] measures against drug abuse,[24] and the desirability of providing treatment.[25] For example, Article 38 stipulates that state parties 'shall give special attention to and take all practicable measures for the prevention of abuse of drugs and for the early identification, treatment, education, after-care, rehabilitation and social reintegration of the persons involved'. These articles are more of a general nature, presumably because it was understood that states should have leeway to translate these articles into practice in ways that were in accordance with their respective situations, legal traditions, and cultures.

Advocates of drug liberalisation are quick to argue that the 1961 Convention focuses (and the international drug control conventions in general focus) predominantly on measures to reduce the supply of drugs (supply reduction), at the expense of prevention and other measures to reduce demand (demand reduction). For example, the Transnational Institute (TNI) argues that from the outset, 'supply control was dominant'[26] in the international approach, with a reduction in the illicit market sought via the 'drying up' of excess capacity. The TNI dismisses Article 38 of the 1961 Convention as 'little more than a passing nod in the direction of the demand side of the drug issue ... The treaty, both original and amended, reflected the long-standing habit of the international community to privilege supply-side approaches in the belief that this would eliminate non-medical and non-scientific drug use.'[27] There is some truth to this argument. When the 1961 Convention was drafted and adopted, the international consensus was that resupply reduction would be sufficient in addressing the problem of drugs. It is relatively recent—in particular at the first Special Session of the General Assembly in 1998—that states have also recognised the important role of demand reduction. Nevertheless, there is little justification for the statement that Article 38 was but a 'passing nod', and it is misleading to suggest that there is nothing about demand reduction in the conventions.

It is also worth noting that, when the 1961 Convention was drafted and the estimates system was created, diversion from the licit market was in

[23] 1961 Convention, Article 35.

[24] 1961 Convention, Article 38.

[25] 1961 Convention, Article 36(1)b.

[26] David Bewley-Taylor and Martin Jelsma, 'Fifty Years of the 1961 Single Convention on Narcotic Drugs: A Reinterpretation' (Amsterdam, Transnational Institute, 2011) 4.

[27] Bewley-Taylor and Jelsma, 'Fifty Years of the 1961 Single Convention on Narcotic Drugs' (n 26) 6.

fact the main source of illicit drugs. It was widely believed that the sort of technical approach towards regulating licit supply established under the 1961 Convention would be effective, and it has been—as even its critics admit, INCB has largely been successful in administering the estimates system so that diversion from the licit market has been virtually eradicated. McAllister notes:

> [Regulating licit markets] has actually worked rather well. There is little diversion from licit channels into illicit traffic; many now campaign for fewer fetters to be placed on pain-management options for patients, but the cost of the analgesics themselves is not a significant factor in the debate. In sum, it is precisely because the original design of the system was as devoted to cost-effective access as to limiting illicit supplies that demand-side issues were shunted to the background, in hopes of reducing the matter to a 'simple' police problem.[28]

The global drug problem now is somewhat different, in that the source of illicit drugs, at least internationally, is overwhelmingly illicit, though what INCB calls 'diversion' from the licit market continues to take place at the national level.[29] The illicit manufacture of psychotropic substances such as amphetamines is also widespread, and the ability to manufacture these substances on a small scale, eg at home, makes accurate assessments of the scale of the problem extremely difficult. Illicit cultivation and manufacture, of course, falls outside the estimates and assessment system administered by INCB, making these systems ineffective in addressing the situation. This is not an argument for dismantling these systems, as they continue to serve an important purpose—rather, it is a recognition that systems designed in 1961 and 1971 are not useful in dealing with problems that had not been foreseen at that time.

The 1988 Convention and Criminalisation

It was mainly the recognition that new international efforts were needed against the illicit trafficking of drugs that led to the drafting of the third convention of the international drug control regime, namely the 1988 UN Convention against the Illicit Traffic in Narcotic Drugs and Psychotropic Substances (the 1988 Convention).[30] As noted in the title, the main aim of the 1988 Convention is to combat illicit trafficking, and as such, there is a much stronger emphasis on law enforcement matters,

[28] McAllister (n 14) 401/2572.

[29] See eg 'Other opioids, such as buprenorphine, fentanyl and methadone, are available in illicit markets in Western and Central Europe. For example, fentanyl and buprenorphine are the main opioids used in Estonia and Finland, respectively. In some instances, these substances account for a significant proportion of overdose deaths, as in the case of fentanyl in Estonia.' UNODC, *World Drug Report 2015* (Vienna, 2015) 49.

[30] See eg UNODC (n 20) 68.

including extradition[31] and mutual legal assistance.[32] The 1988 Convention also establishes a system of international control of precursor chemicals used in the production and manufacture of narcotic drugs and psychotropic substances, which includes a system of pre-export notification. This system is also administered by INCB, though the wide range of legitimate uses of these chemical substances has necessarily resulted in a considerably weaker control system, rendering it somewhat less effective than that of narcotic drugs and psychotropic substances. Nevertheless, UNODC notes that the convention has been successful in encouraging action on the part of states, stating 'very few countries had implemented precursor legislation prior to the 1988 Convention'.[33]

The 1988 Convention also goes further than the 1961 or 1971 Conventions in obligating state parties to criminalise not only actions related to drug trafficking, but also abuse itself (or at least possession for the purposes of abuse). Article 3(2) states that:

> Subject to its constitutional principles and the basic concepts of its legal system, each Party shall adopt such measures as may be necessary to establish as a criminal offence under its domestic law, when committed intentionally, the possession, purchase or cultivation of narcotic drugs or psychotropic substances for personal consumption.

This is stronger than Article 36 of the 1961 Convention, which states that 'possession' and 'purchase' of illicit drugs 'shall be punishable offences when committed intentionally', but, unlike the 1988 Convention, does not specify that sanctions should be taken under criminal law. Article 22 of the 1971 Convention contains nearly identical wording to the 1961 Convention.

Advocates of drug liberalisation cite Article 3 to describe the 1988 Convention as 'the most prescriptive and punitive of the three' international drug control conventions,[34] and while this is a value judgment on their part, as a statement of fact it is correct. One of the key impetuses behind the inclusion of this article was the insistence of developing countries (so-called drug producing countries), many of whom felt they were being shouldered with an unfair burden by the supply reduction focus of the international drug control regime. Since the bulk of illicit cultivation of narcotic drugs takes place in the developing world, emphasising supply reduction meant that governments of those countries (who often are starved of capacity) must play the leading role—a role which, they argued, is made impossible so long as demand in developed countries

[31] 1988 Convention, Article 6.
[32] 1988 Convention, Article 7.
[33] See eg UNODC (n 20) 69.
[34] Barrett and Nowak (n 4) 455.

remains high. Therefore, many developing countries demanded that the developed world play their part, through strict enforcement of the prohibition of drug abuse (which was, rightly or wrongly, understood to bring down demand).[35] The traditional dichotomy between 'consumer countries' (located in the industrialised world) and 'producer countries' (which are comprised solely of developing countries) has in recent years shifted, in particular with rises in abuse in many developing countries.[36] However, during the drafting of the 1988 Convention, this dichotomy was still very present, if only as a political distinction, and Article 3 was included.

The situation surrounding the drafting of Article 3 is representative of an uncomfortable truth for the advocates of drug liberalisation, namely that their positions are based overwhelmingly on the outlook of people in only a small number of advanced Western states. In recent years, Latin American countries have been vocal in advocating an end to drug control, and it is certainly notable that a major 'producing country', Colombia, is part of this call. Nevertheless, the initial impetus for these calls in that region—indigenous rights of traditional consumption of particular substances, as well as resistance to what is perceived as American imperialism—is different from that of the Western legalisation movement, which is based largely on a perceived inevitability of widespread drug abuse. In any case, by and large, the legalisation movement is not a global movement, and is not representative of populations outside of these two regions.

Though, with caveats, the 1988 Convention does require state parties to criminalise the possession of illicit drugs for personal abuse, it goes on to stipulate that state parties need not necessarily punish persons found guilty only of drug abuse. Article 3(4)d states clearly that:

> Parties may provide, either as an alternative to conviction or punishment, or in addition to conviction or punishment of an offence [of possession, purchase or cultivation for personal consumption] measures for the treatment, education, aftercare, rehabilitation or social reintegration of the offender.

Therefore, while the 1988 Convention does require that states make the abuse (or at least the possession) of drugs a criminal offence, it does not necessarily require that people convicted of this offence be subject to incarceration or other punishment. States can fulfil their obligations through providing treatment for the individual, to encourage them to stop abusing drugs. Interestingly, Article 3 also has identical language regarding trafficking offences, indicating that state parties can refrain from conviction or punishment in such cases as well, with the proviso that this would be

[35] See UNODC, Commentary on the United Nations Convention against Illicit Traffic in Narcotic Drugs and Psychotropic Substances (Vienna, 1998) para 3.1. See also David R Bewley-Taylor and Cindy Fazey, 'The Mechanics and Systems of the UN System for International Drug Control' (Forward Thinking on Drugs, 2003) 28.

[36] See eg UNODC (n 29).

'in appropriate cases of a minor nature'.[37] The lack of this proviso in relation to cases of possession for abuse suggests that the drafters recognised that most, perhaps all, cases of that nature would in fact be minor, and that it would be appropriate to provide for treatment for such individuals, not punishment.

Regardless of whether Article 3 of the 1988 Convention is strictly applied, it is clear that state parties to this convention are required to criminalise the abuse of drugs. The 1988 Convention also contains in Article 14(4) a provision requiring that state parties:

> ... adopt appropriate measures aimed at eliminating or reducing illicit demand for narcotic drugs and psychotropic substances, with a view to reducing human suffering and eliminating financial incentives for illicit traffic.

This language is somewhat buried in an article otherwise on eradicating illicit cultivation, and can hardly be said to be sufficient in addressing the issue of demand reduction.

All of the three conventions have achieved nearly universal ratification. As of 1 September 2015, the 1961 Convention as amended by the 1972 Protocol has 185 state parties; the 1971 Convention has 183; and the 1988 Convention has 189. Countries become state party to an international convention for a variety of different political reasons, both international and national—however, it is worth noting the level of international consensus behind the three international drug control conventions.

The Treaty Monitoring Regime of International Drug Control

As noted above, INCB is the body charged with the monitoring of the three international drug control conventions. Arguably, INCB is first and foremost a technical body, staffed in Vienna mainly with statisticians and other technical experts who administer the estimates and other systems that regulate the licit flow of controlled substances. However, in the 1990s, INCB also began to pronounce itself on policy issues, mainly stating its concern when approaches adopted by member states fell foul (in the eyes of INCB) of their obligations under the conventions. As shall be examined later, some of these interpretations by INCB have proved controversial, though this is to be expected in the highly polarised environment that surrounds some of these issues. The controversies surrounding some of the

[37] 1988 Convention, Article 3(4)(c). Article 36(1)(b) of the 1961 Convention also states that 'when abusers of drugs have committed such offences, the Parties may provide, either as an alternative to conviction or punishment or in addition to conviction or punishment, that such abusers shall undergo measures of treatment, education, after-care, rehabilitation and social reintegration'. There is no requirement of the offence having been a 'minor' one in this text.

positions taken by INCB are arguably no greater than those surrounding statements made by similar bodies in human rights—the reality is that countries are generally not happy with being told what to do, and often react negatively towards international bodies that attempt to do so. What is different is that in the field of human rights, most international NGOs appreciate the pro-active positions of human rights bodies. This is not the case in drug control, where many international NGOs that have the resources to make their case heard in international fora are included within the network of advocates of drug liberalisation and, therefore, on the opposite side of the fence from INCB.

The main intergovernmental policy making body in drug control is the Commission on Narcotic Drugs (CND), a commission of the Economic and Social Council, with 53 member states. The CND meets in Vienna annually, usually in March, and adopts resolutions on relevant policy issues. The CND is provided secretariat services by the UN Office on Drugs and Crime (UNODC), an organisation of the UN Secretariat which is also governed by the CND—though the history of UNODC has resulted in a somewhat complex governing structure, whereby activities related to crime prevention (as opposed to drug control) activities are governed by a different intergovernmental commission, the Commission on Crime Prevention and Criminal Justice.[38]

Like many UN organisations, UNODC is heavily reliant on voluntary contributions by states, meaning that the agency must request states, often on an ad hoc basis, for funds for its activities. In 2014, the organisation received 89.3 percent of its budget through voluntary contributions, 98 percent of which were 'earmarked' for specific purposes.[39] Though UNODC states that its donor profile is changing markedly,[40] the fact remains that this funding structure leaves UNODC extremely vulnerable to political pressure by states, in particular wealthy and powerful states. In 2004, a letter was sent by the Executive Director of UNODC to the government of the United States (US), seemingly suggesting that UNODC would change certain organisational positions in response to pressure from the United States, and would cease from using the term 'harm reduction' in some of its documents.[41] The letter was leaked and subsequently widely criticised by advocates of drug liberalisation, who said it was proof that

[38] See eg UNODC, *Annual Report 2014* (Vienna, United Nations, 2015).

[39] UNODC, 'Funds and partners', www.unodc.org/unodc/en/donors/index.html?ref=menutop.

[40] Ibid.

[41] Letter from Antonio Maria Costa, Executive Director, United Nations Office on Drugs and Crime, to Robert Charles, Assistant Secretary, International Narcotics and Law Enforcement Affairs (11 November 2004), available at www.encod.org/info/IMG/pdf/LETCOSTA2004.pdf. The issue of 'harm reduction' will be examined later in this study.

'UNODC … is not capable of defending the interests of citizens. Not only does it possess extremely poor knowledge of facts, it also operates as an agency that is more faithful to financial and political pressure than to scientific evidence.'[42]

INCB does not rely on voluntary contributions from states and is, therefore, not vulnerable in the same manner as UNODC. INCB's funds come completely from the regular UN budget, which is made up of assessments from member states and allocated at the Fifth Committee of the General Assembly. A state could easily stop its voluntary contributions to UNODC, and the threat of this happening from an important donor acts as a major handicap on the independence of that agency. However, for a state to attempt to do this to INCB is technically almost impossible, since all state assessments are pooled for the regular budget. Of course, states communicate with INCB regularly, and powerful states arguably have more resources with which to make their case—nevertheless, the fact is that INCB is shielded from political pressure in a way that UNODC is not.

Human rights treaty bodies—bodies in the human rights field with mandates to monitor application of human rights conventions, in a manner somewhat similar to INCB—are also mainly funded (though not completely) from the regular UN budget. According to information published by the Office for the High Commissioner for Human Rights (OHCHR), the regular budget accounted for 76 percent of the treaty bodies' expenditure for 2010–11.[43] There is little indication that the 24 percent of the treaty bodies' budget that does come from voluntary contributions has resulted in a lack of political independence for any of the treaty bodies in human rights. Nevertheless, NGO advocates of drug liberalisation that stress the 'independent role' of the human rights treaty bodies, and who cry foul when states make statements disagreeing with the treaty bodies' views or otherwise fail to comply with them, are at the same time highly critical of INCB's 'lack of responsiveness' to state parties. This lack of consistency on the part of these advocates is, as shall be shown, a persistent theme throughout this area.

A provision exists in the 1961 Convention further solidifying the independence of INCB. Article 16, titled 'Secretariat', states that '[t]he secretariat services of the Commission and the Board shall be furnished by the Secretary-General. In particular, the Secretary of the Board shall be appointed by the Secretary-General in consultation with the Board.'

[42] Joep Oomen, 'UN Does not Support Harm Reduction' (Antwerp, European Coalition for Just and Effective Drug Policies, May 2007). See also Transnational Institute, 'US Pressure Against Harm Reduction Backfires at CND' (Amsterdam, March 2005).

[43] UN Secretary General, 'United Nations Reform: Measures and Proposals—Note by the Secretary General' (New York, UN index A/66/860, 26 June 2012) 26.

This provision appears to have the intention of shielding the independence of INCB from political interference from the UN. The Commentary on the 1961 Convention, prepared by the UN, states that, while there was controversy on this point, the view that INCB 'needs a separate secretariat for the independent performance of its tasks, which include judicial functions' was eventually adopted.[44]

The idea that INCB should be independent from UNODC permeates much of its daily work as well. INCB staff, including the Secretary, are in theory UN staff and are, therefore, subject to the same administrative regulations, and the same chain of command, as any other UN bureaucrat. However, they are trained to receive substantive instructions only from INCB, and not from the Executive Director of UNODC.

The Enforcement Powers of INCB

As the body tasked with monitoring the application of the three international drug control conventions, INCB evaluates the global drug control situation, and, when states adopt or implement policies that INCB believe violate the conventions, INCB takes steps to encourage that state to rectify the situation. This is done through a variety of means. INCB may dispatch a mission to the country concerned to engage in a dialogue with government officials. INCB sends missions to approximately 20 countries per year, though the criteria for choosing which countries to visit are neither public nor clear. Nevertheless, INCB does appear to make a point of sending missions to countries with which it has disagreements. INCB also has occasional bilateral meetings with government officials in Vienna, sometimes inviting a government to send a delegation to a meeting with the Board during one of its sessions.[45]

INCB does express concerns regarding particular country situations in public, though usually it would attempt the above methods first. INCB publishes an Annual Report, which contains an overview of the estimates and assessments from the preceding year, but which also examines the global drug control situation. INCB uses this Annual Report to pronounce its position on various drug control issues of the day, and also, at times, to condemn particular states that it believes are falling deviant of their obligations under the conventions. In some cases, INCB will issue a statement on a particular development in a country, without waiting for the Annual

[44] UN Secretary General, *Commentary on the Single Convention on Narcotic Drugs, 1961* (Vienna, United Nations, 1973) 204.

[45] For example, INCB invited a delegation of Switzerland for discussions at the INCB session in May 2008, and a delegation of Bolivia to the session at November 2008. See INCB, *Annual Report 2008* (Vienna, 2009) paras 217–222.

Report—though this is unusual, with the most recent example being the statement on Uruguay in December 2013.[46]

In addition to denouncing a country in this manner, INCB is bestowed with quite potent powers to ensure compliance with the conventions. Under Article 14(1)a of the 1961 Convention, INCB has the right to propose formal consultations with a state party if it has:

> objective reasons to believe that the aims of this Convention are being seriously endangered by reason of the failure of any Party … to carry out the provisions of this Convention [or if] a Party or a country or territory has become, or if there exists evidence of a serious risk that it may become, an important centre of illicit cultivation, production or manufacture of, or traffic in or consumption of drugs …

If the consultations do not lead to improvement, INCB can call upon the international community to take further action:

> If the Board finds that the Government concerned has failed to give satisfactory explanations … or has failed, to adopt any remedial measures which it has been called upon … or that there is a serious situation that needs co-operative action at the international level with a view to remedying it, it may call the attention of the Parties, the [Economic and Social Council] and the [CND] to the matter. The Board shall so act if the aims of this Convention are being seriously endangered and it has not been possible to resolve the matter satisfactorily in any other way. It shall also so act if it finds that there is a serious situation that needs cooperative action at the international level …

Though the language used is relatively strong, the notion that INCB can consult with governments and make recommendations for strengthening drug control is uncontroversial—as noted above, the body does so frequently. What is surprising is that the 1961 Convention bestows upon INCB the power to recommend that the international community take sanctions against the recalcitrant government, through an embargo of licit drugs. The article goes on to state:

> The Board … may, if it is satisfied that such a course is necessary, recommend to Parties that they stop the import of drugs, the export of drugs, or both, from or to the country or territory concerned, either for a designated period or until the Board shall be satisfied as to the situation in that country or territory.[47]

Article 19 of the 1971 Convention contains similar wording to Article 14 of the 1961 Convention, essentially allowing INCB the same prerogatives.

INCB has instigated formal dialogues under Article 14/Article 19 with regard to a number of countries, though as a rule it does not make public

[46] INCB, 'Uruguay is breaking the International Conventions on Drug Control with the Cannabis Legislation approved by its Congress' UNIS/NAR/1190, 12 December 2013.

[47] 1961 Convention, Article 14(2).

which countries have been subject to the procedure.[48] In its Annual Report, INCB states the number of countries with which it has dialogues under this Article, and an examination of past Annual Reports shows that in nearly all the cases, the formal activation of the mechanism was quickly discontinued, after the state in question changed its policies.[49] It is difficult to make an informed judgment regarding this, since both Articles 14 and 19 stipulate that the subject matter of the consultations is confidential. It may be that, in the majority of cases, the articles were invoked for relatively minor issues. In any case, the procedure appears to have been, on the whole, quite successful.

The significant exception remains Afghanistan, which is the only country that INCB has publicly stated (with the agreement of the government) is under the Article 14 procedure. INCB first instigated the procedure with regard to Afghanistan in 2000, and, after confidential consultations did not lead to progress, publicly called the attention of the international community to the activation of Article 14 in its Annual Report issued in early 2002.[50] Afghanistan remains the only country currently under the procedure, though with little progress, as evidenced by UNODC's estimates of the continuing huge scale of illicit opium cultivation in that country—in 2015, the organisation announced that cultivation had reached 'historic levels'.[51] Though it is arguable that INCB has managed to maintain an international focus on Afghanistan through the continuing application of Article 14, the wording of the Article would seem to suggest that it is to be used in cases where a government is intentionally flouting its obligations, as opposed to a situation where the government does not control vast portions of the country's territory and does not have the capacity to improve the situation in any meaningful way (as is the case with Afghanistan). This being the case, it remains questionable how effective the Article could be with regard to the current situation in Afghanistan.

As noted above, Article 14 grants INCB the power to recommend to the Economic and Social Council (ECOSOC) sanctions against a particularly defiant country. Understandably, INCB has never yet taken this extreme step. The convention states only that INCB can 'recommend' sanctions, leaving open the possibility that ECOSOC could, of course, reject INCB's recommendation. Being a political body made up of state representatives, it would be interesting to see what would happen if INCB recommended sanctions against a state, in particular a wealthy and politically

[48] Article 14(1) states: '… the Board shall treat as confidential a request for information and an explanation by a Government or a proposal for consultations and the consultations held with a Government'. Article 19(1) of the 1971 Convention has similar wording.

[49] See eg INCB, *Annual Report 1999*, (Vienna, 2000) paras 173–175.

[50] INCB, *Annual Report 2001* (Vienna, 2002) paras 231–234.

[51] See eg UNODC (n 29) 41.

powerful country, such as the Netherlands or Switzerland (both countries with which INCB has longstanding and fundamental policy disagreements, including 'coffee shops' in the Netherlands and injection rooms in Switzerland). In 2004, INCB appeared close to activating the Article 14 procedure against Switzerland, when that country seemed poised to adopt a law allowing for the legalisation of cannabis cultivation and consumption. After heated debate within the Swiss parliament, the bill was rejected.[52]

INCB, UNODC, and Human Rights

INCB has come under heavy criticism from advocates of drug liberalisation for what they portray as failing to be cognisant of human rights standards in examining states' performance under the drug control conventions, or, more fundamentally, ignoring human rights altogether. This is evident, so advocates of drug liberalisation argue, in INCB's failure to condemn governments when they violate human rights in their enforcement of drug control laws (which, these advocates say, is an inevitable result of the 'prohibitive' nature of international drug control), and in that body's ignorance of the importance of 'harm reduction'. Both of these issues will be examined in depth later on in this study.

Advocates of drug liberalisation are quick to argue that INCB refuses to discuss human rights issues.[53] INCB has been described as 'closed to reason'[54] and on an 'erratic crusade',[55] a body that 'abuses results of research at will. Repeatedly, the Board chooses to quote scientific research only when it serves the Board's purpose to push for strict adherence to the Conventions as defined by the Board itself.'[56] The Open Society Foundation (OSF) states that '[i]n the field of human rights the Board's comments and actions are so shockingly out of line with international norms that it calls into question its credibility—if not its competence.'[57] Csete argues that:

> INCB [should] prioritise in its work countries where health services for people who use drugs are compromised because of moral judgments and stigma they face ... If the INCB were doing the job of overseeing adherence to the drug

[52] See eg Diane Steber Buechli and Ruth Dreifuss, 'Swiss Drug Policy in International Context—Fought, Ignored, Admired', in LSE Ideas (ed) (n 14).

[53] See also Barrett and Nowak (n 4) 457.

[54] Canadian HIV/AIDS Legal Network and Open Society Institute, 'Closed to Reason: the International Narcotics Control Board and HIV/AIDS' (Toronto, 2007).

[55] Transnational Institute, 'The Erratic Crusade of INCB' (Amsterdam, 2003) 1.

[56] Ibid 4.

[57] OSF, 'The International Narcotics Control Board Strains its Limited Credibility' (London, LSE Ideas, March 2013).

> conventions in their fullness, these concerns would have high priority. Instead, the Board's concern for treating drug dependence, and other health services for people who use drugs, seems consistently overshadowed by a scientifically unjustified bias in favour of abstinence at all costs and by support for harsh policing.[58]

INCB's views on harm reduction issues, often mischaracterised, will be examined later in this study.

While it is arguably true that INCB refrained from pronouncing itself on human rights for longer than was the case with many other UN and UN-affiliated bodies, it has addressed the importance of human rights in a general sense on several occasions, starting with its Annual Report 2007. In this Annual Report, INCB dedicated its thematic chapter to the issue of 'the principle of proportionality in drug-related offences', and made multiple references to the need to respect human rights in drug law enforcement. In a relatively clear statement, the report noted: 'Due respect for universal human rights, human duties and the rule of law is important for effective implementation of the international drug control conventions. Non-respect for them can prejudice the ability of the criminal justice system to enforce the law, can lead to discriminatory disproportionate responses to drug offending and can undermine the conventions.'[59] This is echoed in the INCB's report for 2014, which states:

> … it is clear that the human rights conventions form an important cluster of binding international legislation that needs to be taken into consideration while implementing any international treaty, be it related to drugs, corruption or the environment, among other things … Member States should give due consideration to the human rights norms relevant in the context of each element of a comprehensive, integrated and balanced approach, according to their legal obligations. They should also, if necessary, seek out the advice of human rights treaty bodies for the implementation of such norms.[60]

There seems to be little controversy regarding this point, and, in principle, little disagreement between INCB and its critics.

Of course, INCB has a different view from advocates of drug liberalisation as to what respect for human rights may or may not have in the way of concrete implications for the international drug control regime. At his address to the 2009 session of CND, Hamid Ghodse, then President of INCB, cited the Annual report 2007 and stated that:

> Controlling drugs and protecting human rights are not opposites but go hand in hand … Drug control policies cannot be successful in the long term if they

[58] Joanne Csete, 'Overhauling Oversight: Human Rights at the INCB', in LSE Ideas (ed) (n 14) 2370, 2381/2572.

[59] INCB, *Annual Report 2007* (Vienna, 2008) para 38.

[60] INCB, *Annual Report 2014* (Vienna, 2015) paras 35, 38.

> are carried out at the expense of human rights and respect for the rule of law. The principle that all human beings are equal in dignity and rights, which is enshrined in the United Nations Universal Declaration on Human Rights, should guide all Governments, intergovernmental organisations and non-governmental organisations in their actions against the drug problem. … while an approach towards drug control that is cognisant of human rights is important … the exercise of the individuals' rights and freedoms does not include the right to abuse drugs. Drug abuse is neither harmless nor victimless and causes serious damage to both individuals and society. In addition, drug abuse is often in conflict with the due recognition of the rights and freedoms of others and in meeting the requirements of health, public order and the general welfare in a democratic society.[61]

Unsurprisingly, this position of the INCB has come under criticism by advocates of drug liberalisation. Barrett and Veerman cite Ghodse's statement and assert that:

> … the way in which [human rights were cited] was questionable … its contention in this regard was that 'Controlling drugs and protecting human rights are not opposite but go hand in hand.' This, however, is far from clear cut. There are areas of convergence … but whether drug control measures contribute to the realisation of these rights is always open and should inform policy decisions. There are also areas of unresolved conflict, including interferences with privacy, religious freedom and indigenous and cultural rights which require focused human rights scrutiny.[62]

Barrett and Veerman do little in the way of explaining their criticisms, however, and it is difficult to find fault with Ghodse's words, unless one believes, as many advocates of drug liberalisation appear to, that there is (or should be) an internationally recognised 'right to abuse drugs'.

UNODC has made more detailed pronouncements on human rights, noting, as with other UN organisations, that human rights form an integral part of its work. Though, like INCB, the organisation had remained silent on the issue for some years, Antonio Costa, the Executive Director at the time, delivered a somewhat surprising statement at the 2008 session of the CND, where he argued that:

> Our work is guided first and foremost by the UN Charter that commits signatories to fundamental freedoms, and by the Universal Declaration of Human Rights … In Article 25 of the Universal Declaration, health is listed as a basic human right. As we emphasize the health aspects of drug control, it stands to

[61] Hamid Ghodse, 'Statement by Professor Hamid Ghodse, President, International Narcotics Control Board, at the high-level segment of the 52nd session of the Commission on Narcotic Drugs on 11 March 2009, Vienna-Austria' (Vienna, 2009) 3.

[62] Damon Barrett and Philip E Veerman, *A Commentary on the United Nations Convention on the Rights of the Child: Article 33: Protection from Narcotic Drugs and Psychotropic Substances* (Leiden, Martinus Nijhoff, 2012) 10, 11.

reason that implementation of the drug Conventions must proceed with due regard to human rights. Thus far, there has been little attention paid to this aspect of our work. This definitely needs to be amended.[63]

The Executive Director then went on to focus on the specific issue of the death penalty for drug-related offences, stating that '[a]lthough drugs kill, I don't believe we need to kill because of drugs ... today I propose that Member States ... give serious consideration to whether the imposition of capital punishment for drug-related crimes is a best practice.'[64] At the same CND, for the first time, a draft resolution was submitted on ensuring respect for human rights standards in drug control policy. After intense debate, the text that was adopted (resolution 51/12), states that the CND:

> Reaffirms that countering the world drug problem ... requires an integrated and balanced approach and that it must be carried out in full conformity with the purposes and principles of the Charter of the United Nations and other provisions of international law ... and all human rights and fundamental freedoms and on the basis of the principles of equal rights and mutual respect.[65]

In 2010, Costa submitted a note to the CND, outlining his views on some of the issues, and putting forward proposals for strengthening the mainstreaming of human rights work in UNODC. The note touches on many of the arguments put forward by advocates of drug liberalisation, and while accepting that human rights considerations must play a role in assessing drug control efforts by states, it rejects implicitly many of those advocates' sweeping assertions. While noting that '[r]esponses to drugs, crime and terrorism that are based on the rule of law must therefore also incorporate human rights law and principles. Too often, law enforcement and criminal justice systems themselves perpetrate human rights abuses and exclude and marginalise from society those who most need treatment and rehabilitation',[66] the note proceeds to state flatly:

> ... such statements do not mean that international human rights law can support a general 'right to abuse drugs'. The issue is rather whether drug control legislation constitutes an unlawful and disproportionate infringement of

[63] Antonio Maria Costa, 'The 51st session of the Commission of Narcotic Drugs, UNODC Executive Director Antonio Mario Costa' (Vienna, UNODC, 2008), available at www.unodc.org/unodc/en/about-unodc/speeches/2008-03-10.html.

[64] Ibid.

[65] Commission on Narcotic Drugs Resolution 51/12,'Strengthening cooperation between the United Nations Office on Drugs and Crime and other United Nations entities for the promotion of human rights in the implementation of the international drug control treaties', in Commission on Narcotic Drugs, *Report on the fifty-first session (28 November 2007 and 10–14 March 2008)* (Vienna, UN index E/CN.7/2008/15, 14 March 2008) 32.

[66] Antonio Maria Costa, 'Drug control, crime prevention and criminal justice: A Human Rights perspective: Note by the Executive Director, United Nations Office on Drugs and Crime' (Vienna, UN index E/CN.7/2010/CRP.6–E/CN.15/2010/CRP.1, 3 March 2010) para 2.

> human rights and fundamental freedoms. The answer to this question essentially depends on the context … [A] number of human rights-based drug law cases (including cases engaging the right to property and the right to freedom of religion) have found drug-related criminal laws to be legitimate limitations necessary to protect public safety, order, health or morals in the individual, at least in the individual circumstances of the case. This is not inconsistent.[67]

Citing statements from INCB and others, Costa also makes it clear that the international drug control conventions do not require that states engage in disproportionate punishment for drug-related offences—refuting what is, as shall be examined in this study, an important pillar of the arguments of advocates of drug liberalisation. Costa notes that:

> … the drug-control conventions generally require parties to establish a wide range of drug-related activities as criminal offences under their domestic law. Nonetheless, they permit parties to respond to them proportionally, including through alternatives to conviction or punishment for offences of a minor nature. Serious offences, such as trafficking in illicit drugs, must be dealt with more severely and extensively than offences such as possession of drugs for personal use. In this respect, it is clear that the use of non-custodial measures and treatment programmes for offences involving possession for personal use of drugs offer a more proportionate response and the more effective administration of justice.[68]

On the other hand, in recent years, there appears to have been a shift within UNODC, towards a direction favoured by advocates of drug liberalisation. What this shift is due to is difficult to gauge, but, like OHCHR, UNODC has been the target of intense lobbying by advocates of drug liberalisation, and it may well be that the human rights language has been effective in convincing UNODC staff.

In December 2013, Yury Fedotov, who had been appointed Executive Director of UNODC in July 2010, submitted a paper to the high-level review of progress towards the UN General Assembly Special Session on Drugs (UNGASS) goals decided in 2009 (see below on UNGASS). While endorsing the recommendations made in the 2009 document as '[remaining] valid today',[69] there is a somewhat subtle change in the manner in which the document describes the international drug control conventions. Fedotov states that '[t]he conventions are not about waging a "war on drugs" but about protecting the "health and welfare of mankind".

[67] Costa, 'Drug control, crime prevention and criminal justice' (n 66) para 19.

[68] Costa (n 66) para 23.

[69] Yury Fedotov, 'Contribution of the Executive Director of the United Nations Office on Drugs and Crime to the high-level review of the implementation of the Political Declaration and Plan of Action on International Cooperation towards an Integrated and Balanced Strategy to Counter the World Drug Problem, to be conducted by the Commission on Narcotic Drugs in 2014' (Vienna, UN index UNODC/ED/2014/1, 6 December 2013) para 48.

They cannot be interpreted as a justification—much less a requirement—for a prohibitionist regime but as the foundation of a drug control system where some psychoactive substances are permitted solely for medical and scientific purposes.'[70] The paper then goes on to warn against dismantling the drug control regime, stating that 'would hardly achieve the ultimate goal of the system, which, as stated in the conventions, is to protect the 'health and welfare of mankind'. Uncontrolled access to drugs would increase their accessibility, thereby creating the risk of a considerable increase in harmful drug use'.[71] Nevertheless, the attempt at characterising the conventions as 'not justifying a prohibitive regime' in essence appears to accept the idea of the advocates of drug control, namely that drug control, at least as implemented today globally, has metamorphasised into a 'prohibitive' regime, and by extension, a problematic one.

The paper then goes on to encourage member states to:

> … reconfigure responses to the world drug problem, so as to balance the drug control system focusing on health and respect for human rights, emphasizing evidence-based prevention and treatment and giving due considerations to the needs of drug-dependent persons, countering cultural stereotypes, stigma and discrimination—all of which limit drug users' access to services.[72]

Numerous aspects of this statement would appear to be lifted out of the playbook of the advocates of drug liberalisation, including the characterisation of current drug control approaches as 'lacking balance', the notion that persons who abuse drugs are vulnerable to 'cultural stereotypes' and discrimination, and the idea that member states are being reticent in providing 'evidence-based' treatment. Fedotov then makes the somewhat uncontroversial statement that states should 'implement drug control policies and programmes within the framework of the rule of law and fully in line with human rights standards. When fighting drug trafficking or illicit drug use, fundamental human rights must be respected.'[73]

In October 2015, UNODC prepared a briefing paper titled 'Decriminalisation of Drug Use and Possession for Personal Consumption' for submission to the annual International Harm Reduction Conference in Malaysia. Astoundingly, this paper states that 'decriminalising drug use and possession for personal consumption is consistent with international drug control conventions and may be required to meet obligations under international human rights law'[74]—a position that is not only problematic in

[70] Fedotov, 'Contribution of the Executive Director of the UNODC' (n 69) para 50.
[71] Fedotov (n 69) para 51.
[72] Fedotov (n 69) para 52(a).
[73] Fedotov (n 69) para 52(c).
[74] UNODC, 'Briefing paper: Decriminalisation of Drug Use and Possession for Personal Consumption' (Kuala Lumpur, October 2015) 1.

its substance, but would amount to a major policy shift for the organisation charged with implementing the international drug control regime.

The paper is rife with sweeping generalisations that have clearly been taken practically verbatim from the advocates of drug liberalisation. It asserts that:

> The threat of arrest and criminal sanctions have been widely shown to obstruct access to lifesaving health services ... The heavy emphasis on criminalisation has fueled high levels of discrimination against people who use drugs, including exclusion from workplace, from education, from child custody and from health care. People who use drugs, especially women who use drugs, are particularly vulnerable to sexual, physical and psychological abuse ... Large numbers of people who use and inject drugs are held in compulsory drug detention centres without their informed consent ... Worldwide, millions of people are imprisoned for minor, non-violent drug-related offences.[75]

As shall be examined in this study, some of the above human rights issues are very real, but they are not necessarily global issues, and certainly not dictated by the international drug control regime.

Noting the language in the 1988 Convention that stipulates that state parties must establish as a criminal offence the possession of illicit drugs '[s]ubject to its constitutional principles and the basic concepts of its legal system', the paper encourages states to take advantage of this proviso, stating that 'states can opt out of the requirement to criminalise possession for personal consumption if it would be unconstitutional (based on, eg, the right to privacy or liberty) or otherwise contrary to their legal systems.'[76] However, the right to privacy has never, at least at an international level, been interpreted to include a right to abuse drugs—and there is no 'right to liberty' in international human rights law, at least not in the general sense that appears to be suggested in this paper.[77]

Perhaps even most problematic is the statement in the paper that '[r]estrictions on certain rights may be imposed if they are prescribed by law, non-discriminatory and proportionate—that is, no more than is necessary to achieve a legitimate aim. The state has the burden to justify that criminalisation meets this test.' While this reading of international human rights law is correct, this statement is based on the premise that abusing drugs is a 'right', subject to restriction only for legitimate purposes—a premise that has no foundation in law.

The circumstances surrounding this paper remain somewhat murky. Within hours, Richard Branson, a flamboyant advocate of drug

[75] UNODC, 'Briefing paper' (n 74) 1.

[76] UNODC (n 74) 2.

[77] The term 'liberty' appears in international human rights legal texts within the context of the right to be free from arbitrary detention. See International Covenant on Civil and Political Rights, Article 9.

liberalisation and a member of the Global Commission on Drug Policy (GCDP), released the paper to the media, stating that it had been provided to him and a small number of other select individuals.[78] The briefing paper received wide attention in the international media,[79] and UNODC quickly issued a somewhat meek statement that the paper had been:

> … intended for dissemination and discussion at a conference in Kuala Lumpur, [and] is neither a final nor formal document from [UNODC] … UNODC regrets that, on this occasion, there has been an unfortunate misunderstanding about the nature and intent of this briefing paper. UNODC emphatically denies reports that there has been pressure on UNODC to withdraw the document. But, it is not possible to withdraw what is not yet ready.[80]

This statement by UNODC notwithstanding, it would appear that UNODC is at least giving serious consideration to a quite dramatic change of course, taking the international debate to a new dimension. Transform notes that:

> … if, as the UNODC says, it was merely 'intended for dissemination and discussion' at the Kuala Lumpur conference, then why was the document withdrawn at all? Why not release it so that it could be discussed, as it was supposedly meant to be? It all points to an outside intervention … [W]hatever has gone on behind the scenes, the UNODC are now answerable to a document that is very much in the public domain. If they are suggesting there are flaws in the analysis, or that they don't agree with any of it, then they will need to say why.[81]

II. HUMAN RIGHTS

The philosophical underpinnings of human rights concepts are often traced to such documents as the American Declaration of Independence, the French Declaration of the Rights of Man, and even Magna Carta. However, human rights as a modern legal body of law was born from widespread revulsion at the abuses that took place during the Holocaust, and from an international consensus that laws should be adopted to

[78] Richard Branson blog, 'Finally—a change in course in drug policy' (19 October 2015), www.virgin.com/richard-branson/finally-a-change-in-course-on-drug-policy.

[79] See eg Newsweek, 'Richard Branson Leaks UN Draft Paper on Decriminalizing Drugs', 19 October 2015; The Guardian, 'UN denies Richard Branson's claim it is poised to call for drug decriminalization', 19 October 2015.

[80] UNODC, 'UNODC Spokesperson statement', 19 October 2015, www.unodc.org/unodc/en/press/releases/2015/October/statement-by-the-spokesperson-for-the-un-office-on-drugs-and-crime.html.

[81] Transform, 'The truth behind the UNODC's leaked decriminalisation paper', (London, 20 October 2015).

ensure that such widespread, systematic violations of human dignity do not take place again.[82]

The bedrock of modern human rights law is what is commonly referred to as the International Bill of Human Rights, consisting of three legal standards: the Universal Declaration of Human Rights (UDHR) (adopted by the UN General Assembly in 1948 and reaffirmed on countless occasions since); the International Covenant on Civil and Political Rights (ICCPR); and the International Covenant on Economic, Social, and Cultural Rights (ICESCR) (the latter two having been adopted in 1966).

From practically the outset, the development of international human rights law, as is the case with international drug control law and with all bodies of international law, has been captive to geopolitical considerations and strains in international relations. As is the case with drug control, this is not to suggest that these bodies of law have no value, but merely to state the fact—international law is made by states in what is inherently a political process, and to expect it to be somehow pure and free of such banal considerations is naïve.

The Universal Declaration is made of 30 operative articles, enumerating a wide range of rights that must be protected. These include rights that could be classified as civil and political rights eg the right to freedom of expression (Article 19), the right to be free from torture (Article 5), the right to 'full equality to a fair and public hearing by an independent and impartial tribunal' (Article 10), as well as economic, social, and cultural ones eg the right to education (Article 26), the right to an adequate standard of living (Article 25), and the right to work (Article 23). After the adoption of the Universal Declaration in 1948, the plan was to swiftly prepare and adopt a binding treaty on human rights, that would set out in legal obligations the aspirations outlined in the Declaration. However, this plan quickly fell aground in the context of the Cold War, with the two global camps separating on ideological grounds. The Western bloc, led by the US, argued that only civil and political rights were true human rights, and balked at the prospect of a binding document obligating states to provide for economic and social rights. The Eastern bloc, lead by the Soviet Union, on the other hand, argued that economic and social rights should come first, and that would lead to a natural progression in civil and political rights.[83]

[82] Many also count as one of the founding documents the judgment of the Nuremberg Tribunal. Some scholars argue that there was in fact no connection between the Holocaust and the creation of modern international human rights law: see eg Stephen Hopgood, *The Endtimes of Human Rights* (Ithica, Cornell University Press, 2013).

[83] See eg Philip Alston (ed), *The United Nations and Human Rights: a Critical Appraisal* (Oxford, Clarendon, 1995).

In the end, it was decided to have two conventions, one for each category of rights—hence the two covenants. It should be noted that the degree of protection afforded in the ICCPR is considerably stronger than that of the ICESCR. Obligations under the ICCPR are immediate—upon ratification, states must immediately comply with the provisions or risk being accused of not fulfilling their treaty obligations. Obligations under the ICESCR, on the other hand, are progressive, with state parties required only to '[undertake] to take steps ... to the maximum of its available resources, with a view to achieving progressively the full realization of the rights'.[84] The Committee on Economic, Social, and Cultural Rights (CESCR—see next section) has elaborated on the progressive nature of these obligations, stating 'even where the available resources are demonstrably inadequate, the obligation remains for a State party to strive to ensure the widest possible enjoyment of the relevant rights under the prevailing circumstances',[85] and stressing also that efforts must not be discriminatory.

For many decades, economic, social, and cultural rights were considered by many to be less important than civil and political rights. The factors for this are many, and go far beyond the scope of this book—by their nature these rights were considered aspirational or not attributable to individuals, they were not recognised as justiciable in a court of law, they went against the dominant ideology of economic neoliberalism, amongst others. Nevertheless, the Declaration and Programme of Action adopted at the World Conference on Human Rights in Vienna in 1994 states clearly that '[a]ll human rights are universal, indivisible and interdependent and interrelated. The international community must treat human rights globally in a fair and equal manner, on the same footing, and with the same emphasis',[86] language that has been reiterated in numerous subsequent international relations and declarations.

As clear as the above understanding is on paper, it of course does not clarify the fundamental issue of the differing levels of obligations between the two covenants. This has been allowed to stand, most probably due to the lengthy process that would be required in attempting to revise any multilateral treaty.

Both covenants count the majority of states as state parties, though the number of ratifications is not quite as high as with the international drug control conventions. As of 2 September 2015, ICCPR had 168 state parties, and ICESCR 164. The UDHR, being a declaration, is of course not

[84] ICESCR, Article 2(1).

[85] CESCR, 'General comment No. 3: The nature of States parties' obligations' (Geneva, UN index E/1991/23, 1991) para. 11.

[86] Vienna Declaration and Programme of Action (Adopted by the World Conference on Human Rights in Vienna on 25 June 1993) para 5.

subject to ratification. Some scholars argue that the UDHR has passed into the realm of customary international law, through its constant reaffirmation as a standard for all states and in particular its use as a justification for various international policies.[87] The veracity of these arguments notwithstanding, it is difficult to see much practical value in this idea, in the absence of any kind of serious enforcement mechanism.

Besides the above three documents, there is a large number of human rights treaties, generally covering specific human rights issues or groups. Already before 1966, some conventions were adopted that covered topics that were thought to be relatively uncontroversial even in the Cold War context: the Convention on the Prevention and Punishment of the Crime of Genocide (the Genocide Convention, which was adopted a day before the UDHR), and the International Convention on the Elimination of All Forms of Racial Discrimination (ICERD, 1965). Arguably, the Genocide Convention has been subject to the most spectacular failures, as the situations in Bosnia, Cambodia, and perhaps occupied Palestine attest. However, the Genocide Convention became one of the philosophical underpinnings for the adoption of the Rome Statute of the International Criminal Court in 1998.

Since the late 1980s, a large number of human rights conventions has been adopted. The Office of the High Commissioner on Human Rights (OHCHR) lists nine of them as 'core international human rights conventions'. Besides the ICCPR, the ICESCR, and ICERD, the Convention on the Elimination of all Forms of Discrimination against Women (CEDAW), the Convention against Torture and other Cruel, Inhuman or Degrading Treatment or Punishment (CAT), the Convention on the Rights of the Child (CRC), the International Convention on the Protection of the Rights of all Migrant Workers and their Families (ICPMW), the International Convention for the Protection of All Persons from Enforced Disappearance (CPED), and, the Convention on the Rights of Persons with Disabilities (CRPD) are all listed as core conventions, as are several optional protocols to these conventions.[88] One article of the CRC is particularly relevant to the drug control issue, and will be examined in detail.

There has also been a plethora of declarations and resolutions on human rights over the years, covering a wide range of topics. Some of these issues are longstanding and clearly relevant to a wide segment of humanity, such as the rights of indigenous people and the right to development. Some,

[87] For a general discussion on this subject, see eg Bertrand G, Ramcharan (ed), *Human Rights. Thirty Years after the Universal Declaration* (Amsterdam, Springer, 1979); also Jochen von Bernstorff, 'The Changing Fortunes of the Universal Declaration of Human Rights: Genesis and Symbolic Dimensions of the Turn to Rights in International Law' (2008), in 19 *European Journal of International Law* 5 at 903.

[88] OHCHR, 'The Core International Human Rights Instruments and their monitoring bodies', www.ohchr.org/EN/ProfessionalInterest/Pages/CoreInstruments.aspx.

on the other hand, are somewhat 'niche' issues, such as the human rights implications of toxic waste,[89] and the use of mercenaries,[90] amongst others. This is not to belittle the human rights implications of some of those issues, but to state that the usefulness of human rights as a tool to address those developments can be questioned. Concern has been raised regarding the seemingly constant generation of new standards and new topics in the field, and some have argued for a greater focus on implementation of existing standards. Others, on the other hand, note that 'the international human rights regime has been strong on declarations and weak on implementation [because that] reflects the interests of the principal international actors: *states*.' (emphasis in original).[91] In any case, the important role that NGOs play in the human rights field in channeling new concerns and issues into international policy making fora means that new issues will surely continue to be raised on a regular basis.

Human rights have also expanded through what could be termed as acquisition of standards in other fields. These other standards were not made as human rights standards as such, but, due to their focus on protecting the welfare of particular groups of vulnerable persons, they have been widely used by the human rights community to the extent that they are often categorised as human rights conventions. Included among these are the 1951 Convention related to the Status of Refugees and modern standards of humanitarian law, ie the Four Geneva Conventions of 1949 on the conduct of war and their two 1977 Additional Protocols. All of these conventions were drafted and adopted in specialised international fora outside of the human rights framework, and were not initially conceptualised as human rights treaties (as evidenced by the fact that they are formulated in terms of the treatment states should afford individuals in accordance with that treaty, not in the standard language of human rights, where the starting point is that individuals are entitled to certain rights by virtue of the fact that they are human beings).

Both the expansion in the number and breadth of standards and the acquisition of standards from other fields is a testament to the success of human rights as a social movement. To paraphrase Donnelly, human rights has given a language to the oppressed of the world—a language in which to express their need for dignity, freedom, and good governance.[92]

[89] See eg OHCHR, 'Special Rapporteur on the implications for human rights of the environmentally sound management and disposal of hazardous substances and wastes', www.ohchr.org/EN/Issues/Environment/ToxicWastes/Pages/SRToxicWastesIndex.aspx.

[90] See eg OHCHR, 'Working Group on the use of mercenaries as a means of violating human rights and impeding the exercise of the right of peoples to self-determination', www.ohchr.org/EN/Issues/Mercenaries/WGMercenaries/Pages/WGMercenariesIndex.aspx.

[91] Michael Freeman, *Human Rights,* 2nd Edition (London, Polity Press, 2011) 59.

[92] As Donnelly says: 'Human rights is the language of victims and the dispossessed'. See Jack Donnelly, *International Human Rights*, Fourth Edition (Boulder, Westview Press, 2013) 20.

As Freeman has noted, the very existence of the human rights regime in the current state-governed international system is 'astonishing'.[93] As the human rights movement has expanded over the decades, it was perhaps inevitable that groups with specific claims that may not have fallen under the purview of human rights as initially conceptualised would start using the human rights framework as a tool for advocacy. This can be seen in other areas as well, the example of human rights being used in the anti-globalisation movement being a good example.

One can say, therefore, that insofar as oppression continues in any shape or form, the human rights framework contains the potential for constant expansion. In principle, this is not undesirable, since individuals and communities need to be able to pursue their claims for justice, and, within limits, legal standards should be flexible enough to adjust to new realities. At the same time, it is submitted that viewing human rights as a panacea, a 'catch all' solution for all social ills can be fraught with difficulties. It is important that the limits of human rights are recognised; it is a set of standards of minimum conduct, predominantly (though not solely) for government authorities—not a tool to win social justice in each and every way. If human rights stands for everything, it stands for nothing.

The above notwithstanding, it is an oft repeated truism that human rights has revolutionalised international law. Before the advent of human rights, states were the subjects of international law, not individuals. Treaties outlined the obligations of states towards each another, not to individuals, and certainly not to a state's own nationals. Some international agreements included provisions regarding the treatment of particular groups of individuals, but these were limited to foreign nationals (or minority populations with a special connection to another state). Even if a state failed to treat these groups in accordance with the agreement, individuals had no legal standing—they could only appeal to other state parties to the agreement to take up their case. Treatment of a state's own citizens was considered a sovereign prerogative, not to be interfered with or commented on by other states. Certainly the notion that an individual could appeal to an international tribunal regarding his treatment at the hands of his own state was inconceivable.

With human rights, the above changed dramatically. A state's treatment of its own citizens is a legitimate international concern, and can and often does lead to widespread international condemnation. In addition, grieved individuals can and do appeal to international bodies, claiming rights violations by their own (and other) states. None of this is to oversimplify the debates that take place surrounding human rights, or the time and difficulty it takes to ensure that states actually implement

[93] Freeman (n 89) 60.

human rights obligations. The point is that, despite the many political and social challenges, human rights as a legal framework is no less than revolutionary.

The International Human Rights Regime

The international human rights regime has actors similar to that of the international drug control regime. There is an intergovernmental forum for policymaking, the Human Rights Council, which in many ways operates in a manner akin to the Commission on Narcotic Drugs and other international bodies within the UN system and elsewhere. A UN organisation, the Office of the High Commissioner for Human Rights (OHCHR), exists to promote human rights globally, and is governed by the Human Rights Council. Finally, there is a monitoring system established by the individual human rights treaties themselves. In theory, the official treaty monitoring framework is separate from the above UN bodies, but the relevant bodies operate in close synchronisation with relevant actors within the entire regime, including OHCHR and specialised mechanisms of the Human Rights Council (the 'Special Procedures', which shall be examined in this section).

The monitoring system in place for the human rights conventions is in many ways strikingly similar to that of the international drug control conventions. The model is that of an independent committee, made up of experts who are elected by states at the UN Economic and Social Council but perform their functions in an individual capacity, ie without receiving instructions from their or any other state. These committees—called 'treaty bodies' in the human rights field—are provided with secretariat services by the UN Secretary General (in the case of human rights, by OHCHR), and operate in a quasi-judicial manner, sitting several (usually three) times a year and reviewing state performance in implementing their obligations. State parties to the conventions provide data on their implementation on a regular basis, though the nature of the subject matter (as well as the fact that the provisions of the human rights conventions are much broader and more general than the technical ones of the international drug control conventions) means that the bulk of the information tends to be more of a policy-based, general nature than the numerical data that is required by INCB.[94] State parties to the

[94] Human rights treaty bodies do request various statistical data from state parties. See OHCHR, 'Guidelines on the form and content of the reports to be submitted by state parties to the international human rights treaties' (Geneva, UN index HRI/GEN/2/Rev.6, 6 June 2009).

international human rights conventions are required to provide information to the relevant committee on a much less frequent basis than for INCB, eg once every four years for ICCPR. This may also be due to the difference in substance—it can take much longer for new policies in human rights to show results than it does to perform the simple task of tallying stockpiles of particular controlled substances.

One of the most significant differences between the treaty monitoring regimes of human rights and drug control is that each human rights convention has a separate monitoring committee, each with its own members, its own sessions, and its own reporting requirements. Thus, the ICCPR is monitored by the Human Rights Committee (HRC), the ICESCR by the Committee on Economic, Social and Cultural Rights (CESCR), and so on. Relatively recent human rights conventions have also created their own, independent monitoring committees.[95] All of this is in contrast to drug control, where INCB was successively charged with monitoring the 1971 and 1988 Conventions.

The above situation means that, for example, a state party to the ten core conventions must submit a report once every four years on implementation of the ICCPR, every five years on implementation of the ICESCR, every two years on implementation of the ICERD, every four years on implementation of CEDAW, every four years on implementation of CAT, every five years on implementation of CRC, and so on. Understandably, this has resulted in considerable frustration on the part of state parties, many of which complain they are overburdened with a never-ending stream of production of reports, and, many of which concurrently do not submit reports on time. The system is also characterised by long delays in the consideration of state reports, since the increase in state ratification of the conventions has not been accompanied by an increase in frequency or length of the monitoring committee sessions—arguably an impossible task in any case, since most of the treaty body members have other commitments outside of their (unpaid) roles as treaty body members. Some commentators have noted that the system itself relies on delays in states submitting their reports, because it is not logistically feasible for any of the treaty bodies to review the reports in a timely manner.

Many note that the system is unsustainable, and proposals have been made to revamp the system entirely through the creation of a 'super treaty body' that would sit on a full-time basis.[96] Progress with this proposal,

[95] OHCRH, 'The Core International Human Rights Instruments' (n 88).

[96] See eg OHCHR, 'Concept Paper on the High Commissioner's Proposal for a Unified Standing Treaty Body' (Geneva, HRI/MC/2006/CRP.1, 2006); Michael O'Flaherty and Claire O'Brien, 'Reform of UN Human Rights Treaty Monitoring Bodies: A Critique of the Concept Paper on the High Commissioner's Proposal for a Unified Standing Treaty Body' (2007) in 7 *Human Rights Law Review* 1, 141.

however, has been hampered by various political and technical factors, including the significant resource implications and the perceived difficulties in finding highly qualified members able to commit to a full-time position of that nature. In 2009, OHCHR launched an initiative aimed at garnering political support towards 'rationalizing' and 'streamlining' the treaty body machinery, within the parameters of the current system.[97] This initiative led to a resolution by the General Assembly that decided, inter alia, to increase the meeting time of the treaty bodies and to provide for capacity building for states to assist them in treaty reporting. The resolution also establishes a word limit for reports submitted to treaty bodies (and, in turn, for documentation produced by treaty bodies).[98]

Human Rights Treaty Bodies and INCB

The working methods of the human rights treaty bodies are similar to one another, and differ in some important respects to that of the INCB's. As noted above, state parties are required to submit a regular report on the implementation of the convention in question. This report is not to be a dry, bland listing of laws or policies, but an in-depth exploration of the effects of state actions and the actual human rights situation on the ground. As OHCHR puts it:

> both the *de jure* and the *de facto* situation with regard to the implementation of the provisions of the treaties … Reports should not be confined to lists or descriptions of legal instruments adopted in the country concerned in recent years, but should indicate how those legal instruments are reflected in the actual political, economic, social and cultural realities and general conditions existing in the country.[99]

How in-depth the reports actually are naturally depends on the resources of the state, as well as the seriousness with which it approaches the process, but they can be more than 100 pages in length.[100]

After some written exchanges to clarify the information required, the treaty body then invites a delegation of the state for an in-person dialogue during the session. This is an interactive process whereby members of the

[97] OHCHR, 'The High Commissioner's Treaty Body Strengthening Initiative Information Note' (Geneva, 15 March 2012).

[98] UN General Assembly, 'Strengthening and enhancing the effective functioning of the human rights treaty body system' (New York, UN index A/RES/68/268, adopted on 9 April 2014).

[99] OHCHR, 'Guidelines on the form and content of the reports' (n 94) at para 25.

[100] The guidelines issued by OHCHR state that, 'if possible, initial reports should not be longer than 140 pages, and subsequent, periodic reports a maximum of 120 pages': OHCHR (n 94) para 19.

treaty body ask questions of the delegation, which is expected to provide clarifications and any other relevant information. After this dialogue, which typically lasts a full day or more, the treaty body deliberates and adopts its concluding observations on the country's performance. These concluding observations generally contain a significant number of recommendations to the country as to how to better implement its human rights obligations.[101] The treaty body will normally follow up on these recommendations, in particular, at the occasion of the next state report.

The role of NGOs in the treaty body process is a large one, a fact readily and regularly recognised by the treaty bodies themselves.[102] Put diplomatically, state reports are rarely full pictures of the human rights situation in that country, and information is also welcomed from NGOs, many of which submit what are commonly known as 'shadow reports' to the treaty bodies. Indeed, some treaty bodies strongly encourage state parties to draft their reports on the basis of consultation with NGOs[103]—though, unsurprisingly, cases where this actually happens appear to be relatively rare.[104]

Many treaty bodies also have briefing sessions, either formal or informal, with NGOs before the actual review of the state report, where NGOs can once again highlight their key concerns. For example, 'CESCR holds a pre-sessional briefing that is open to NGOs, who can pre-send oral or written submissions. Some of the treaty bodies, such as CAT for example, allow for NGO representatives to brief committee members orally during its formal session.'[105] In the case of other treaty bodies, NGOs can request OHCHR to facilitate informal meetings.[106]

The formal dialogues between treaty bodies and state delegations are open to the public and generally well attended by NGOs and media representatives, and though only treaty body members and the state delegation are allowed to speak, it is submitted that the fact that the dialogue is publicised is an added incentive for states to be responsive to concerns. Indeed, the entire treaty body process is very open, with all documents (including the state report, all exchanges between the state and the treaty body, information submitted by NGOs, and the concluding observations) publicised on the OHCHR website.

[101] It was by no means a given that the treaty bodies would make such recommendations: see eg Torkel Opsahl, 'The Human Rights Committee', in Philip Alston (ed) (n 83).

[102] See eg International Service for Human Rights, 'Simple Guide to the UN Treaty Bodies' (Geneva, 2010) 35.

[103] See eg Committee against Torture, 'Guidelines on the form and content of initial reports under article 19 to be submitted by States parties' (Geneva, UN index CAT/C/4/Rev.3, 2–21 May 2005).

[104] See eg International Service for Human Rights, 'Simple Guide' (n 102) 36.

[105] See eg International Service for Human Rights (n 102) 39.

[106] See eg ibid.

The open and inclusive nature of the treaty body process has certainly been effective in ensuring its utilisation as an advocacy tool for human rights activists worldwide. The spectacle of a state regularly being brought in front of a UN committee of experts and judged on its human rights record arguably energises human rights NGOs, as well as many journalists. In addition, the public process strengthens the sense of accountability for the state party being reviewed—though whether this has translated, or at least has contributed, to actual improvements in state practice is debatable.

These working methods are in stark contrast with those of INCB, which operates in an extremely closed and secretive manner. All INCB sessions are closed, not only to the public (including NGOs), but to governments, and even to UNODC (ie non-INCB secretariat) staff. Documents reviewed and discussed at the sessions are also restricted to members of the INCB and the secretariat. As noted above, governments are occasionally invited to specific segments of INCB sessions, to engage in discussions regarding specific concerns INCB might have—however, this is a rare occurrence, and certainly not every government that is criticised by INCB in its Annual Report or elsewhere is afforded this opportunity.

As might be expected, INCB has been subject to strong criticism by advocates of drug liberalisation, in particular those NGOs part of this network, for these working methods. Criticism is particularly stark with regard to the lack of serious engagement on the part of INCB with NGOs. Barrett and Nowak, for example, argue that:

> The INCB has specifically stated that it will not engage with civil society, and conducts the vast majority of its work behind closed doors … Dealings with governments are strictly private, with relevant information being kept from the public, though tax payers cover their expenses through the UN, and even from other States parties to the Conventions (a practice that appears to be ultra vires the contractual nature of the treaties). Transparency, accountability and participation at the INCB are therefore weak to the point of absence.[107]

Likewise, the International Harm Reduction Association (IHRA) notes that:

> The INCB has chosen secrecy, while the human rights treaty bodies have chosen open engagement. The INCB's choice is becoming an increasing worry for the international community. Rather than working behind closed doors, the INCB should instead learn from the methods used by the human rights treaty bodies to develop a dialogue with civil society.[108]

[107] Barrett and Nowak (n 4) 474.

[108] IHRA, 'Unique in International Relations? A comparison of the International Narcotics Control Board and the UN human rights treaty bodies' (London, 2008) 6.

Some of these NGOs may be used to the open practices of the human rights treaty bodies, and—rightly or wrongly—expect that INCB should follow suit. Of course, human rights treaty bodies also hold some deliberations behind closed doors—to say that everything with human rights treaty bodies is open is a fallacy—but certainly NGOs are justified in pointing out that INCB does not provide adequate information regarding how it reaches its policy decisions, in particular, its evaluations of state policies, and there is little to no opportunity for NGOs to influence this process, like they do with human rights treaty bodies. Displeasure with this secrecy has also been expressed by member states: INCB (like all UN bodies) is funded completely by states, and yet, states are often not given the chance to rebut any criticism before it is made public.[109]

Advocates of drug liberalisation are certainly correct in arguing that transparency is itself important. At the same time, it is worth noting that the criticisms of advocates of drug liberalisation do not truly stem from the fact that the policy formulation process within INCB is opaque; rather, they are unhappy because INCB adopts positions that they are against. Advocates of drug liberalisation criticise INCB for relying almost predominantly on information provided by states, and argue (correctly) that the involvement of civil society is:

> [an] essential check and balance against the information provided by states and against their assertions relating to the implementation of treaty obligations … [C]ivil society organisations and NGOs are important sources of information and advice, as well as a link to affected communities, within many UN agencies and processes.[110]

At the same time, they are critical of INCB for not being responsive to states (mainly Western European ones) that they see to be their allies.

Indeed, there is an interesting dynamic at play in international drug control, whereby some NGOs reiterate and strengthen the concerns of states that share their position on the issues, acting as a representative for these governments. The International Drug Policy Consortium, for example, criticises the INCB for not giving government rebuttals to INCB's position adequate coverage in the Annual Report:

> The balance and tone of the Annual Report could be greatly improved by ensuring that explanations by governments are duly represented. The INCB has to ensure that the outcome of a dialogue with Member States, not just the Board's side of the argument, is genuinely reflected in the Annual Report.[111]

[109] See eg Buechli and Dreifuss (n 52).

[110] IHRA, 'Unique in International Relations?' (n 108) 10.

[111] IDPC, 'The International Narcotics Control Board: Current Tensions and Options for Reform' (London, 2008) 20.

It is extremely difficult to imagine an NGO arguing that a human rights treaty body should ensure that their observations on a state need to be 'balanced' in this manner. It would appear that to advocates of drug liberalisation, it is not so much that INCB does not listen to the positions of states, but rather that they refuse to listen to the 'right kind' of states.

The above notwithstanding, it is difficult to understand why INCB insists on retaining these secretive practices. Certainly there is nothing in the drug control conventions that require this—Article 11(1) of the 1961 Convention merely states that INCB 'shall adopt its own rules of procedures', and it appears that it is only these internal rules that remain the obstacle to greater openness. INCB has made some efforts in recent years, for example through the holding of meetings with NGOs at sidebar sessions during the annual meeting of the CND.[112] INCB has also published a regular newsletter since 2008, though this publication is generally of a promotional nature, and does not give any substantive indication as to the information INCB bases its decisions on. Though the criticisms of INCB by advocates of drug liberalisation on the substance of INCB positions may or may not be misguided, the aforementioned International Drug Policy Consortium report is correct in pointing out that:

> The view that the independence of the Board would be compromised by interactions with governments, other UN agencies and civil society organisations, is ... unfounded and contradicts the general principle that access to sources of information and conversations with all sectors involved enhance integrity and independence.[113]

A more open approach is surely called for.

In addition to their concluding observations on particular countries, human rights treaty bodies also adopt General Comments on particular provisions of their conventions. General Comments interpret legal provisions so as to aid state parties in implementing them, and though, as with Concluding Observations, they are not in and of themselves binding, they provide an authoritative interpretation of the articles and the obligations in the conventions. Besides being used by NGOs and advocates worldwide, General Comments are relied upon heavily by the Treaty Bodies themselves, which cite them in their dialogue with states and recommend consulting them in the formulation of policy. Since they are essentially interpretative guides of particular provisions, General Comments are as

[112] Csete notes that: 'When questioned about the closed nature of the Board at these sessions, INCB officials have repeatedly cited security concerns and the need for confidentiality associated with sensitive drug control measures. Can it be impossible, however, for the INCB to engage with civil society if the Security Council can do so with the delicate and potentially explosive issues that it considers?' Csete (n 58) 67.

[113] IDPC (n 111) 20.

a rule not focused on a particular country: however, many of them are detailed, and do provide guidance for states (and advocates) on whether specific approaches are compatible with that convention—as shall be examined later, the General Comment of the HRC on the death penalty is a case in point.

INCB does not issue General Comments, or similar interpretative guides. As noted above, it does make statements on current policy issues, and from time to time pronounces its positions on whether certain approaches are in compliance with the drug control conventions. However, these positions tend to be extremely short and lack the reasoning behind them, stating merely whether, in the view of INCB, a particular measure is in compliance with the drug control conventions. This is not to say that the positions are necessarily mistaken, but that it is difficult to make any kind of reasoned critique without more elaboration on the part of INCB. For example, the INCB's position on injection rooms (as shall be shown, easily one of the most contentious of its positions) is only a couple of short paragraphs. It has no detailed explanation, save to say that the approach is in contravention of the drug control conventions, making it somewhat difficult to have a reasoned argument with the body regarding the righteousness of their argument.

On the other hand, it is only relatively recently that the General Comments of human rights treaty bodies have become lengthy, detailed pronouncements. For example, the most recent General Comment of the HRC, Number 35 on Article 9 (liberty and security of person), adopted in December 2014 is over 19 pages[114]—but earlier comments are much shorter, and not decidedly longer than the positions of INCB. For example, the aforementioned General Comment on the right to life adopted in 1982, is seven paragraphs, with only two directly related to the death penalty.[115]

For some years, critics of INCB pointed to the lack of trained international lawyers amongst its members as one of the factors behind this reluctance to cite authorities for their arguments.[116] However, this is no longer the case; its membership as of January 2015 includes three members listed as having been trained in law.[117] In any case, it is not entirely clear that

[114] HRC, 'General Comment No. 35: Article 9 (liberty and security of person)' (Geneva, UN index CCPR/CG/35, 16 December 2014).

[115] HRC, 'General Comment No. 6, Article 6 (right to life)' (Geneva, 1982). At tbinternet.ohchr.org/_layouts/treatybodyexternal/Download.aspx?symbolno=INT%2fCCPR%2fGEC%2f6630&Lang=en.

[116] See eg Barrett and Nowak (n 4) 457.

[117] The members with legal training are Marc Moinard, Ahmed Samak, and Werner Sipp. See International Narcotics Control Board, 'INCB Membership', at www.incb.org/incb/en/about/membership.html.

having more legal expertise would lead to a change in either INCB's positions or their working methods, and this conflict between INCB's modus operandi and the demands of NGOs and some governments looks set to continue.

Unlike the drug control conventions, the international human rights conventions make very little provision for ensuring expertise in any particular field, with the text on membership in each convention generally only stating that members must have 'high moral character and recognised competence',[118] or some variation thereof. The ICCPR does state that 'consideration [should be] given to the usefulness of the participation of some persons having legal experience',[119] but, unlike the drug control conventions with regard to medical expertise, there is no specific mechanism to this effect.

As with INCB, the human rights treaty bodies are in theory not UN entities, but committees created by the particular conventions that are provided secretariat services by the UN Secretary General. However, the human rights conventions contain no provisions regarding the independence of their respective Secretaries or Secretariats vis-à-vis the UN, and in practice the treaty bodies operate in a much more synchronised manner with other human rights bodies and with the rest of OHCHR: there is, for example, an annual meeting between the treaty bodies and other human rights mechanisms.[120] Staff and information flow relatively freely between treaty bodies and the rest of OHCHR, to a far greater extent than within the hallways of UNODC. Though INCB frequently includes recommendations to UNODC in its Annual Reports, it would be extremely odd for a human rights treaty body to issue a formal recommendation to OHCHR. The issues in the field of human rights are at least as politicised as in drug control, yet there is no information to suggest that this closer working relationship has resulted in any obstacles for either OHCHR or the treaty bodies. The importance of maintaining such an 'arms length' distance between the bodies responsible for drug control seems somewhat questionable.

The human rights conventions contain no enforcement provisions similar to that of Articles 14/19 of the 1961/71 Conventions. This is wholly unsurprising—indeed, it is the far-reaching powers bestowed upon INCB (as of yet unused by that body) that are highly unusual in international law.[121] The tools the human rights treaty bodies have to influence

[118] ICCPR Article 28(2).

[119] Ibid.

[120] International Service for Human Rights (n 102) 47.

[121] In response to criticism from journalists at a press conference in 2007, the Secretary of INCB once made the statement that that INCB was 'unique in international relations'. Unsurprisingly, this comment became the subject of considerable scorn at the hands of advocates

state behaviour are limited to their persuasive authority and their ability to express public concern—often known in the human rights field as 'naming and shaming'. This is common to all UN human rights bodies, and in many ways the lack of the ability to force countries to protect human rights is a recurring theme throughout the decades of the human rights movement.

Charter-Based Bodies—The Human Rights Council

The main policy-making body in human rights is the Human Rights Council, which meets in Geneva three times a year. The Human Rights Council is made up of 47 member states who are elected for a three-year term, though all UN member states are invited to the Council and can speak at its meetings. The Human Rights Council was created in 2006 as a successor to the Commission on Human Rights, which was abolished with the Council's creation. Though the General Assembly resolution creating the Council (and abolishing the Commission) does not specify this, it is widely understood that one of the main impetuses behind abolishing the Commission was that it had become highly politicised and dysfunctional.[122] Whether the Council is significantly better in those respects is highly questionable, but changing a commission into a council is in effect a promotion within the UN system.

Establishment of the Council also brought with it the Universal Periodic Review, a new peer review procedure for the review of states' human rights performance. Since it is a review of state practice by other states, there is always the potential for the 'glass house' effect, and the Universal Periodic Review came into being amidst a high level of skepticism. Nevertheless, it has proved more effective at highlighting human rights concerns than many had thought, not least because all UN member states are subject to the procedure, not just those party to particular conventions.[123]

The Council also inherited procedures from its predecessor, the most relevant for this study being what are usually referred to in human rights

of drug liberalisation. See eg IHRA (n 108) 11. Nevertheless, though this statement would seem to be questionable on its face, there is a case to be made that the significant enforcement powers granted to INCB under Articles 14 and 19 of the 1961 and 1971 Conventions respectively are in fact unique.

[122] For a general discussion of the creation of the Human Rights Council, see eg Rosa Freedman, *The United Nations Human Rights Council: a Critique and Early Assessment* (London, Routledge, 2013).

[123] See eg Emma Hickey, 'The UN's Universal Periodic Review: Is it Adding Value and Improving the Human Rights Situation on the Ground?' (2013) 7 Vienna Journal of International Constitutional Law 4, 1.

as the Special Procedures. The Special Procedures is a mechanism by which the Council (and the Commission before it) retains independent expertise to report to the Council on a particular human rights issue (or a country situation) on a regular basis, normally annually. According to OHCHR, as of March 2015 there were 41 thematic and 14 country mandates.[124] Special Procedures mandate holders are independent experts that are appointed for this purpose—like members of treaty bodies and of INCB, they are appointed for their expertise in the issue and do not represent their or any other state. Unlike treaty body and INCB members, however, Special Procedure mandate holders are not elected through a political process—there is an open application process, with candidates assessed and chosen by the Bureau of the Council. Though there are some notable exceptions, for example the Working Group on Arbitrary Detention, Special Procedures mandates are generally that of a lone Special Rapporteur—an independent expert on a particular theme or country. Though individual Special Rapporteurs have terms, eg three years, the mandates themselves tend to continue, leading to the appointment of successive Special Rapporteurs.

Being independent experts, Special Rapporteurs have wide ranging latitude in the performance of their functions. Treaty bodies in principle exist mainly to respond to the state reports and to the information they receive from NGOs, giving them an inherently reactive character. Special Rapporteurs, on the other hand, are able to shape the contours of their work with much more liberty, and can choose the topics they wish to focus on in their reports with considerable freedom. Special Rapporteurs do engage in a semblance of mutual co-ordination, with a Co-ordination Commission established for this purpose, and the OHCHR staff assigned as assistants to each Special Rapporteur attempt to ensure continuity.[125] Nevertheless, Special Rapporteurs can and do choose their own issues and their own approaches, and it is not uncommon for them to insist on personally preparing the text of their reports (as opposed to allowing the civil servants of OHCHR to do the bulk of the work).

The reports of Special Rapporteurs are submitted to the Council, which as a rule adopts them through a resolution. The reports, and the recommendations to particular countries contained therein, are not legal standards as such, and are clearly not binding in and of themselves. The fact that the Council adopts a particular report would seem to suggest that it supports the recommendations of the Special Rapporteur, and this would seem to mean that states should give the same attention to them

[124] OHCHR, 'Special Procedures of the Human Rights Council', at www.ohchr.org/EN/HRBodies/SP/Pages/Welcomepage.aspx.

[125] For a general discussion of co-ordination amongst Special Procedures, see eg Marc Limon and Ted Piccone, 'Human Rights Special Procedures: Determinations of Influence' (Washington, Brookings, 2014).

as it would be expected to do with any other resolution of the Council. However, the standard formulation of this type of resolution merely 'welcomes' the report of the Special Rapporteur, and '[u]rges all Governments to cooperate fully with the Special Rapporteur and to respond favourably to his requests to visit their countries and to provide him with all necessary information to enable him to fulfill his mandate even more effectively'[126]—not necessarily a resounding show of support for the recommendations themselves.

That neither the reports of the Special Procedures nor the recommendations contained therein are definitive statements of international law is recognised first and foremost by the Special Rapporteurs themselves. For example, Juan Mendez, the current Special Rapporteur on Torture and other Cruel, Inhuman or Degrading Treatment of Punishment (Special Rapporteur on Torture), has stated that:

> … reports from mandate-holders like me are not submitted for adoption by the Council but only for a free and open discussion … The nature of these thematic reports is of a vehicle to generate a discussion among States and interested civil society on standards that the mandate believes are necessary to cover issues and practices for which the existing normative framework is ambiguous or unclear. My thematic reports are not meant to be read as the ultimate word on the international law governing the issues I choose to deal with, but rather to initiate a discussion about what international law should provide for regarding those matters.[127]

Of course, the reports of Special Procedures mandate holders are not meaningless. They are reports prepared by an expert in the field commissioned by the Council, so they carry authoritative weight, and the reports are cited by human rights advocates worldwide. Nevertheless, as with the views of the human rights treaty bodies, they are not binding in and of themselves.

Finally, the Council is the governing body of OHCHR, the UN agency responsible for human rights issues. Like UNODC, OHCHR is an organisation of the UN secretariat and, therefore, has limited budgetary freedom. However, it receives 40 percent of its funding from the regular UN budget,[128] meaning that it has considerably more ability to resist political pressure than UNODC. Of the remaining 60 percent of OHCHR's budget in 2014, 47 percent was earmarked for specific

[126] See eg HRC, 'Freedom of religion or belief' (Geneva, UN index A/HRC/25/L.19, 21 March 2014) para 14.

[127] Juan Mendez, 'Letter to Dr Jeffrey Lieberman, President American Psychiatric Association; Dr Pedro Ruiz, President World Psychiatric Association; and Dr Saul Levin, CEO/Medical Director American Psychiatric Association' (Geneva, 22 January 2014) 1.

[128] OHCHR, *Annual Report 2014* (Geneva, 2015) 62.

purposes[129]—a significantly smaller proportion than UNODC, again allowing OHCHR more independence. Of course, being UN agencies governed by states means that neither OHCHR nor UNODC can ever be completely free from state influence, and, as with civil services everywhere, senior staff of both organisations must often walk a fine line between the principles of the organisation they serve and the demands of their political masters of the time.

The Office of the High Commissioner on Human Rights (OHCHR)

OHCHR was silent on the issue of human rights and drugs until Navanethem Pillay, the High Commissioner at the time, made a statement in 2009, on the occasion of the international review of progress made since the 1998 UNGASS (see below). In her statement, Pillay seemed to repeat the arguments of advocates of drug liberalisation, stating that:

> Too often, drug users suffer discrimination, are forced to accept treatment, marginalized and often harmed by approaches which over-emphasize criminalization and punishment while under-emphasizing harm reduction and respect for human rights. This is despite the longstanding evidence that a harm reduction approach is the most effective way of protecting rights, limiting personal suffering, and reducing the incidence of HIV.[130]

Going on to suggest that the current international drug control regime was out of date, Pillay then stated that:

> It is too late for us to return to earlier, outdated approaches to drug use. We cannot deny that those suffering from addiction require medical care. We must opt for treatment that is evidence-based, and be responsive to the views of those in need of treatment. We must do our utmost to reduce harm to individuals related to drug use, including exposure to HIV. We must ensure at all times that every individual's inalienable rights are respected, protected and fulfilled.[131]

Though not calling directly for an end to the drug control regime, the High Commissioner appeared to agree with some of the main tenets of the advocates of drug liberalisation: the current drug control regime is out of date and must be shifted to one centering on harm reduction, and persons who abuse drugs are at risk of being 'marginalised'. These arguments (harm reduction and persons who abuse drugs as a marginalised or vulnerable group) shall be examined later in this study.

[129] Ibid.
[130] OHCHR, 'High Commissioner calls for focus on human rights and harm reduction in international drug policy' (Geneva, 2009).
[131] Ibid.

Since the 2009 statement, OHCHR, and in particular Pillay, have made several statements suggesting broad agreement with the advocates of drug liberalisation on several points. At a side event of the Human Rights Council in June 2014, the High Commissioner stated that she:

> [has] advocated on several occasions for human rights to be taken into account in international drug control policy … [H]uman rights violations continue to occur in the context of States' implementation of drug control policies … I urge all States to reconsider from a human rights perspective the decades-old approach to drug control based on repression.[132]

She encouraged states to consider decriminalisation:

> A number of States no longer incarcerate persons for minor drug offences, and some have decriminalised minor drug offences. It is also possible, and consistent with current international drug control treaties, to re-frame some drug-related conduct as administrative offences, followed with a social and medical response.[133]

This characterisation of the provisions of the drug control conventions is, as shall be examined in this study, correct, and the human rights violations she raises in her statement are certainly within the parameters of her mandate. Nevertheless, it is submitted that the general framing of drug control as 'repressive' and 'outdated', which is along the lines of the arguments of the advocates of drug liberalisation, is problematic and unfortunate.

Of course, it is not at all surprising that the UN human rights agency would be influenced by the human rights arguments of the advocates of drug liberalisation. As already noted, these advocates include prominent human rights organisations, such as Human Rights Watch (HRW), who engage in a wide range of policy-related discussions with OHCHR on a regular basis. Many individuals in the human rights field, as in other fields, will have studied for their advanced degrees in the same university (sometimes together), and it is not uncommon for persons to move between positions at different organisations (including OHCHR). Other organisations may not be as personally familiar with OHCHR, but nevertheless have mastered the human rights framework to the extent that they speak the 'same language' as staff in that organisation, leading to the same sense of familiarity and collegiality.

Therefore, the fact that OHCHR has advanced—or been pulled—in the same direction as advocates of drug liberalisation follows a general pattern in the field of human rights. Nevertheless, it is submitted that it is somewhat disappointing that the UN organisation dedicated to the protection of human rights would not take greater care in examining what

132 OHCHR, 'Side event: World Drug Problem on Human Rights' (Geneva, 16 June 2014) 1.

133 OHCHR, 'Side event' (n 132) 2.

may look at first glance to be human rights arguments, but at their core have little relevance to the High Commissioner.

At the March 2015 session, the Human Rights Council adopted a resolution requesting OHCHR to prepare a study on the 'impact of the world drug problem on the enjoyment of human rights, and recommendations on respect for and the protection and promotion of human rights in the context of the world drug problem, with particular consideration for the needs of persons affected and persons in vulnerable situations'.[134] Though the language of the resolution itself is neutral in its description of the international drug control regime, that the resolution was adopted is clearly significant, and is arguably another indicator of the inroads that advocates of drug liberalisation have made into international human rights fora.

Nevertheless, the resulting report by OHCHR is relatively tame. It does recommend that states give '[c]onsideration … to removing obstacles to the right to health, including by decriminalizing the personal use and possession of drugs; moreover, public health programmes should be increased',[135] suggesting agreement with the position of advocates of drug liberalisation that criminalisation hampers a person's access to harm reduction programmes. However, by and large, the report avoids the kind of sweeping mischaracterisations that are a feature of statements by advocates of drug liberalisation, and does not state that drug control inevitably leads to human rights abuses. Rather, the report limits itself mainly to a listing of the violations that commonly take place in connection with enforcement of drug control laws, without tying those to the drug control regime itself (with the exception of the issue of indigenous rights, see below on Bolivia). Whether this is a new approach adopted by the recently appointed High Commissioner remains to be seen,[136] but it is submitted that it is encouraging to see OHCHR adhere more strictly to its mandate.

III. ARTICLE 33 OF THE CONVENTION ON THE RIGHTS OF THE CHILD

Like most bodies of international law, international human rights law and international drug control law have developed largely in isolation from

[134] HRC, 'Contribution of the Human Rights Council to the special session of the General Assembly on the world drug problem of 2016', Geneva, UN index A/HRC/28/L.22, 23 March 2015) para 1.

[135] OHCHR, 'Study on the impact of the world drug problem on the enjoyment of human rights' (Geneva, UN index A/HRC/30/65, 4 September 2015) para 61.

[136] Zeid Ra'ad Al Hussein was appointed as High Commissioner in June 2014, to replace Pillay. See OHCHR, 'High Commissioner', at www.ohchr.org/EN/AboutUs/Pages/HighCommissioner.aspx.

each other. However, Article 33 of the Convention on the Rights of the Child (CRC) is a notable, and important, exception.

Whereas most other human rights conventions before CRC tended to focus predominantly on either civil and political rights or economic, social, and cultural rights—and most usually the former category—CRC stipulates obligations under both categories.[137] For example, CRC contains provisions on freedom of expression (Article 13), freedom of association (Article 15), and juvenile justice (Article 40), while also stipulating the child's right to education (Article 28), an adequate standard of living (Article 27), and social security (Article 26). This omnibus quality, alongside with the fact that it is the most ratified convention in all of international law—only the US has yet to become state party[138]—makes it an oft cited example by advocates of the universality and indivisible nature of human rights. The rights are not divided into categories within the CRC, but, to aid states in reporting, the Committee on the Rights of the Child (Committee), the treaty body charged with monitoring application of the convention, has divided the articles into 'clusters', to '[reflect] the Convention's holistic perspective of children's rights: that they are indivisible and interrelated, and that equal importance should be attached to each and every right'.[139]

CRC was adopted in 1989, which is worthy of note since it was being prepared at the same time as the 1988 Convention. CRC Article 33, which is included in the 'special protection measures' cluster under 'children under situations of exploitation',[140] states:

> States Parties shall take all appropriate measures, including legislative, administrative, social and educational measures, to protect children from the illicit use of narcotic drugs and psychotropic substances as defined in the relevant international treaties and to prevent the use of children in the illicit production and trafficking of such substances.

This is not only a clear reference to the international drug control conventions, but an unambiguous reaffirmation of states' obligations in drug control. Indeed, the official *Legislative History of the Convention on the Rights of Children* notes that the two committees that were drafting the CRC and the 1988 Convention respectively were in contact on this article, and the text was finalised on the basis of suggestions from the UN Narcotics Drugs Division,

[137] The Convention on the Elimination of All Forms of Discrimination against Women (CEDAW), adopted in 1979, also contains provisions on both 'categories' of rights. However, it is not as comprehensive as the CRC.

[138] The US has signed the convention. See OHCHR, 'Status of Ratification', at http://indicators.ohchr.org, viewed 2 September 2015.

[139] CRC, 'General Guidelines for Periodic Reports' (Geneva, UN index CRC/C/58 20 November 1996) para 9.

[140] Ibid para155.

the predecessor of UNODC.[141] It is also worth noting that Article 33 draws from the preamble of the 1988 Convention, which expresses:

> ... [deep concern] ... particularly by the fact that children are used in many parts of the world as an illicit drug consumers market and for purposes of illicit production, distribution, and trade in narcotic drugs and psychotropic substances, which entails a danger of incalculable gravity.[142]

Article 33 is, understandably, the focus of much more attention by those who, with this author, argue that there is no conflict between human rights and drug control. Ghodse, the President of INCB at the time, referred to Article 33 in his address to the CND in 2009, where he noted that:

> ... the exercise of the individuals' rights and freedoms does not include the right to abuse drugs. Drug abuse is neither harmless nor victimless and causes serious damage to both individuals and society ... Children deserve special protection from drug abuse and from being involved in the production and distribution of drugs, as outlined in article 33 of the Convention on the Rights of the Child. This treaty obligation should be respected at all times.[143]

Raymond Yans, who succeeded Ghodse as President, reiterated this in his Foreword to the Annual report 2013, stating that:

> Drug abuse causes a disproportionate amount of harm to those most vulnerable: children, whose right to be protected from drug abuse is enshrined in the Convention on the Rights of the Child. Prenatal exposure to drugs can cause emotional, psychological and physical disorders, and even death ... Children exposed to drugs—whether through actual consumption or by living in an environment of drug abuse—may be exposed to a higher risk of physical and sexual abuse and are more likely to suffer anxiety and depression, have educational and attention problems, commit delinquent acts and become involved in crime and drug abuse. Urgent action must be taken to protect society's most precious resource—its children—from drug abuse and its effects.[144]

Dahlgren and Stere argue that Article 33 not only requires a firm stance against drugs with regard to children, ie restrictions to ensure that children are directly protected from drugs, but also that, given the effects on children brought about by drug abuse by adults in their community, Article 33 requires a strict approach against drug abuse in general. Though the Committee has not issued any General Comment on Article 33, it has issued

[141] OHCHR, *Legislative History of the Convention of the Rights of the Child*, Volume II (Geneva, UN index HR/PUB/07/1, 2007) 709711.

[142] 1988 Convention, Preamble para. 2.

[143] Ghodse (n 61) 3.

[144] INCB, *Annual Report 2013* (Vienna, 2014) at iv. Though not citing Article 33 directly, INCB also referred to its substance in its press release on the 2011 Annual Report. INCB, 'Youth have a right to be protected from drug abuse and dependence' (Vienna, 28 February 2012).

one on Article 19, on the right of the child to be free form any form of violence. Article 19 contains similar language[145] to Article 33, and Dahlgren and Stere note that the General Comment on that Article, therefore, provides guidance on some of the terms. This includes the language 'shall take all appropriate measures, including legislative, administrative, social and educational measures', on which the Committee states in its General Comment:

> 'Shall take' is a term which leaves no leeway for the discretion of States parties. Accordingly, States parties are under strict obligation to undertake 'all appropriate measures' to fully implement this right for all children … 'Appropriate' cannot be interpreted to mean acceptance of some forms of violence.[146]

Dahlgern and Stere argue that:

> … in the context of Article 33 'appropriate' would refer to a … multi-sectoral set of measures which would prevent and protect children from illicit drug use … and cannot be interpreted to mean the normalisation or acceptance of such phenomena … We conclude that the matter of illicit drugs is a protection measure which States Parties must take as seriously as any other special protection matter … Hence, the full implementation of the UN drug conventions is indispensable for prevention and the creation of a protective environment against illicit drugs.[147]

This would be the normal reading of Article 33. Unsurprisingly, advocates of drug liberalisation oppose this interpretation. Barrett and Veermann launch a somewhat convoluted and unconvincing argument, stating:

> The CRC Committee has [stated] … that '[a]ppropriate' *cannot* be interpreted to mean acceptance of some forms of violence [emphasis in original]. Does the same finding apply to article 33? Certainly on the use of children in the drug trade (as a form of exploitation), but what about drug use among children and young people? While the wording is the same in each article (all appropriate measures … to protect the child from …), they relate to qualitatively different issues. One relates to violence inflicted upon children, the other to behaviours among them, and a category, for some, of vulnerability. The context is important.

[145] Article 19(1) states: 'States Parties shall take all appropriate legislative, administrative, social and educational measures to protect the child from all forms of physical or mental violence, injury or abuse, neglect or negligent treatment, maltreatment or exploitation, including sexual abuse, while in the care of parent(s), legal guardian(s) or any other person who has the care of the child.'

[146] Committee on the Rights of the Child, 'General comment No. 13 (2011), The right of the child to freedom from all forms of violence' (Geneva, UN index CRC/C/GC/13, 18 April 2011) paras 37, 38.

[147] Stephan Dahlgren and Roxana Stere, *The Protection of Children from Illicit Drugs—a Minimum Human Rights Standard: a Child Centred vs a User Centred Drug Policy* (Stockholm, Fri Foerlag in co-operation with World Federation against Drugs, the Swedish Society for Sobriety and Social Upbringing and the Swedish Carnegie Institute, 2012) 19, 20, 22.

> That drug use among children is not to be accepted is clear from the wording. But what does this mean in practice? What if a lack of acceptance translates into stigma and social marginalisation, as seen in relation to people who use drugs [in] many parts of the world?'[148]

They then go on to assert, without providing any justification:

> … appropriate measures must take into account other provisions more conducive to the realisation of the rights of the child … This, in turn … raises the question of the role of the international drug conventions and whether these are conducive to the realisation of the rights of the child.[149]

Barrett and Veermann go on to argue that recreational drug abuse by children is in fact not a cause for concern:

> Many drugs now used by children and young people did not exist in 1989. Far fewer children and young people were using drugs. The internet, when CRC was adopted, was still an experiment. Today, 'legal highs' are widely available for purchase online. Today's world for children is very different in myriad ways. Our reading of article 33 and our consideration of 'appropriate measures' must be able to take this into account.[150] … Labeling of a child as a 'drug user' can have negative impacts on education and psychological wellbeing while drug tests fail to distinguish between recreational drug use (which would not require treatment intervention) and problematic use or dependence.[151]

Essentially, the intent appears to be to ignore the connection between Article 33 and the international drug control conventions, and to define 'appropriate measures' out of existence.

Barrett and Veerman also criticise the aforementioned address of the INCB President, stating:

> While the INCB's formulation of article 33 was not a problem, the way in which it was used was questionable … The INCB's use of article 33 was to defend against any claims of a 'right to use drugs', a rather inaccurate, simplistic caricature of these concerns, and an apparent assertion that article 33 blandly supports the status quo and justifies these restrictions on other fundamental rights. Like the [CND], the INCB has also equated article 33 with efforts to prevent drug use—a somewhat trite position that fails to do justice to the full potential of the article.[152]

There is no indication as to what exactly Barrett and Veerman believe the 'potential' of Article 33 to be, and there is no elaboration as to why exactly the argument of Ghodse against any 'right to abuse drugs' is indeed 'inaccurate and simplistic'.

148 Barrett and Veerman, *A Commentary on the United Nations Convention on the Rights of the Child* (n 62) 38, 39.
149 Barrett and Veerman (n 62) 39.
150 Barrett and Veerman (n 62) 44.
151 Barrett and Veerman (n 62) 50.
152 Barrett and Veerman (n 62) 10, 11.

The Committee has examined drug control issues on numerous occasions in its review of state reports, though generally not in great detail. Often the Committee merely reiterates Article 33, together with an expression of concern regarding the phenomenon of drug abuse in the country under review.[153] A notable exception was when it reviewed the country report of Ukraine in 2011. The Committee stated its deep concern at:

> … the increasing practice of drug injection among children … It is deeply concerned at the lack of specialized youth-friendly services aimed at treatment and rehabilitation for these at-risk children, and that legal and attitudinal barriers impede access to such services … The Committee is also concerned that the State party's drug strategy 2010–015 fails to take these issues sufficiently into account and that new regulations relating to personal possession of drugs may bring more at-risk adolescents into contact with the criminal justice system … [T]he State Party should … [e]nsure that criminal laws do not impede access to such services, including by amending laws that criminalize children for possession or use of drugs.'[154]

This would appear to indicate that the Committee's position is for a regime based on decriminalisation, though there has been no consistency in recommending this before or after this review of Ukraine.

In any case, even advocates of drug liberalisation admit that the Committee's pronouncements on drug issues have been uneven, with the topic not featuring in most reviews of state reports. Barrett and Veerman note with some disappointment that:

> Aside from notable exceptions … the Committee's Concluding Observations on drug use have often been very general, sometimes no more than a restatement of article 33 itself, a call to 'combat' drug abuse, or an expression of the Committee's concern about the high number of children who consume drugs in the State Party, followed by a recommendation of a general nature. There has been a lack of focus on recreational drug use, with concerns and recommendations relating mainly to problematic drug use, injecting, and drug dependence.[155]

It is unclear why the attention given by the Committee to issues surrounding Article 33 has been uneven—as noted above, human rights treaty bodies do discuss positional issues behind closed doors, much like INCB does, and it is impossible to know if Article 33 has been the subject of any internal debate. In any case, however, the somewhat creative

[153] See eg CRC, 'Concluding Observations on Grenada' (Geneva, UN index CRC/C/15/Add.121, 28 February 2000) para 27; 'Concluding Observations on South Africa' (Geneva, UN index CRC/C/15/Add.122, 22 February 2000) para 38.

[154] CRC, 'Concluding Observations on Ukraine' (Geneva, UN index CRC/C/UKR/CO/3-4, 21 April 2011) paras 60, 61.

[155] Barrett and Veerman (n 62) 35.

reading of Barrett and Veerman aside, the language of Article 33 appears to be clear in its linkage with the international drug control conventions, and in its general presentation of drug abuse as something extremely harmful that children should be protected from. This being the case, the argument of Barrett and Veerman that Article 33 somehow has 'potential' to justify a right of children to engage in what they term as 'recreational drug use' seems highly questionable. Indeed, Article 33 on its own would appear to disprove the general contention of advocates of drug liberalisation that international human rights law and international drug control law are in conflict.

3

UNGASS and Developments in Latin America

OUTSIDE OF THE specific legal frameworks of human rights and drug control, the UN has examined drug control within the framework of special sessions of the General Assembly, commonly known as UNGASS (UN General Assembly Special Sessions). A Special Session on drug control will be held in March 2016, and there is expected to be heated, if not even acrimonious debate, on some of the issue outlined in this study, in particular whether the current international drug control regime is cognizant of human rights.

Besides UNGASS, there have been particularly important developments in Latin America, which will be examined in this chapter.

I. UNGASS

The UN General Assembly can hold special sessions on particular issues, with a view towards garnering international attention on a particular global issue of concern. These Special Sessions generally result in the adoption of a declaration and an international plan of action. As with all resolutions of the General Assembly, those are not binding on states; nevertheless, they are an expression of international consensus, and provide at least authoritative guidance for states on the issues elaborated in them.

The General Assembly has held Special Sessions on drug abuse in 1990, on the 'World Drug Problem' in 1998, and will hold a third in 2016. To hold a third special session on essentially the same issue is highly unusual, though not unprecedented,[1] and arguably is indicative of the lack of significant progress—though to suggest, as advocates of drug liberalisation tend to do, that there has been no discernable progress whatsoever

[1] The General Assembly has held three sessions on the question of disarmament, in 1978, 1982, and 1988, and two on Palestine, in 1947 and 1948. See eg UN, 'Special Sessions of the General Assembly', at www.un.org/en/ga/sessions/special.shtml.

against drug abuse and trafficking would be incorrect. UNODC noted in 2008:

> Major successes were registered in reducing the area under coca cultivation, for instance, in Peru and Bolivia in the 1990s, and in Colombia after 2000. Morocco reduced its cannabis resin production significantly from 2003–2005. Major successes were also achieved in South-East Asia, notably by Myanmar and the Lao PDR, in reducing opium production, following the achievements made by Thailand over the previous three decades, although these successes were dwarfed by opium production in Afghanistan.[2]

Advocates of drug liberalisation, naturally, see things differently. Jelsma states regarding the review in 2009:

> One could hardly ignore the elephant in the room: that none of those targets were being met. In fact, it was difficult to develop a credible discourse that any progress had been achieved at all. Nonetheless, acknowledging failure was a politically unacceptable admission for most governments.[3]

Progress or no, the UNGASS sessions have clearly stressed the need to combat drug abuse and trafficking. The 1998 UNGASS Political Declaration starts by noting that:

> Drugs destroy lives and communities, undermine sustainable human development and generate crime … Drugs are a grave threat to the health and well-being of all mankind, the independence of States, democracy, the stability of nations, the structure of all societies, and the dignity and hope of millions of people and their families; therefore: We, the States Members of the United Nations …. Reaffirm our unwavering determination and commitment to overcoming the world drug problem through domestic and international strategies to reduce both the illicit supply of and demand for drugs.[4]

The 1998 Special Session was particularly significant in that it highlighted the importance of demand reduction, with the adoption of the Declaration on the Guiding Principles of Drug Demand Reduction. In outlining the Guiding Principles, the Declaration states that they must be viewed 'in accordance with the principles of the Charter of the United Nations and international law, in particular … human rights and fundamental freedoms and the principles of the Universal Declaration of Human Rights'.[5] There is also a reference to CRC Article 33 as one of several 'Supplementary

[2] UNODC, 'UNGASS: Ten years On' (Vienna, 2008) 2.

[3] Martin Jelsma, 'UNGASS 2016: Prospects for Treaty Reform and UN System-Wide Coherence on Drug Policy' (Washington, Brooking Institution, 2015) 10.

[4] Special Session of the General Assembly Devoted to Countering the World Drug Problem Together 8–10 June 1998, 'Political Declaration' (New York, June 1998), preamble para 1.

[5] Special Session of the General Assembly Devoted to Countering the World Drug Problem Together 8–10 June 1998, 'Declaration on the Guiding Principles of Demand Reduction' (New York, 1998) para. 8.

Reference Material for Governments Considering National Drug Control Strategies'.[6] In a somewhat veiled reference to 'harm reduction', the Declaration states that demand reduction policies should '[a]im at preventing the use of drugs and at reducing the adverse consequences of drug abuse'. The contentious issue of 'harm reduction' shall be examined below.

On the occasion of the hundred year anniversary of the Shanghai Conference, in 2009, a high-level segment of the Commission on Narcotic Drugs examined progress with the 1998 plan of action. At this segment, the Executive Director of UNODC stated that while the drug problem had certainly not been eradicated, international efforts had been successful at containing the phenomenon. Making reference to advocates of drug liberalisation as wishing to 'throw the baby out with the bathwater', he stated that:

> Drugs are not harmful because they are controlled—they are controlled because they are harmful. The fact that certain unlawful transactions are hard to control doesn't mean that they should be made legal. Should humanity accept pedophilia, human trafficking, or arms smuggling out of a naïve sense of market inevitability or intractability? Lifting the controls on drugs would reveal a state's impotence to fight organized crime or protect the health of its citizens ... We should invest in the solid middle ground between: (a) criminalization of drug users and (b) legalization of its use, by framing our collective efforts against drugs less like a war, and more like an effort to cure a social disease.[7]

There was significant controversy at the 2009 meeting, with a group of 24 European countries, Bolivia, and Saint Lucia making an interpretative statement to the effect that 'harm reduction' measures had been endorsed by the 1998 Political Declaration and Plan of Action. Countries traditionally against drug liberalisation, such as the United States, Japan, and Russia, objected to the statement.[8] In the end, the segment adopted the 'Political Declaration and Plan of Action on International Cooperation towards an Integrated and Balanced Strategy to Counter the World Drug Problem'. Advocates of drug liberalisation deride this new Declaration as only setting more targets that are, in their eyes, unrealistic and undesirable.[9]

[6] Ibid Appendix para 3.

[7] UNODC, 'Political Declaration and Plan of Action on International Cooperation towards an Integrated and Balanced Strategy to Counter the World Drug Problem, High-level Segment, Commission on Narcotic Drugs, Vienna, 11–12 March 2009' (Vienna, 2009) 3.

[8] Commission on Narcotic Drugs, 'Report on the Fifty-Second Session' (Vienna, UN index, E/CN.7/2009/12, March 2009) paras 157–63.

[9] Jelsma states that there was 'no call to alter the basic course of action and yet once again [set] another 10-year target, now for 2019, "to eliminate or reduce significantly and measurably" the illicit drugs market.' (n 3) 13.

As might be expected, and, as with the previous UNGASS sessions, advocates of drug liberalisation have been making great efforts towards advancing their agenda on the occasion of the 2016 Special Session. The Open Society Foundation (OSF), for example, states somewhat dramatically:

> Never before have so many governments voiced displeasure with the international drug control regime … For the first time, there is significant dissent at the local, national, and international levels. UNGASS 2016 is an unparalleled opportunity to put an end to the horrors of the drug war and instead prioritise health, human rights, and safety … In advance of UNGASS, our partners are working with civil society groups and governments to promote real debate on drug law reform. This work includes coordinating meetings between governments and grassroots organizations, publishing reports on priorities for international debate, organizing days of action to draw attention to the damages of the drug war, and holding events that will engage policymakers.[10]

Nevertheless, even some of the most staunch advocates of drug liberalisation have admitted that there is little prospect of success, at least radical success. Jelsma of the Transnational Institute notes that:

> Present divides in global drug policy preclude any significant progress on a new UNGASS political declaration through consensus-driven negotiations. Controversial issues like cannabis regulation and treaty reform are unlikely to appear prominently on the UNGASS 2016 agenda … A concerted effort is being made to keep the contentious treaty revision issue off the UNGASS 2016 agenda and to preserve the façade of the global consensus … Except for the small minority of daring dissenters … avoiding any debate on the conventions is politically convenient for most countries.[11]

What exactly will come out of the third UNGASS remains to be seen, and it is submitted that, given the current political climate, there is a real possibility that the debate could be overshadowed by other issues.

II. LATIN AMERICA: REGIONAL DEVELOPMENTS

Besides UNGASS, there have been important developments at the regional and international level related to drug control and human rights in Latin America. Over recent years, several prominent figures in the region, including sitting and former Presidents, have emerged as prominent

[10] OSF, 'Explainers: What Is UNGASS 2016?', at www.opensocietyfoundations.org/explainers/what-ungass-2016.
[11] Jelsma (n 3) 1, 17.

proponents of drug liberalisation. One example is Otto Perez Molina, the current President of Guatemala, who has written that:

> ... the prohibition paradigm that inspires mainstream global drug policy today is based on a false premise: that the global drug markets can be eradicated. We would not believe such a statement if it were applied to alcoholism or tobacco addiction, but somehow we assume it's right in the case of drugs. Why? ... To suggest liberalisation—allowing consumption, production and trafficking of drugs without any restriction whatsoever—would be, in my opinion, profoundly irresponsible ... Our proposal, as the Guatemalan government, is to abandon any ideological position (whether prohibition or liberalisation) and to foster a global intergovernmental dialogue based on a realistic approach—drug regulation. Drug consumption, production and trafficking should be subject to global regulations, which means that consumption and production should be legalised but within certain limits and conditions.[12]

Human rights have not necessarily been at the forefront of these arguments, but it has often been cited as one of the reasons the current regime should be revised, and many of these prominent individuals have worked together with NGOs and other advocates of drug liberalisation—for example, through participation in the Global Commission on Drug Policy (GCDP). As with other advocates of drug liberalisation, the international drug control regime is portrayed with negative generalisations such as 'prohibitionist'[13] and 'repressive',[14] with little explanation of what these terms actually mean. Policies of decriminalisation and harm reduction, on the other hand, are 'evidence based', 'humane', and also, so the proponents argue, cognizant of human rights.

A prominent vehicle for such arguments in Latin America was the Latin American Commission on Drugs and Democracy, a group comprising of prominent intellectuals and high ranking politicians. Three former Presidents co-chaired the Commission: Fernando Henrique Cardoso (Brazil), César Gaviria (Colombia) and Ernesto Zedillo (Mexico). The Commission, which was funded partially by the OSF,[15] was the subject of considerable media attention,[16] partially because it seemed to indicate an increasing willingness of historically somewhat subservient Latin American countries to stand up to the United States, at least in the area of drug policy. Nevertheless, while there may have been political significance in the

[12] Otto Perez Molina, 'We have to find new solutions to Latin America's drugs nightmare', The Guardian, 7 April 2012.

[13] Latin American Commission on Drugs and Democracy, 'Drugs and Democracy: toward a paradigm shift', 2009, 5.

[14] Ibid 7: 'Limits and undesirable effects of repressive strategies'.

[15] OSF is listed as one of the funders in the report. See Latin American Commission on Drugs and Democracy, 'Drugs and Democracy' (n 13) inside front cover.

[16] See eg Alma Guillermoprieto, 'An end to the war on drugs?', New York Review of Books, 12 April 2012.

endeavour, the Commission appears to have accomplished little more than the publication of one, relatively short report.

In its report, the Commission states that '[p]rohibitionist policies based on the eradication of production and on the disruption of drug flows as well as on the criminalization of consumption have not yielded the expected results',[17] and that:

> Current drug repression policies are firmly rooted in prejudices, fears and ideological visions. The whole issue has become taboo which inhibits public debate. The association of drugs with crime blocks the circulation of information and segregates drug users in closed circles where they become even more exposed to organized crime. Hence, breaking the taboo and acknowledging the failure of current policies and their consequences is the inescapable prerequisite for opening up the discussion …[18]

However, the Commission stops short of calling for a complete abandonment of the international drug control regime, stating it does not support:

> [an] outright rejection of policies that combat the narcotics trade … Nor [do we] detract in any way from the urgent priority to strengthen the struggle against cartels and drug traffickers. The way forward lies in acknowledging the insufficient results of current policies and, without dismissing the immense efforts undertaken, launching a broad debate about alternative strategies.[19]

Though not entirely clear, the Commission appears to be arguing for a form of decriminalisation of the abuse of drugs, at least for cannabis, while maintaining criminal penalties for drug trafficking. It states that countries must:

> Change the status of addicts from drug buyers in the illegal market to that of patients cared for in the public health system … [T]he State must establish the laws, institutions and regulations enabling those who have become addicted to drugs to stop being buyers in an illegal market and to become patients of the health care system …[20]

and

> [Evaluate] from a public health standpoint and on the basis of the most advanced medical science the convenience of decriminalizing the possession of cannabis for personal use.[21]

Notwithstanding any political significance of the work of the Commission, or the media attention garnered by its work, the arguments of advocates of drug liberalisation that drug control violates human rights has, to date,

17 Latin American Commission on Drugs and Democracy (n 13) 5.
18 Ibid 6.
19 Ibid.
20 Ibid 8.
21 Ibid.

not yet made significant inroads in Latin America. After a high-level debate of OAS countries on drug policies in Colombia in 2012, the topic essentially went nowhere. Armenta and others note that:

> … high expectations [on the part of advocates of drug liberalization] were quickly tempered to a general approval that the topic had been discussed at this level at all. The summit's outcome can be called both a failure and a success: no alternatives to prohibition were discussed …[22]

In June 2013, the Organization of American States (OAS) General Assembly at Antigua, Guatemala, adopted a declaration titled 'For a Comprehensive Policy against the World Drug Problem in the Americas'. Though expectations were high amongst advocates of drug liberalisation that this meeting would provide a dramatic breakthrough, the text that was adopted in the end was relatively tame.

In this declaration, the OAS states it will 'continue to advance in a coordinated manner in the search for effective solutions to the world drug problem with a comprehensive … approach with full respect for human rights and fundamental freedoms …'.[23] OAS member states appear to signal their sympathy for the arguments of advocates of drug liberalisation, by stating '[they] encourage the consideration of new approaches to the world drug problem in the Americas based on scientific knowledge and evidence,'[24] and that 'drug policies must have a crosscutting human rights perspective consistent with the obligations of parties under international law … in order to promote and achieve, inter alia, the well-being of individuals, their social inclusion, access to justice and health'.[25] At the same time, the member states also stressed '[t]he importance of fully implementing the three international drug control conventions … which constitute the framework of the international drug control system',[26] '[t]heir commitment to make greater efforts to effectively reduce demand for drugs',[27] and '[t]heir commitment to strengthen efforts at reducing the illicit supply of drugs'.[28] There are several paragraphs outlining a law enforcement centred approach to combat organised crime,[29] but nowhere is there any mention of legalisation or decriminalisation of drugs.

[22] Amira Armenta, Pien Metaal, and Martin Jelsma, 'A breakthrough in the making? Shifts in the Latin American drug policy debate' (Amsterdam, Transnational Institute, 25 June 2012).

[23] OAS, 'For a Comprehensive Policy against the World Drug Problem in the Americas' (Antigua, 6 June 2013) para 1.

[24] OAS, 'For a Comprehensice Policy' (n 23) para 2.

[25] OAS (n 23) para 10.

[26] OAS (n 23) para 4.

[27] OAS (n 23) para 12.

[28] OAS (n 23) para 13.

[29] OAS (n 23) para 14.

III. LATIN AMERICA: DEVELOPMENTS AT THE NATIONAL LEVEL

Though developments at the regional level have not been as dramatic as advocates of drug liberalisation might have hoped, in recent years, two Latin American countries, Bolivia and Uruguay, have announced policies that might prove to have ramifications throughout the international drug control regime.

Bolivia

For some years, the situation in Bolivia had been the subject of some controversy within drug policy circles, due to the longstanding tradition in many farming communities (including indigenous populations) in that country of coca leaf chewing. Coca leaf is included in Schedule 1 of the 1961 Convention, and naturally chewing the substance for other than medical or scientific purposes is prohibited. Nevertheless, Article 49 allows state parties to permit coca leaf chewing 'to the extent that [this was] traditional … and [was] permitted on 1 January 1961', for a limited period of 25 years, if they make a reservation to that effect upon 'signature, ratification, or accession' to the convention.[30] However, Bolivia did not make such a reservation upon its ratification in 1976, and in any case the 25-year period would have elapsed in 1996.

Also relevant is Article 14(2) of the 1988 Convention, which states that efforts against the eradication of illicit cultivation of narcotic drugs 'shall respect fundamental human rights and shall take due account of traditional licit uses, where there is historic evidence of such use, as well as the protection of the environment'. This provision was inserted during the drafting of the 1988 Convention upon the insistence of Bolivia, and, upon signing the 1988 Convention, Bolivia also lodged a reservation to Article 3(2):

> [declaring] the inapplicability to Bolivia of those provisions [that would establish] as a criminal offence the use, consumption, possession, purchase or cultivation of the coca leaf for personal consumption … [that would be] contrary to principles of [the Bolivian] Constitution and basic concepts of its legal system which embody respect for the culture, legitimate practices, values and attributes of the nationalities making up Bolivia's population. Bolivia's legal system recognizes the ancestral nature of the licit use of the coca leaf which, for much of

[30] This article also makes provisions for the traditional use of, inter alia, opium smoking and the use of cannabis, though also for only a limited period (15 years with regard to opium smoking and 25 with regard to cannabis).

> Bolivia's population, dates back over centuries. In formulating this reservation, Bolivia considers that [the] coca leaf is not, in and of itself, a narcotic drug or psychotropic substance ...[31]

There is nothing to indicate that any state had objections to this reservation of Bolivia at the time. Nevertheless, INCB states flatly that:

> The provisions of the 1988 Convention, including reservations made under that Convention, do not absolve a party of its rights and obligations under the other international drug control treaties. It is therefore important that States fulfill their obligations under those treaties in spite of any reservations they may have made.[32]

The argument of INCB, therefore, was that the reservation of Bolivia to the 1988 Convention was without any practical effect, since the country was obligated under the 1961 Convention to prohibit coca leaf chewing.

The issue remained unresolved until it came to the forefront with the election in 2005 of President Evo Morales. Himself a member of the indigenous community and a former coca farmer, Morales stated his objection to the international prohibition on coca leaf chewing and, in 2009, he led a diplomatic effort to have coca leaf removed from the international control schedule. The effort was unsuccessful, with 18 state parties filing formal objections to the amendment, thereby ensuring that it did not go forward.[33] It is notable that the states objecting to Bolivia's proposal included not only countries commonly known to be supportive of the international drug control regime, such as the United States, the United Kingdom, Russia, and Sweden, but also countries that are often at the forefront of efforts to reform the regime, such as Germany and Italy.

The disagreement has been put forward by many advocates of drug liberalisation as yet another example of how the drug control regime violates human rights—in this case, the right of indigenous peoples to maintaining their cultural practices. There is of course no international treaty stipulating the rights of indigenous peoples but, in 2007, the UN General Assembly adopted the UN Declaration on the Rights of Indigenous Peoples, which enumerates rights such as self-determination, autonomy, and

[31] This reservation was confirmed by Bolivia upon ratification of the 1988 Convention in 1990. United Nations Treaty Collection, 'Reservation made by Bolivia (Plurinational State of) upon signature and confirmed upon ratification of United Nations Convention against Illicit Traffic in Narcotic Drugs and Psychotropic Substances' (New York, 20 August 1990), at treaties.un.org/Pages/ViewDetails.aspx?src=TREATY&mtdsg_no=VI-19&chapter=6&lang=en.

[32] INCB, *Annual Report 2007* (Vienna, 2008) para 220.

[33] In chronological order: United States, Sweden, United Kingdom, Latvia, Japan, Canada, France, Germany, Bulgaria, Slovakia, Denmark, Estonia, Italy, Mexico, Russian Federation, Malaysia, Singapore, and Ukraine. See Transnational Institute, 'Objections and support for Bolivia's coca amendment', at www.druglawreform.info/index.php?option=com_flexicontent&view=items&cid=96:unscheduling-the-coca-leaf&id=1184:objections-and-support-for-bolivias-coca-amendment&Itemid=33.

the 'right to maintain and strengthen … distinct political, legal, economic, social and cultural institutions' (Article 5) to be protected. The Transnational Institute, for example, states that 'the provisions in the Single Convention are clearly at odds' with this declaration.[34] In 2009, the Permanent Forum on Indigenous Issues, a UN advisory body to the Economic and Social Council, 'recognize[d] the cultural significance and medical importance of the coca leaf in the Andean and other indigenous regions of South America', and 'recommend[ed] that those portions of the [1961 Convention] regarding coca leaf chewing that are inconsistent with the rights of indigenous peoples to maintain their traditional health and cultural practices … be amended and/or repealed.'[35]

In June 2011, Bolivia took the unprecedented step of denouncing the 1961 Convention, with the intent of re-acceding with a reservation under Article 49. INCB issued a damning statement that it was:

> … of the opinion that while this step by Bolivia may be in line with the letter of the Convention, such action is contrary to the Convention's spirit. The international community should not accept any approach whereby Governments use the mechanism of denunciation and re-accession with reservation, in order to free themselves from the obligation to implement certain treaty provisions. Such approach would undermine the integrity of the global drug control system, undoing the good work of Governments over many years to achieve the aims and objectives of the drug control conventions, including the prevention of drug abuse which is devastating the lives of millions of people … The Board requests the Bolivian Government to consider very seriously all the implications of its actions in this regard, and invites it to do so in the context of the shared responsibility of all countries in dealing with the universal drug problem.[36]

In December 2011, INCB sent a mission to Bolivia to hold discussions on the issue, and sent a letter to the government reiterating its views in early 2012.[37]

The Bolivian government had harsh words for INCB. In its response to the letter, the Foreign Minister states:

> Bolivia would like to call your attention, with deep regret, to the biased character and inferences of your note and to reject unacceptable judgments … The fact that, according to your note, the purpose of the mission was to analyze 'the grave consequences for international drug control' of our political decision makes it clear that the mission apparently arrived in our country already prejudiced … Bolivia … feels forced to express its utmost rejection of the

[34] Transnational Institute, 'Coca leaf: Myths and Reality' (Amsterdam, 5 August 2014).

[35] Permanent Forum on Indigenous Issues 'Report of eight session (18–29 May 2009)' (New York, UN index E/2009/43, May 2009) para 89.

[36] INCB, 'International Narcotics Control Board Regrets Bolivia's Denunciation of the Single Convention on Narcotic Drugs' (Vienna, 5 July 2011).

[37] INCB, 'Focus on international drug control, October–December 2011' (Vienna, 2011) 1.

> disqualifications expressed in your note, which fail to ponder on the conclusive and unprecedented results of the Bolivian commitment to control the surplus coca cultivation and the illicit drugs trade.[38]

In January 2013, Bolivia re-acceded to the 1961 convention, with the according reservation to Article 49. As less than a third of state parties objected to the reservation, it stood, and the 1961 Convention once again came into force—minus the provision—for Bolivia in February 2013.[39] Throughout the controversy, many advocates of drug liberalisation took the opportunity to mock INCB, with one organisation stating:

> INCB's latest salvo against Bolivia to be further evidence of the Board's stubborn combination of incompetence and overreach. The INCB's harsh response to Bolivia begs the question of why the Board is so afraid ... Why does the Board consider the international drug Conventions to be so fragile? ... How do one country's legitimate efforts to reconcile its treaty obligations with its own constitutional requirements represent an existential threat to the entire system in the eyes of the INCB?[40]

Likewise, the Transnational Institute stated upon Bolivia's re-accession that '[t]oday the Plurinational State of Bolivia can celebrate a rightful victory, as the country can become formally a party again to the 1961 Single Convention on Narcotic Drugs'.[41] Ironically, these statements could be viewed as recognition of the lasting strength and importance of the international drug control regime—precisely what advocates of drug liberalisation state their opposition to in other contexts.

As noted above, the Permanent Forum on Indigenous Issues has expressed its objection to the relevant portions of the 1961 Convention. Though the Permanent Forum is not a human rights body as such, its pronouncement is clearly based on the UN Declaration, and this would appear to be one issue—in the view of this author, perhaps the only issue—on which human rights standards do in fact conflict with the actual provisions of the international drug control conventions, as opposed to how those provisions are interpreted by some states. Indeed, in its 2015 study on drug control and human rights, OHCHR refers to this issue (though without specific mention of Bolivia) and concludes that

[38] Unofficial translation from Spanish produced by Transnational Institute, available at http://druglawreform.info/en/issues/unscheduling-the-coca-leaf/item/3229-response-of-bolivia-to-the-international-narcotics-control-board-incb.

[39] UNODC, 'Bolivia to re-accede to UN drug convention, while making exception on coca leaf chewing' (Vienna, January 2013). The 1961 Convention lists the Articles which a country may make reservations to upon ratification, but also goes on to state in Article 50(3) that states that wish to make reservations to other Articles may do so, unless one-third or more of the states parties to the Convention at the time object.

[40] Washington Office on Latin America, 'UN Drug Board Attacks Bolivia: Drug Control Regime under Strain' (Washington, 28 February 2012).

[41] Transnational Institute, 'Bolivia wins a rightful victory on the coca leaf' (Amsterdam, 15 January 2013).

'[i]ndigenous peoples have a right to follow their traditional, cultural and religious practices. Where drug use is part of these practices, the right of use for such narrowly defined purposes should in principle be protected, subject to limitations provided for in human rights law.'[42] Pillay, the High Commissioner for Human Rights, in her statement at a side event of the Human Rights Council in 2014 (one of her last functions before retiring in the summer of that year), went even further and even seemed to endorse the Bolivian approach when she indicated that '[s]tates should seek solutions—including through interpretation of the existing international legal framework; by entering reservations when ratifying a treaty; or by denouncing an applicable treaty and re-ratifying it with the appropriate reservation.'[43] It is somewhat astounding that a senior policy-maker of the UN would encourage states to take actions arguably aimed at demeaning particular international treaties.

Nevertheless, the extrapolation of this one particular issue to make a universal judgment of the international drug control regime seems strained at best. It may be the case that the relevant provision in the 1961 Convention should be revisited in light of new understandings of the rights of indigenous communities—though, legally speaking, the notion that a treaty is automatically superseded by a declaration is hardly a given. In any case, that hardly serves as an argument against the entire drug control framework—an argument that, it should be stressed, even the Bolivian government was not attempting. Throughout its statements, the government stresses its commitment to the regime and, indeed, in the reservation it delivered upon re-accession to the 1961 Convention, Bolivia states it 'will continue to take all necessary measures to control the cultivation of coca in order to prevent its abuse and the illicit production of the narcotic drugs which may be extracted from the leaf.'[44] Bolivia itself, therefore, does not appear to have fundamental objections to the principle of drug control; indeed, if it had, it would probably not have re-acceded to the 1961 Convention.

Uruguay

In December 2011, Uruguay became the first country since the advent of modern international drug control to legalise cannabis at the national level, not only removing criminal penalties for consumption, but also

[42] OHCHR, 'Study on the impact of the world drug problem on the enjoyment of human rights' (Geneva, UN index A/HRC/30/65, 4 September 2015) para 67.

[43] OHCHR, 'Side event: World Drug Problem on Human Rights' (Geneva, 16 June 2014) 2.

[44] UN Secretary General, 'Instrument of accession of Bolivia (Plurinational State of) to the Single Convention on Narcotic Drugs, 1961, as amended by the Protocol Amending the Single Convention on Narcotic Drugs, 1961' (New York, UN index C.N.94.2013.TREATIES-VI.18 (Depositary Notification), 22 January 2013) 2.

creating a legal market for the drug.[45] The country's parliament voted to allow licensed production and distribution through pharmacies, as well as small-scale cultivation by individuals for personal use. As of the writing of this study, the implementing regulations for the law had yet to be finalised.

As with the case of Bolivia, a heated debate with INCB followed. Yans, President of INCB, issued a statement condemning the Uruguayan Parliament, stating INCB was:

> … surprised that a legislative body that has endorsed an international law and agreements, and a Government that is an active partner in international cooperation and in the maintenance of the international rule of law, knowingly decided to break the universally agreed and internationally endorsed legal provisions of the treaty … the decision of the Uruguayan legislature fails to consider its negative impacts on health since scientific studies confirm that cannabis is an addictive substance with serious consequences for people's health. In particular, the use and abuse of cannabis by young people can seriously affect their development.[46]

In response, the President of Uruguay told a Colombian journalist:

> Tell this old guy not to lie … Any guy in the street can meet with me. Let him come to Uruguay and meet with me whenever he wants … He thinks that because he's in an international position, he can tell whatever lie he wants.[47]

Human rights have been advanced in the arguments of the Uruguayan government for the legalisation of cannabis, though not, it seems, in any kind of structured or coherent manner. There appears to have been no in-depth discussion as to why bringing an end to the 'prohibitive' and 'repressive' current system of drug control is necessarily in synch with human rights, and the references to human rights are somewhat passing, as if the connection was self-evident. Some observers state that it was intentional that the vote in the upper house of the Uruguayan Parliament was scheduled for 10 December, the day commemorating the adoption of the UDHR,[48] and Uruguay has been active in international policy fora such as the CND in calling for drug control efforts to be more cognizant of human rights.[49]

[45] The Parliament of Switzerland debated a bill with similar provisions in 2004, but the bill was eventually rejected. See eg INCB, *Annual Report 2004* (Vienna, 2005).

[46] INCB, 'Uruguay is breaking the International Conventions on Drug Control with the Cannabis Legislation approved by its Congress' (Vienna, 11 December 2013).

[47] Cited in Roque Planas, 'Uruguay's Prez Rips Into U.N. Official Over Marijuana Law: "Stop Lying"', Huffington Post, 13 December 2013.

[48] Jeremey Daw, 'Uruguay to Become First Country to Legalize Cannabis', Cannabis Now, 10 December 2013.

[49] See eg Transnational Institute, 'Drug Law Reform in Latin America: Overview of drug policy, drug law and legislative trends in Uruguay' (Amsterdam), www.druglawreform.info/en/country-information/latin-america/uruguay/item/5667-uruguay.

As might be expected, developments in Uruguay have been greeted with euphoria by advocates of drug liberalisation. Nevertheless, it is worth noting, as even some of the advocates admit, that public opinion in Uruguay is firmly against cannabis legalisation, with as much as 66 per cent of the public negative about the new law.[50] The answer, according to advocates of drug liberalisation, is to educate the masses:

> [T]he average Uruguayan lacks a firm sense of the reasoning behind [the new law] ... despite efforts by drug policy reformers to promote the law as a public health measure, the largest bloc of respondents (37 per cent) said they believe that the goal of the law is to prevent crime and combat drug trafficking ... 10 per cent believed it was passed to bring in money, 5.5 per cent said it was an attempt to get an electoral boost, and 12.3 per cent gave other responses, which included 'other interests' and that it 'seeks to distract people from real problems.' All of this shows that the new administration would benefit from launching a coordinated communications campaign to better educate the public on what the law does, and does not, aim to achieve. If the public persistently misconstrues the law's purposes, it will be difficult to demonstrate success...[51]

While this author is not an expert on the workings of Uruguayan domestic politics, the above analysis, provided as it is by two non-Uruguayans, would seem to betray a somewhat condescending attitude towards the Uruguayan electorate. It is also generally indicative. The drug policy 'experts' purport to know best what would benefit the Uruguayan people (ie cannabis legalisation), and it is the people who must be 'educated' to understand. Of course, this type of loftiness is hardly unique to the field of international drug policy, and can be seen in most other fields of international development and similar issues (including human rights).[52]

Outside influence in the process may not have been limited to the advice of so-called technical experts. According to some reports, foreign funds were also heavily involved in the campaign for cannabis legalisation. One journalist states that:

> ... the government got help from a national TV campaign and other lobbying efforts supporting [sic] by billionaire currency speculator and philanthropist George Soros and his Open Society Foundation and Drug Policy Alliance. In September, Mujica met with Soros and billionaire David Rockefeller in New York to explain his 'experiment.' These deep-pocketed connections drew criticism from Mujica's opponents. 'I would say to Mr. Soros, to Mr. Rockefeller,

[50] John Walsh and Geoff Ramsey, 'Uruguay's Drug Policy: Major Innovations, Major Challenges' (Washington, Washington Office on Latin America, 2015) 2.

[51] Walsh and Ramsey, 'Uruguay's Drug Policy' (n 50) 15.

[52] For a general discussion of this topic, see eg Barbara Harrell-Bond, *Imposing Aid* (Oxford, Oxford University Press, 1986).

> and to the president of the republic that you don't experiment with the Uruguayans. We are not guinea pigs'.[53]

It is of course difficult to verify such claims, but they are indicative of a power dynamic that can be seen throughout this issue: public debate can be influenced, and even shaped, with skilled lobbyists at the right places and an adequate amount of funding.

[53] Leonardo Haberkorn and Michael Warren, 'Uruguay Legalizes Marijuana Trade', Huffington Post, 10 December 2013.

4

Drug Control: Violating Human Rights?

ADVOCATES OF DRUG liberalisation have advanced numerous human rights-based arguments to argue for revising the international drug control regime fundamentally, or even discarding it altogether. The arguments aim at creating, and expanding, the idea that the current drug control regime, and, indeed, drug control itself, is incompatible with human rights. Scrapping the current system is, advocates of drug liberalisation argue, the only way to ensure that human rights, in particular the human rights of persons who abuse drugs, are protected. A handful of Special Rapporteurs have played a large role in promoting this view, together with some human rights NGOs, including Human Rights Watch (HRW), one of the leading and most influential international human rights NGOs. OHCHR and UNODC have also made statements that seem to agree in part with the arguments of advocates of drug liberalisation.

In particular, two successive Special Rapporteurs on the Right of Everyone to the Enjoyment of the Highest Attainable Standard of Physical and Mental Health (Special Rapporteur on the Right to Health) have been vocal promoters for drug liberalisation. This started with Paul Hunt (Special Rapporteur from August 2004 to July 2008), who, for example, stated in an address to a conference of the International Harm Reduction Association (IHRA) in 2008 that:

> It is imperative that the international drug control system … and the complex international human rights system that has evolved since 1948, cease to behave as though they exist in parallel universes. The UN human rights system must give closer attention to the international drug conventions, the issue of drug control, and the plight of those who use drugs. Equally, the international drug control system must be respectful of human rights. This is not an option. It is a legal requirement.[1]

[1] IHRA, 'Human Rights, Health, and Harm Reduction: State Amnesia and Parallel Universes' (London, 2008) 10.

Nevertheless, Hunt's work on this issue in his capacity as Special Rapporteur was somewhat limited, concentrating mainly on one country mission to Sweden in 2006.[2] Rather, it was Anand Grover (Special Rapporteur from August 2008 to July 2014) who used his position as Special Rapporteur to the fullest extent to argue for drug liberalisation. Grover's 2010 report to the Human Rights Council is a veritable treatise for advocates for drug liberalisation: he argues that the 'criminalization of drug use', required by the international drug control conventions, is the source of all the problems with the current regime, and that a 'human rights based approach to drug control' (as opposed to the 'criminalization approach') must be adopted as a matter of urgency. His report is worth citing at length, as it is indicative of the arguments of most advocates of drug liberalisation.

Grover's description of the international drug control regime, which is the starting point of his critique, is questionable at best. After noting the (somewhat obvious) fact that persons have the right to the highest attainable standard of health regardless of whether they abuse drugs,[3] Grover asserts: 'People who use drugs and people who are dependent on drugs possess the same freedoms and entitlements guaranteed by international legal instruments, and both groups experience violations of their rights under the current international drug control regime.'[4] It would appear from this description that people who abuse drugs are automatically victimised because of that abuse—as shall be examined, a common theme with the arguments of advocates of drug liberalisation in general. Grover goes on to state that the international drug control conventions '[criminalise] virtually every aspect of the unauthorized production and distribution of [internationally controlled] substances',[5] seemingly suggesting that it is in and of itself something undesirable. There is no doubt where Grover stands on the criminalisation of drugs; he states:

> Criminalization of drug use and possession are implicated in violation of several human rights, including the right to health. Other infringements of the right to health are less direct, but occur as by-products of the skewed focus of

[2] Paul Hunt, 'Report of the Special Rapporteur on the right of everyone to the enjoyment of the highest attainable standard of physical and mental health, Mission to Sweden' (Geneva, UN index A/HRC/4/28/Add.2, 28 February 2007).

[3] Anand Grover, 'Report of the Special Rapporteur on the right of everyone to the enjoyment of the highest attainable standard of physical and mental health' (Geneva, UN index A/65/255, 6 August 2010) paras 7, 8: 'The enjoyment of the right to health of all people who use drugs—and are dependent on drugs—is applicable irrespective of the fact of their drug use … [A]n individual's use of drugs cannot constitute grounds for curtailing her/his rights, irrespective of whether she or he has a recognized dependence syndrome or whether the applicable drug control regime allows for imprisonment or other sanctions.'

[4] Grover, 'Report of the Special Rapporteur' (n 3) para 8.

[5] Grover (n 3) para 9.

> the international drug control regime: for instance, insufficient access to essential medications. The Special Rapporteur considers that each of these violations is traceable ultimately to a disproportionate focus on criminalization and law enforcement practices at the expense of the enjoyment of the right to health and reduction of harms associated with drugs.[6]

Grover's report is full of sweeping and unsubstantiated assertions that drug control and human rights inevitably conflict, and that the current drug control regime must be revised fundamentally to ensure compliance with human rights:

> When the goals and approaches of the international drug control regime and international human rights regime conflict, it is clear that human rights obligations should prevail.[7] … Despite this, explicit consideration of human rights is absent in the treaties and has lacked priority among the implementing bodies.[8] … [I]t is clear that significantly more must be done to make human rights central to drug control.[9]

As is the case with many reports by advocates of drug liberalisation, the majority of Grover's citations are of papers issued by other advocates, engaging in a circle of mutual substantiation that has the result (intended or not) of creating an ever-increasing mass of impressive looking but somewhat repetitive documentation. Indeed, Grover also takes a dim view of law enforcement in general (not just in the sphere of drug control), and appears to believe that human rights and law enforcement inevitably conflict. He states:

> Law enforcement approaches are ingrained institutionally in the international drug control regime, as drug control is housed within UNODC, which leads the United Nations efforts on organized crime. This association between law enforcement and drug control, in part, precludes adoption of a human rights-based approach and interaction with the human rights bodies of the United Nations.[10]

Like most advocates of drug liberalisation, Grover conflates all of drug control with the general and undefined expression 'war on drugs':

> Unfortunately, the current approach to global drug control maintains that drugs are an undisputable 'evil', which the international community has a 'duty to combat'. The concept of a war on drugs is used to justify extreme policies and practices. The links drawn between drug production and the funding of armed groups, for example between opium growers and the Taliban in Afghanistan, have further justified a zero-tolerance approach, even though such policies are

[6] Grover (n 3) para 18.
[7] Grover (n 3) para 10.
[8] Grover (n 3) para 11.
[9] Grover (n 3) para 13.
[10] Grover (n 3) para 48.

> increasingly shown to be ineffective in reducing the supply of and demand for drugs. Therefore, this approach not only fails to achieve its primary stated aim—preventing health-related harms of drug use—but also fails to achieve genuine drug control.[11]

Grover makes the sweeping, and extremely questionable, assertion that:

> … people invariably continue using drugs irrespective of criminal laws, even though deterrence of drug use is considered the primary justification for imposition of penal sanctions.[12]

He then makes the bold statement that:

> Drug use may have harmful health consequences, but the Special Rapporteur is concerned that the current drug control approach creates more harm than the harms it seeks to prevent. Criminalization of drug use, designed to deter drug use, possession and trafficking, has failed.[13]

As an immediate measure, Grover asserts that drugs should be decriminalised, stating that:

> … the continuing imposition of criminal penalties for drug use and possession perpetuates many of the major risks associated with drug use. [The Special Rapporteur] advocates for consideration of less restrictive approaches to drug control, including decriminalization or de-penalization.'[14]

In what arguably may be an attempt to make his recommendation more politically acceptable, Grover notes (correctly) that decriminalisation is not synonymous with legalisation; nevertheless, a few pages later, Grover essentially states that he is in fact in favour of legalisation—albeit, it would seem, with some measure of regulation. He states:

> The Special Rapporteur considers that there is a need in the long term to consider alternatives to the current drug control system. One such alternative model may be the Framework Convention on Tobacco Control, in which certain controlled medicines would be regulated in a manner similar to tobacco. The purpose of the Framework Convention is to reduce the social, environmental and public health harms of tobacco smoke … It represents a paradigm shift in developing a regulatory strategy to address addictive substances, which protects the rights of people who use and are dependent on drugs while minimizing associated harms … The non-prices measures of the Framework Convention on Tobacco Control provide the best examples of the protections and regulations that may

[11] Grover (n 3) para 14.

[12] Grover (n 3) para 15. The effect of law as a deterrence of drug abuse, and of criminal behaviour in general, is of course a topic of debate. See eg Raymond Paternoster, 'How Much Do We Really Know About Criminal Deterrence' (2010) 100 *Journal of Criminal Law and Criminology* 765; also Paul Robinson and John Darley, 'Does Criminal Law Deter? A Behavioural Science Investigation' (2004) 24 *Oxford Journal of Legal Studies* 173.

[13] Grover (n 3) para 16.

[14] Grover (n 3) para 62.

> replace the existing enforcement-based framework. Such measures include regulation of drug content, education and awareness-building, and measures concerning dependence reduction and cessation. Implementation of these measures would secure the right to health by, inter alia, ensuring supply of unadulterated drugs, increasing individual and community awareness to minimize risk, and ensuring access to appropriate treatment, where necessary. There generally are high levels of implementation among Parties to the Framework Convention on Tobacco Control on nearly all of these measures, suggesting similar possibilities for currently controlled drugs.[15]

Another Special Rapporteur who has engaged in sustained criticism of the international drug control regime for violating human rights and has promoted liberalisation of drug control, is Manfred Nowak, Special Rapporteur on Torture from 2004 to October 2010. Juan Mendez, appointed Special Rapporteur after Nowak, has also continued examining the issue, though in a less concentrated manner.

Nowak has written more forcefully on this subject outside of his official duties as Special Rapporteur, but he does dedicate an entire chapter to the subject in his report to the Human Rights Council in 2009, and his perspective is clear from the outset. He starts by stating that:

> The linkages between drugs and the right to personal integrity and human dignity have not previously been exposed in a systematic way, in particular not from a torture/ill-treatment perspective. One of the factors contributing to this is the limited access to justice for drug users, which goes hand in hand with the criminalization and marginalization to which they are subjected in many contexts.[16]

The examples of abuses connected with drug control he continues with, such as 'the use of drugs to blunt fear and pain in child soldiers, or drugging to make people compliant or to obtain information'[17] are uncontroversial in their human rights implications and their clear lack of legitimacy. However, the report then continues as an argument against drug control in general. Nowak states that 'in the course of several of his country visits, [he] has noted the challenges posed to criminal justice systems by punitive drug policies … [in Indonesia,] the use of, and dealing in, drugs within correctional institutions constitutes a major problem',[18] suggesting that it is punitive drug control policies, not the inability of the authorities to control drug abuse in prisons, that is at the heart of the issue.

[15] Grover (n 3) paras 73, 74.

[16] Manfred Nowak, 'Report of the Special Rapporteur on torture and other cruel, inhuman or degrading treatment or punishment' (Geneva, UN index A/HRC/10/44, 14 January 2009) para 54.

[17] Nowak, 'Report of the Special Rapporteur' para 54.

[18] Nowak (n 17) para 55.

Nowak rightly expresses concern regarding the possibility of persons who abuse drugs suffering withdrawal symptoms while in prison, without having access to adequate care.[19] Though this would appear to be somewhat of an isolated example, related more than anything to the quality of health care in prisons, Nowak then proceeds on the assumption that there are 'many tensions' between the international drug control regime and human rights, recommending that:

> To address [these] tensions between the current punitive approach to drug control and international human rights obligations, including the prohibition of torture and cruel, inhuman and degrading treatment, the Special Rapporteur calls on the Human Rights Council to take up the question of drug policies in the light of international obligations in the area of human rights at one of its future sessions.[20]

The above chapter notwithstanding, as noted above, Nowak has tended to write more strongly against drug control outside of his official capacity as Special Rapporteur. The papers that Nowak has written for the Human Rights Council have tended to be relatively subdued in this regard. For example, Nowak's further recommendations to the Special Session of the General Assembly in 2009 are arguably uncontroversial, stating mainly that '[s]tates should ensure that their legal frameworks governing drug dependence treatment and rehabilitation services are in full compliance with international human rights norms' and that they should 'ensure that drug dependence treatment … are accessible in all places of detention and that drug dependence treatment is not restricted on the basis of any kind of discrimination'.[21] This is in stark contrast to Grover, as seen above.

It is more in his capacity as academic that Nowak has written against the international drug control regime, and this is also the case with Hunt. Of course, in engaging in academic and other activities outside of the UN, none of the Special Rapporteurs hide their status as Special Rapporteur, and, on the contrary, appear to cite their title freely. Under such circumstances, even if statements are made in an individual capacity, one's status as a Special Rapporteur clearly adds considerable weight to those views. This arguably raises broader questions about the multiple 'hats' that these independent experts have, and the grey areas between their various capacities. There is a Code of Conduct for Special Procedures Mandate Holders,

[19] 'One of the questions in this context concerns withdrawal symptoms and to what extent they may qualify as torture or ill-treatment. There can be no doubt that withdrawal symptoms can cause severe pain and suffering if not alleviated by appropriate medical treatment, and the potential for abuse of withdrawal symptoms, in particular in custody situations, is evident … Moreover, if withdrawal symptoms are used for any of the purposes cited in definition of torture enshrined in article 1 of the Convention against Torture, this might amount to torture.': see Nowak (n 17) para 57.

[20] Nowak (n 17) para 73.

[21] Nowak (n 17) para 74.

but it covers only activities taken during the exercise of the mandate, not actions taken in the mandate holder's private capacity.[22]

In a paper co-written with Barrett, for example, Nowak extrapolates human rights issues in a few countries, generalising them as if they are universal and inevitable results of the international drug control regime, stating merely that: 'While the drug conventions do not directly result in the human rights abuses detailed above, they also cannot be divorced from these and other violations, as their influence on domestic drug control policy and legislation is considerable.'[23] No actual evidence that the international drug control conventions influence domestic policy and encourage human rights abuses is provided, save one sole judgment of a court in Indonesia, where the court stated (wrongly) that the 1988 Convention supported the death penalty for drug offenders.[24]

Nevertheless, this one isolated example is enough for Barrett and Nowak to question the legitimacy of drug control as a whole, stating that '[t]here is a danger that drug control has become an end in itself.'[25] Using the UN Charter to justify an argument that drug control is legitimate only insofar as it puts the 'human being at the centre of policies',[26] they argue that '[d]rug policy is fundamentally out of step with this basic premise',[27] though, again, there seems to be little justification for this assertion. They continue:

> In our view … international drug policy objectives and activities … should be justified only insofar as they contribute to human development, human security and human rights. … Without … demonstrable results in terms of human rights impact, the international drug policy regime and its current supply and demand reduction approach remain self-justifying and self-perpetuating, and unanswerable for human rights failures. What we are describing is a human rights based approach to international drug policy.[28]

[22] Human Rights Council, 'Code of Conduct for Special Procedures Mandate-holders of the Human Rights Council', UN index A/HRC/RES 5.2, adopted on 18 June 2007. Issues have cropped up from time to time; in 2013, for example, Richard Falk, the Special Rapporteur on Palestine, was subject to intense criticism, including by the Secretary General of the UN and some governments, for comments that he made on his personal blog. See eg 'Richard Falk blasted by American Jewish Committee for linking bombing, Israel', *The Forward*, 25 June 2013.

[23] Damon Barrett and Manfred Nowak, 'The United Nations and Drug Policy: Towards a Human Rights-Based Approach', in Aristotle Constantinides and Nikos Zaikos, eds. *The Diversity of International Law: Essays in Honour of Professor Kalliopi K. Koufa*, (Leiden, Brill/ Martinus Nijhoff, 2009) at 455.

[24] Barrett and Nowak, 'The United Nations and Drug Policy' (n 23) 455.

[25] Barrett and Nowak (n 23) 457.

[26] Barrett and Nowak (n 23) 458.

[27] Barrett and Nowak (n 23) 459.

[28] Barrett and Nowak (n 23) 460.

As noted above, many NGOs have also been vocal in calling for fundamental reform of the international drug control regime. Most prominent in this area are the arguments of Human Rights Watch (HRW), one of the leading and most influential international human rights organisations. Their views are enumerated in detail in its 2014 Annual Report, in which the organisation dedicates an entire chapter, titled 'The Human Rights Case for Drug Reform: How Drug Criminalization Destroys Lives, Feeds Abuses, and Subverts the Rule of Law', to this topic. As with Grover's report, it is worth citing from this chapter in detail.

In this chapter, HRW states that it has adopted an organisational position in 2013 'calling on governments to decriminalise all personal use and possession of drugs … [and to] consider—and eventually adopt—alternative policies on the drug trade to reduce the enormous human rights costs of current approaches.'[29] HRW states that after having spent years documenting human rights violations stemming from what it calls 'wars on drugs':

> … there was a growing sense within [the organisation] that … the problem did not lie merely with ill-considered policies or their abusive execution. Rather, the criminalization of drugs itself seemed to be inherently problematic. Especially when it came to personal possession and use, imposing the full force of the criminal justice system to arrest, prosecute, and incarcerate appeared contrary to the human rights to privacy and personal autonomy that underlie many rights.'[30]

HRW thereby makes a sweeping statement regarding all efforts against drug abuse and trafficking, and then in the sentence following directly afterwards equates those efforts with the incarceration of persons for drug possession. However, the two are not one and the same—the vast majority of countries that outlaw illicit drugs do not engage in mass incarceration for this offence, and it is inaccurate to present international drug control as if it is synonymous with the approach taken in only a handful of countries.

Law enforcement is presented as synonymous with 'abuse' throughout the chapter. HRW states:

> … 'tough' enforcement has created its own nightmare for human rights protection. Thailand's 2003 'war on drugs' resulted in some 2,800 extrajudicial killings by state security forces in its first three months. In Canada, Kazakhstan, Bangladesh, and Ukraine, police have violently mistreated people who use drugs. In Tanzania, police and quasi-official vigilante groups brutally beat people who inject drugs. Russia's policies have resulted in mass incarceration, often in environments that pose high risk of HIV transmission, and detention of

[29] Maria McFarland Sanchez-Moreno, 'The Human Rights Case for Drug Reform: How Drug Criminalization Destroys Lives, Feeds Abuses, and Subverts the Rule of Law', in HRW, *World Report 2014* (New York, 2014) 20.

[30] Sanchez-Moreno, 'The Human Rights Case for Drug Reform' (n 29) 19.

> drug offenders without trial. In countries such as Singapore and Malaysia, drug offenders face the death penalty. Iran imposes a mandatory death sentence for various drug offences. Other countries impose grossly disproportionate punishment in drug cases.'[31]

The reader is left with the impression that all of these human rights violations are a necessary result of drug law enforcement—that enforcing drug laws inevitably results in the above abuses. However, none of those abuses are condoned, much less required, by the international drug conventions. The sort of abuses that HRW cites are not intrinsic to drug control, but rather are features of law enforcement in those countries. They must be condemned, for sure, but they are not inherent in efforts to prevent drug abuse and trafficking.

HRW concludes with the pronouncement that a 'human rights approach to drug control' requires that governments must:

> ... decriminalise personal use and possession of drugs for personal use. Laws criminalizing drug use are inconsistent with respect for human autonomy and privacy rights. ... [L]ike other private behaviour that some may view as immoral (such as consensual homosexual conduct amongst adults), there is no legitimate basis for criminalization.[32]

However, the casual statement that drug control is 'incompatible' with 'respect for human autonomy' is problematic. As shall be examined in this study, there is no definition of 'human autonomy' in international human rights law, or international law in general. What exactly this concept might include in different cultures warrants a large philosophical discussion that is out of the scope of this book, but the notion that prohibiting drug abuse is incompatible with this is hardly self-evident.

Nor is it in any way obvious that drug control violates 'privacy rights'. There is an internationally recognised right to privacy, enumerated for example in Article 17 of the International Covenant on Civil and Political Rights (ICCPR) (though it is not altogether clear that is what is indicated by HRW when it mentions 'privacy rights'). Nevertheless, this right has never been interpreted to include a right to abuse drugs.[33]

HRW goes on to argue that governments must also decriminalise the drug trade itself. According to HRW:

> ... [the] criminalization of the drug trade carries enormous human rights costs, dramatically enhancing the profitability of illicit drug markets and fuelling the

[31] Sanchez-Moreno (n 29) 24.

[32] Sanchez-Moreno (n 29) 26.

[33] Jurisprudence of human rights bodies on this has been limited. In 2004, the European Court of Human Rights ruled inadmissible the application of Wretlund, who had alleged that her right to privacy had been violated by her employer by mandatory drug testing: *Wretlund v Sweden* App No 46210/99, 9 March 2004.

> growth and operations of groups responsible for large-scale violence and corruption. Finding alternative ways to regulate production and distribution and cutting into illicit drug profits would allow governments to weaken the influence of such groups and reduce the various abuses—killings, disproportionate sentencing, torture, and barriers to access to health care—that governments often commit in the name of fighting drugs.[34]

The underlying current of libertarianism is apparent in the arguments of HRW (and other advocates of drug liberalisation). For example, in its submission to OHCHR for that organisation's 2015 report on drug control to the Human Rights Council, HRW argues that:

> Criminalizing personal drug use per se is itself problematic in terms of human rights, as it tramples on the person's right to privacy and basic concepts of autonomy underpinning all rights … The decision to use drugs is a matter of personal choice protected by the right to privacy, a cornerstone of respect for personal autonomy and human dignity. Limitations on autonomy and the right to privacy are justified only if they meet the criteria of legitimate purpose, proportionality, necessity, and non-discrimination. Human Rights Watch believes these criteria can rarely if ever be met for the criminalization of personal drug use or possession of drugs for personal use.[35]

HRW suggests that one of, perhaps the main reason that governments criminalise drugs is due to a perception of morality: 'drug use is seen by many as morally dubious or reprehensible, regardless of whether someone is harmed by it.'[36] This assertion is questionable; while some governments might cite public morals as justification for restricting various types of behaviour, this is generally not the case with drugs, certainly not in international fora. At least taken at face value, statements by governments indicate that they combat drugs because of the grave health and social consequences that they can cause—not because they are 'morally wrong'. There may be underlying moral considerations behind drug policies, as there are for many policies, but the notion that governments act against drugs predominantly because of morality is unsubstantiated.

Proceeding with the assumption that combatting drugs is primarily about morality, HRW makes an analogy with sexual orientation:

> Human rights principles, however, support each individual's autonomy and right to privacy, which encompasses engaging in conduct that the majority may eschew as immoral or indicative of a weak character. Thus, human rights jurisprudence leaves no doubt today that majority public morality, if so inclined,

[34] Sanchez-Moreno (n 29) 27.

[35] HRW, 'Re: Call for Submissions on the Issue of Drugs and Human Rights (the implementation of Resolution A/HRC/28/L.22)' (New York, 15 May 2015) 10.

[36] HRW, 'Re: Call for Submissions on the Issue of Drugs and Human Rights' (n 35) 6.

> cannot justify criminalization of private homosexual conduct by consenting adults. In essence, promoting public morality in the absence of harm to others is not a 'legitimate purpose' for criminalization.[37]

As shall be examined in this study, this comparison with sexual orientation is extremely problematic.

HRW's recommendations in the 2015 submission to OHCHR are somewhat vague, but, as with the 2014 Annual Report, there is a very clear slant towards legalisation of drugs. It recommends that states:

> … [e]nd the criminalization of the personal use of drugs and the possession of drugs for personal use. To deter, prevent, and remedy the harmful use of drugs, states can rely on non-penal regulatory and public health approaches that do not violate human rights.[38]

The organisation also recommends that countries:

> Pursue a process to reform the international drug conventions to ensure that they do not prohibit or discourage states from adopting policies, in line with the above, that would enable them to fulfill their human rights obligations and reduce the human rights costs of current policies.[39]

There is no evidence in the document produced by HRW how the organisation believes the international drug control conventions encourage states to violate human rights, and why they believe the conventions require reform. Rather, it is taken as self-evident that the drug control conventions require an overly punitive and prohibitive approach, which violate human rights (or 'personal autonomy').

HRW concludes by stating that it:

> … [recognises] that reform of existing strategies for drug control may raise legitimate concerns about unintended social or health costs, such as a significant increase in drug abuse. Governments should implement reforms based upon evidence of effective ways to reduce the harms to others that can accompany drug use and drug control.[40]

The message appears to be that HRW recognises that drug abuse will increase significantly if drugs are legalised (or decriminalised), but believes simply that states should prepare for this eventuality through strengthening their harm reduction measures (as opposed to considering whether legalisation is truly the best option). The notion that the costs of legalisation may be too heavy for society to bear is simply not discussed.

[37] HRW (n 35) 6.
[38] HRW (n 35) 10.
[39] Ibid.
[40] Ibid.

This study aims to show that the arguments outlined above, of advocates of drug liberalisation, are fundamentally without foundation. The framing of drug control as a human rights issue appears to have been effective in creating the notion in the minds of many people that efforts to control drugs inevitably violate human rights, and that international human rights obligations necessitate that drug control is terminated. However, when examined closely, the arguments of advocates of drug liberalisation are based on a reading of human rights standards that is selective and highly questionable. Far from being the result of a process of human rights analysis, these arguments depart from the initial premise that persons should be free to abuse drugs, and that efforts on the part of the state to dissuade them from doing so are ipso facto illegitimate. The question, in other words, is not what human rights demands, but rather how human rights can be used to justify this starting premise—the premise that there is a 'right' to abuse drugs. To advocates of drug liberalisation, human rights is not a weapon to fight for social justice, but a mere promotional tool to advance the agenda of drug legalisation.

I. AT FIRST, THERE WAS 'HARM REDUCTION'

To understand the context of how human rights started to be used by advocates of drug legalisation, it is important to examine the context of harm reduction, and its rise to prominence in international drug control policy circles.

Harm reduction is not clearly defined in any international legal text, but it is generally understood to mean a range of measures taken by governments to mimise the health and other risks caused by drug abuse. Harm reduction became prominent in international policy circles in the late 1980s and early 1990s, during the global HIV/AIDS crisis. Since the sharing of contaminated needles was one of the main ways that the HIV virus was being transmitted in many countries, an approach commonly known as 'needle exchange' or 'needle distribution' was implemented, to prevent (or at least attempt to prevent) needle sharing, and the resulting transmission. Essentially, persons who abuse drugs could receive sterile needles and other injection equipment at designated distribution centres, mobile facilities, and sometimes even vending machines situated near known locations of the 'open drug scene'.

Though these measures clearly did nothing towards stopping the drug abuse itself, they aimed towards at least minimising one of the serious negative effects of the abuse—hence the name 'harm reduction'. Needle distribution programmes are implemented in a significant number of countries worldwide—according to IHRA, 90 countries had such programmes in 2014, with five countries (Dominican Republic, Colombia, Jordan, Kenya, and Senegal) having introduced the approach since 2012[41]—and there is general consensus in international fora that they are effective in stemming the spread of HIV. WHO states that there is 'compelling evidence that increasing the availability and utilisation of sterile injecting equipment … reduced HIV infection substantially' and that 'there is no convincing evidence' that such programmes lead to an increase of drug abuse.[42]

As noted above, there is no internationally recognised definition of harm reduction, and, in particular, what measures are included in the term. The IHRA defines the term simply as follows:

> … policies, programmes and practices that aim to reduce the harms associated with the use of psychoactive drugs in people unable or unwilling to stop. The defining features are the focus on the prevention of harm, rather than on the prevention of drug use itself, and the focus on people who continue to use drugs.[43]

Barrett has a more sweeping definition of harm reduction, stating that '[h]arm reduction is an area of practice, science and policy that has been proven to reduce the health and social harms of drug use.'[44] Building on this somewhat expansive definition, he continues to tie it in with a critique of INCB, as shall be seen below. This definition is clearly too broad to be truly meaningful.

Strict definitional matters aside, harm reduction is generally understood to include measures such as the aforementioned needle exchange or needle distribution, pill testing at rave parties and other venues, and, more controversially, so-called 'injection rooms', where persons can abuse illicit drugs under official supervision. Substitution treatment, ie the prescription of opiates besides heroin (usually methadone) to heroin addicts, is also often included as a harm reduction approach. What is important to stress is that, as elaborated clearly in the above definitions proposed by advocates of drug liberalisation, harm reduction approaches do not aim at stopping drug abuse—that is not their objective. Harm reduction strives only at reducing the harm caused by drug abuse.

The above is, on its own, of course not undesirable, and given the serious difficulties in overcoming drug addiction that many people exhibit,

[41] IHRA, 'Global State of Harm Reduction 2014' (London, 2015) 16. This is a significant increase from the 60 countries that operated such progammes in 2007, see WHO, UNODC, and UNAIDS, 'Guide to starting and managing needle and syringe programmes' (Geneva, 2007) 5.

[42] WHO, 'Effectiveness of sterile needle and syringe programming in reducing HIV/AIDS amongst injecting drug users' (Geneva, 2004) 28.

[43] IHRA, 'What is Harm Reduction? A Position Statement', at http://www.ihra.net/what-is-harm-reduction.

[44] Damon Barrett and Philip E. Veerman, *A Commentary on the United Nations Convention on the Rights of the Child: Article 33: Protection from Narcotic Drugs and Psychotropic Substances* (Leiden, Martinus Nijhoff, 2012) 85.

such measures are clearly called for. The question is whether it should be accepted as sufficient. In other words, should harm reduction be viewed as just one component of a comprehensive strategy against drugs, a strategy which has as its ultimate goal the eradication of drug abuse? Or should states abandon efforts to stop drug abuse, accept its inevitability (or even accept that persons should be free to abuse whatever substances they wish), and focus only on reducing the ill effects caused by this abuse? The answer to this question naturally depends on one's position regarding drugs in general.

The answer put forward by the international drug control regime is that harm reduction has an important part to play, but it can only be a stop-gap measure, not a goal in itself. Harm reduction can ensure that persons who abuse drugs avoid at least some of the health risks involved, but it does nothing to address the root cause of these health risks: that is not its goal and that is not how it is designed. Therefore, it cannot replace strategies and measures against drugs—only complement them. INCB has argued this in several of its Annual Reports, noting that harm reduction may be useful:

> ... as a tertiary prevention strategy for demand reduction purposes ... [and] could play a part in a comprehensive drug demand reduction strategy, but such programmes should not be carried out at the expense of other important activities to reduce the demand for illicit drugs, for example drug abuse prevention activities ... [T]he Board drew attention to the fact that 'harm reduction' programmes could not be considered substitutes for demand reduction programmes.[45]

INCB has also stated its 'regret' that:

> ... since some 'harm reduction' measures were controversial, discussions of their advantages and disadvantages had dominated the public debate on drug policy ... [and] that the discussion on some 'harm reduction' measures had diverted the attention (and, in some cases, funds) of Governments from important demand reduction activities such as primary prevention or abstinence-oriented treatment.[46]

UNODC, in a paper issued in 2008, also states that:

> 'Harm reduction' is often made an unnecessarily controversial issue as if there was a contradiction between prevention and treatment on one hand and reducing the adverse health and social consequences of drug use on the other. This is a false dichotomy. They are complementary.[47]

[45] INCB, *Annual Report 2003* (Vienna, 2004) para 219.
[46] INCB, *Annual Report 2003* (n 45) para 220.
[47] UNODC, 'Reducing the Adverse Health and Social Consequences of Drug Abuse: a Comprehensive Approach' (Vienna, 2008) preface.

While noting that harm reduction, 'combined with good-practice treatment facilities may prevent immediate adverse health and social consequences and be effective in the long-term reduction of drug-related harm for individuals and society',[48] UNODC stresses that any harm reduction measure must be in compliance with the drug control conventions,[49] seemingly indicating that INCB's judgement on particular approaches should be accepted as definitive.

In 2015, INCB expanded on its position, arguing that harm reduction was important precisely because drug abuse needed to be combated:

> It is not simply drugs users themselves who are affected, but also their families and immediate communities. The world drug problem affects our entire societies as trafficking, related crime and violence, in some regions, and health and socio-economic impacts worldwide directly or indirectly deteriorate our quality of life as individuals, and as members of our communities.[50]

Unsurprisingly, advocates of drug liberalisation see things differently. Harm reduction is key to the arguments of the advocates of drug liberalisation, who without exception argue for the harm reduction approach. Harm reduction is presented as an approach based on human rights,[51] one that '[exemplifies] human rights in action'.[52] Barrett argues that '[t]he best that can be said is that harm reduction is discretionary under the drug conventions. Banning harm reduction is not permitted.'[53]

Often cited as justification for this notion is ICESCR Article 12, which states that persons have the right to the 'highest attainable standard of physical and mental health'. There is a General Comment on Article 12,[54] adopted in 2000, but it does not provide guidance on these issues (though drug abuse is presented clearly in the General Comment as an undesirable activity that states should at least discourage).[55] Hunt visited Sweden during his term as the Special Rapporteur on the Right to Health. In a passage in his report espousing the benefits of the needle exchange

[48] UNDOC, 'Reducing the Adverse Health and Social Consequences of Drug Abuse' (n 47) 6.

[49] UNDOC (n 47) 5.

[50] INCB, 'The International Narcotics Control Board reviews global availability of medicines and access to treatment' (Vienna, 15 May 2015).

[51] See eg IHRA, 'What is Harm Reduction?' (n 43).

[52] International Federation of Red Cross Societies, 'Out of harm's way: Injecting drug users and harm reduction' (Geneva, December 2010) 2.

[53] Barrett and Veerman, *A Commentary on the United Nations Convention on the Rights of the Child* (n 44) 85.

[54] Committee on Economic, Social, and Cultural Rights (CESCR), 'General Comment number 14: The Right to the Highest Attainable Standard of Health' (Geneva, UN index E/C.12/2000/4/, 11 August 2000).

[55] See eg CESCR, 'General Comment number 14' (n 54) para 37.

programme he visited in that country, Hunt seemingly goes on to extrapolate his conclusions to include all harm reduction services, stating that there is:

> … worldwide experience that harm-reduction programmes, including needle exchange programmes and associated health care, promote and protect the health of drug users [and] are highly cost-effective … The Special Rapporteur emphasizes that the Government has a responsibility to ensure the implementation, throughout Sweden and as a matter of priority, of a comprehensive harm-reduction policy, including counselling, advice on sexual and reproductive health, and clean needles and syringes.[56]

Since it is unclear what in practice harm reduction actually entails, blanket statements of its benefits, and certainly of any 'human right to harm reduction', are of limited value. At its most general, harm reduction aims at reducing the harm associated with drug abuse. As a policy goal, this is difficult to argue against—a fact no doubt not lost on advocates of drug liberalisation—but it is when specific approaches are examined that there is room for debate. The devil is truly in the detail. As noted above, INCB has no principled objections to the harm reduction approach, as long as it does not supplant the ultimate goal of stopping drug abuse. However, INCB has stated its position that certain measures usually included under the harm reduction umbrella violate the international drug control conventions, giving rise to fierce criticism from advocates of drug liberalisation.

INCB's Annual Report 2003 remains the most comprehensive enumeration of INCB's position on specific harm reduction approaches, and it is worth citing the relevant paragraphs at length:

> In a number of countries, Governments have introduced since the end of the 1980s programmes for the exchange or distribution of needles and syringes for drug addicts, with the aim of limiting the spread of HIV/AIDS. The Board maintains … that Governments need to adopt measures that may decrease the sharing of hypodermic needles among injecting drug abusers in order to limit the spread of HIV/AIDS. At the same time, the Board has been stressing that any prophylactic measures should not promote and/or facilitate drug abuse … Many Governments have opted in favour of drug substitution and maintenance treatment as one of the forms of medical treatment of drug addicts, whereby a drug with similar action to the drug of dependence, but with a lower degree of risks, is prescribed by a medical doctor for a specific treatment aim. Although results are dependent on many factors, its implementation does not constitute any breach of treaty provisions, whatever substance may be used for such treatment … In some countries, facilities have been established where injecting drug abusers can inject drugs that they have acquired illicitly. That practice has

[56] Hunt (n 2) para 60.

> been allowed by national drug control legislation or Governments have simply allowed or tolerated such initiatives by local governments or institutions. The Board has stated on a number of occasions … that the operation of such facilities remains a source of grave concern. The Board reiterates that they violate the provisions of the international drug control conventions … [F]rom a legal point of view, such facilities violate the international drug control conventions. In some countries where the abuse of synthetic drugs, mainly amphetamine-type stimulants, has become widespread, authorities have provided facilities for having the composition and quality of the drugs, usually in tablet form, tested and then returned to the drug abusers, informing them about the results of the test, in particular to warn them if the drug is impure or adulterated. The Board has been concerned that such practices conveyed the wrong message on the risks of drug abuse and provided a false sense of safety for drug abusers … The Board notes the announcement of the Government of the Netherlands, one of the first countries where such drug testing had been introduced, that the programme of pill testing at parties and clubs had been terminated in order to avoid the projection of messages counter- productive to drug abuse prevention efforts.[57]

The position of INCB can, therefore, be summarised as follows: it does not oppose needle exchange or distribution; nor does it oppose substitution treatment. INCB is, however, against both pill testing and so-called 'injection rooms'—in particular the latter, which it states clearly is against the international drug control conventions.

Given that there is no disagreement between INCB and advocates of drug liberalisation on needle exchange, this issue would seem to be somewhat redundant. Nevertheless, advocates of drug liberalisation criticise the positions of INCB, essentially arguing that the body doesn't go far enough: IHRA claims that '[INCB's] statements [are] heavily reserved, stating that harm reduction should not promote drug use, and indeed often hostile'[58] to harm reduction as a whole. Advocates of drug liberalisation argue that INCB should take a stronger stance on the issue, promoting needle exchange worldwide,[59] but it is not altogether clear why this should be INCB's role, especially since other UN agencies, such as WHO and UN Aids, already do this. INCB does take note of needle exchange programmes in specific countries in its Annual Reports without any indication of disapproval.[60] Given that, in the eyes of INCB, there is no controversy on the compatibility of needle exchange with the drug control conventions in principle, there does not seem to be much further to say.

The issue of pill testing on the other hand, has generally not been raised by advocates of drug liberalisation in their critiques of INCB.

[57] INCB (n 45) at paras 221 to 226.

[58] IHRA, 'Unique in International Relations? A Comparison of the International Narcotics Control Board and the UN Human Rights Treaty Bodies' (London, 2008) 9.

[59] OSF, 'Selective Concern: The 2005 Report of the International Narcotics Control Board and the Need for Accountability' (New York, 2006).

[60] See eg INCB, *Annual Report 2011* (Vienna, 2012) para 378.

The approach remains politically controversial in many countries,[61] and the number of countries where it takes place remains relatively small. The most comprehensive study on the measure was conducted by the European Monitoring Centre for Drugs and Drug Addiction (EMCDDA) in 2001, at which point the organisation listed only six countries within the European Union where pill testing took place[62]—and, as noted in the passage from INCB's 2007 Annual Report, governments are not always entirely convinced of the utility of the measure either.

The remaining two issues—substitution treatment and 'injection rooms'—remain a source of contention, in particular the latter.

Substitution Treatment

Replacement or substitution treatment, usually using methadone, is widely recognised as an effective means of improving the health situation of opiate (in particular heroin) addicts. In a joint position paper on substitution treatment, UNODC, WHO, and UNAIDS note that '[s]ubstitution maintenance therapy is one of the most effective treatment options for opioid dependence. It can decrease the high cost of opioid dependence to individuals, their families and society at large by reducing heroin use, associated deaths, HIV risk behaviours and criminal activity.'[63] According to IHRA, opiate substitution treatment was available in 80 countries in 2014,[64] with methadone being the most common substance for this treatment.

The utility and general desirability of substitution treatment is not in doubt, and, as noted above, INCB has stated that it is not in violation of the international drug control conventions. This makes sense from the point of view of INCB: unlike most of the other measures usually included as harm reduction, opiate substitution treatment is generally not a one-off intervention, but a sustained process of treatment that involves medical professionals and other interventions aimed at ensuring the individual overcomes his drug dependence. In other words, it is a medical intervention using drugs for a medical purpose, so by definition it would seem to be allowed by the international drug conventions.[65]

[61] See eg 'Nightclub drug tests: saving lives or quality control?', *Channel 4 News*, 30 September 2013.

[62] Austria, Belgium, France, Germany, the Netherlands, and Spain. See EMCDDA, 'On-site pill testing interventions in the European Union' (Lisbon, 2001).

[63] UNODC, WHO, and UNAIDS, 'Substitution maintenance therapy in the management of opioid dependence and HIV/AIDS prevention' (Geneva, 2004) 2.

[64] IHRA (n 41) 16.

[65] On the other hand, INCB also states that countries should not authorise the use of cannabis for medical purposes, as 'the evidence that cannabis might be useful as a medicine

Therefore, as with needle exchange, this is another issue that INCB and advocates of drug liberalisation agree on.[66] Nevertheless, INCB receives heavy criticism from those advocates on this topic. For example, Csete accuses INCB of 'disregarding' the 'internationally accepted norm' of methadone substitution therapy: 'the Board has often sounded the alarm over fast-growing HIV epidemics linked to drug use, but has generally refused to recognise [substitution therapy] as an important HIV prevention tool, as the technical UN bodies have done.'[67] She then cites the 2012 INCB Annual Report, where INCB referred to the methadone substitution programme in Mauritius and '[invited] the Government to increase the provision of psychosocial support and to find ways of guiding drug abuses towards reducing their drug intake so that they may eventually stop abusing drugs.' Ceste states that this statement of the INCB amounts to a 'characterisation of methadone treatment as "abusing drugs" [undermining] this essential therapy in a way that is exactly contrary to the mandate of the INCB.'[68] It is not clear to this author how this was read into this statement of INCB, which appears to be an uncontroversial recommendation to a government to ensure that substitution therapy does not simply continue forever, but is directed at ensuring, over time, that drug abuse discontinues.

IHRA notes that 'In 2012, 78 countries with reported injecting drug use [did] not provide OST [(Opioid Substitution Therapy)] services.'[69] Russia is a prominent, and much criticised example of a country that has serious problems of injecting drug abuse and yet continues to prohibit substitution treatment. As noted by HRW:

> … the virtual absence of humane services to treat drug addiction and the illegality in Russia of methadone and other drugs used elsewhere to treat heroin addiction further compromise HIV prevention among drug users.[70] … [The Russian government should] [r]epeal the ban on use of methadone in replacement or substitution therapy for opiate addiction and make replacement therapy a central element of HIV prevention for opiate users.[71]

is insufficient. Countries should not authorise the use of cannabis as a medicine until conclusive results based on research are available. Sound scientific evidence for its safety, efficacy and usefulness is required to justify its use in medical practice.' INCB, 'US Supreme Court Decision Upholds International Law' (Vienna, 8 June 2005). Nevertheless, it is the role of the WHO, not INCB's, to assess the medical evidence available for particular controlled substances.

[66] HRW, 'Lessons not Learned: Human Rights Abuses and HIV/AIDS in the Russian Federation' (New York, 2004) 6.

[67] Joanne Csete, 'Overhauling Oversight: Human Rights at the INCB', in *Governing the Global Drug Wars*, LSE Ideas (London, London School of Economics, 2012) Kindle version 2350/2572.

[68] Csete, 'Overhauling Oversight' (n 67) 2352/2572.

[69] IHRA (n 41) 16.

[70] HRW (n 61) 3.

[71] HRW (n 61) 6.

INCB has been criticised for not promoting methadone substitution therapy to the Russian government, and for failing to condemn the country for not allowing such treatment: for example, in the same paper as above, Csete states that 'INCB has done nothing to urge Russia, which bans methadone, to lift that ban, or to urge countries with very limited availability to methadone therapy to expand it.'[72] Whether INCB could do more to promote substitution therapy is a legitimate question, and it is understandable that advocates of drug liberalisation would be frustrated with the body's failure to criticise particular states that fail to adopt particular policies. At the same time, to attempt to characterise INCB (or the international drug control regime as a whole) as being against substitution therapy is clearly incorrect.

In a related criticism, Mendez has cited Nowak in stressing the human rights implications of the denial of methadone substitution treatment in situations of detention.[73] That denying methadone treatment to a detainee to force a criminal confession constitutes torture should be relatively uncontroversial, and it would also seem appropriate that effective treatment for drug dependence, including methadone treatment, should be available within prisons. However, Mendez expands this argument even further, asserting that '[s]imilar reasoning should apply to the non-custodial context, particularly in instances where Governments impose a complete ban on substitution treatment and harm reduction measures.'[74]

Though Mendez does not elaborate, it would appear that his argument is that any government that does not allow methadone substitution treatment, not only in custodial settings but in general, is committing ill-treatment against persons who abuse drugs. This would seem to be quite a leap: it is clear that a state that allows particular methods of treatment should authorise it within detention facilities as appropriate, but it is hardly self-evident that the failure of a state to authorise certain harm reduction approaches at all is, as a legal matter, a violation of that state's human rights obligations. Mendez goes on to state that:

> By denying effective drug treatment, State drug policies intentionally subject a large group of people to severe physical pain, suffering and humiliation, effectively punishing them for using drugs and trying to coerce them into abstinence, in complete disregard of the chronic nature of dependency and of the scientific evidence pointing to the ineffectiveness of punitive measures.[75]

[72] Csete (n 67) 2360/2572. See also OSF (n 59) 2.

[73] Juan Mendez, 'Report of the Special Rapporteur on torture and other cruel, inhuman or degrading treatment or punishment' (Geneva, UN index A/HRC/22/53, 1 February 2013) para 73.

[74] Mendez, 'Report of the Special Rapporteur' (n 73).

[75] Mendez, 'Report of the Special Rapporteur' (n 73) para 74.

On the other hand, individual members of INCB have made statements that call into question their personal dedication to INCB's position on opiate substitution treatment. In 2005, Tatyana Dmitrieva, a former Russian Health Minister and then-member of INCB, joined in on the signing of a public memorandum arguing against methadone substitution, published in a widely read Russian medical journal. According to advocates of drug liberalisation, the text of this memorandum:

> ... contained numerous inaccuracies and half-truths about methadone. The memorandum insinuates incorrectly that WHO has opposed methadone therapy for most of its history and that the CND has rejected methadone as a tool for treating heroin addiction. It also recounts deaths from methadone overdose in Lithuania that experts in that country could not corroborate, and cites research by authors whose names could not be found in any medical database. The authors included many assertions of the ineffectiveness or dangers of methadone, without citing evidence to support their claims. Scientists from the United States, the United Kingdom, Iran, the Czech Republic, Italy, Australia, Albania, Switzerland, Croatia, Germany, Canada and France issued a heavily referenced, point-by-point reply to this statement, correcting the article's many errors.[76]

Though Dmitrieva identified herself as a member of INCB in the memorandum, there do not appear to have been any ramifications for her status within that body: she went on to serve in numerous functions in INCB, including two terms as Vice President.[77] Within this context, it is understandable that advocates of drug liberalisation would question INCB's institutional commitment to substitution treatment, and this issue remains unresolved.

The above notwithstanding, it is worthy to note that substitution treatment is not a panacea, and, at least in isolation, is not really treatment as such. Ghodse, in his capacity as an academic, warns against the idealisation of methadone maintenance:

> ... a serious cause for concern is that long-term opiate maintenance is not really treatment in any meaningful sense of the word. It encourages drug-dependent individuals towards a passive acceptance of their condition ... If opiate maintenance is routinely available as a treatment option, it is understandable and to be expected that many will opt for it rather than face the anxieties of being without their drug, and the chance of achieving abstinence is lost—at least for a while. In summary, therefore, long-term methadone maintenance should be regarded very much as the last resort in the management of opiate dependence

[76] Canadian HIV/AIDS Legal Network and International Harm Reduction Development Program of the Open Society Institute, 'Closed to Reason: The International Narcotics Control Board and HIV/AIDS' (Toronto, 2007) 17.

[77] INCB, 'In memoriam', *Annual Report 2010* (Vienna, 2011) iii.

> … Withdrawal should be attempted and repeated, if only to establish that it cannot be tolerated or that the addict's life without drugs becomes increasingly chaotic.[78]

While this does not detract from the general desirability of substitution treatment as an option for persons with problematic opiate abuse problems, its shortcomings should be noted. There is no one size fits all panacea for problematic drug abuse.

Injection Rooms

Probably the most contentious issue between advocates of drug liberalisation and INCB is that of injection rooms. These facilities are referred to using numerous terms, with differing political nuances. Injection room (the term originally used by most to describe the facilities) has negative implications, at least in the mind of most people who use the term, and arguably conjures up images of the opium dens of China before the Opium Wars. Strictly speaking, the term may be incomplete, since most of the facilities have areas for inhalation of drugs, separate from spaces where persons can inject. EMCDDA uses the relatively neutral term 'drug consumption rooms',[79] but other, even more innocuous sounding terms exist, such as 'supervised injection site', the term used in Canada for the one facility in Vancouver.[80]

Injection rooms are facilities run by the state where persons can appear unannounced and abuse their own illicit drugs, under medical supervision. Medical personnel are on hand to ensure that injections are done in a safe manner, and that any overdose is cared for immediately. Social workers are also usually at hand, though the extent to which they actually approach the persons using the facilities naturally depends on a wide range of factors, and it is unrealistic to expect that all individuals who enter injection rooms will be encouraged to avail themselves of treatment

[78] Hamid Ghodse, *Drugs and Addictive Behaviour: a Guide to Treatment*, third edition (Cambridge, Cambridge University Press, 2002) 260, 261.

[79] EMCDDA defines drug consumption rooms as 'professionally supervised healthcare facilities where drug users can consume drugs in safer conditions. They seek to attract hard-to-reach populations of drug users, especially marginalised groups and those who use drugs on the streets or in other risky and unhygienic conditions. One of their primary goals is to reduce morbidity and mortality by providing a safe environment for more hygienic drug use and by training clients in safer drug use. At the same time, they seek to reduce drug use in public and improve public amenity in areas surrounding urban drug markets. A further aim is to promote access to social, health and drug treatment facilities.' EMCDDA, 'Drug consumption rooms: an overview of provision and evidence' (Lisbon, June 2015) 2.

[80] See Vancouver Coastal Health, 'Insite—supervised injection site (SIS)', http://supervisedinjection.vch.ca.

options. Still, proponents of the approach argue that they provide opportunities to access some the most 'hard core' drug addicts, many of whom would otherwise have no connection with social services at all. Proponents also argue that the facilities are successful in reducing public nuisances, such as drug abuse and discarded needles in public spaces.

EMCDDA appears to promote the approach, stating that:

> ... the benefits of providing supervised drug consumption facilities may include improvements in safe, hygienic drug use, especially among regular clients, increased access to health and social services, and reduced public drug use and associated nuisance. There is no evidence to suggest that the availability of safer injecting facilities increases drug use or frequency of injecting. These services facilitate rather than delay treatment entry and do not result in higher rates of local drug-related crime.[81]

EMCDDA even publishes a 'service model' for injection rooms.[82]

Injection rooms exist only in a handful of countries. According to the EMCDDA:

> ... as of June 2015 there are 31 facilities in 25 cities in the Netherlands; 24 in 15 cities in Germany; 12 in two cities in Spain; one in Norway; one in Luxembourg; five in three cities in Denmark; and 12 in eight cities in Switzerland. In a recent development, as of April 2015 a six-year trial of drug consumption rooms was approved in France and it is expected that facilities will be opened in three cities in the coming months. Outside of Europe there are two facilities in Sydney, Australia and one medically supervised injecting centre in Vancouver, Canada.[83]

All of these governments have received stern letters from INCB, and have found themselves on the receiving end of public criticism in INCB's Annual Reports.

In the course of preparing its Annual Report 2003, in which it elaborated its positions on the various harm reduction measures, INCB requested the Legal Department of UNODC to prepare a discussion paper on the legal issues raised by harm reduction and the compatibility of particular approaches with the drug control conventions. Titled 'Flexibility of treaty provisions as regards harm reduction approaches',[84] after its submission to INCB, the paper was subsequently leaked to advocates of drug liberalisation, who present it as a ringing endorsement of all harm reduction approaches (including injection rooms) and further evidence of the stubbornness, or even ignorance, of INCB for refusing even UNODC legal

[81] EMCDDA (n 79) 6.
[82] Ibid.
[83] EMCDDA (n 79) 2.
[84] UNODC Department of Legal Affairs, 'Flexibility of treaty provisions as regards harm reduction approaches' (Vienna, UN index, E/INCB/2002/W.13/SS.5, 20 September 2002).

advice on harm reduction.[85] In fact, the paper does no such thing, and advocates of drug liberalisation usually quote the paper selectively, using text out of context.

For example, the paper includes a brief discussion of whether operation of injection rooms can be considered to constitute incitement to abuse drugs (prohibited specifically in Article 3 of the 1988 Convention), and answers in the negative. The Transnational Institute (TNI), however, takes selective quotes out of this context, and presents them as if UNODC had endorsed the entire injection room approach, which it does not. TNI also makes much of one of the paper's closing remarks, 'It could even be argued that the drug control treaties, as they stand, have been rendered out of synch with reality, since at the time they came into force they could not have possibly foreseen these new threats.'[86] At the same time, TNI fails to note that this statement is followed immediately by language reiterating the need for combating drug abuse:

> Nonetheless, no matter how true those arguments may prove, the legal obligations derived from the international drug control treaties remain. The unfortunate facts that illicit drug markets are taking over parts of urban areas or of drug abusers poisoning themselves with adulterated substances do not invalidate the Parties obligation to combat drug abuse. If anything, these new trends make it all the more urgent for them to find new ways to substantially reduce the illicit demand for drugs. Even leaving the definition of treatment, rehabilitation or social reintegration to Parties, it seems clear that fulfilling their obligations under the treaties should be more comprehensive than just alleviating the harm associated with drug abuse. It seems evident that all-encompassing positions on harm reduction are of very little practical use.[87]

The paper also points out that pill testing is 'perhaps the strategy that is hardest to reconcile with the obligations … [T]he defeatism at the base of this approach, and the misleading message it sends to society at large, run contrary to the spirit of the Convention.'[88] These sections of the letter have been universally ignored by advocates of drug liberalisation, whose goal appears to be to criticise INCB come what may.

Whatever the advice from UNODC may have been, INCB remains vehemently against injection rooms, and occasionally uses passages in its Annual Reports to reiterate its position. For example, in a very strong passage in its Annual Report 2006, INCB:

> [noted] with concern that, despite its ongoing dialogue with the Governments concerned, drug injection rooms, where drug abusers can abuse with impunity

[85] See eg Transnational Institute, 'Flexibility of Treaty provisions', at www.undrugcontrol.info/en/static/item/2307-flexibility-of-treaty-provisions

[86] UNODC Department of Legal Affairs (n 84) paras 36, 37.

[87] Ibid.

[88] UNODC Department of Legal Affairs (n 84) para 33.

> drugs acquired on the illicit market, remain in operation in a number of countries, including Australia, Canada, Germany, Luxembourg, the Netherlands, Norway, Spain and Switzerland. [INCB] regrets that no measures have been taken to terminate the operation of such facilities in the countries concerned, and, in some cases, the number of such rooms has increased … [INCB] wishes to reiterate that the provision of rooms for the abuse of drugs … are contrary to the international drug control treaties … [INCB] believes that any national, state or local authority that permits the establishment and operation of rooms or any outlet to facilitate the abuse of drugs, by injection or any other route of administration, also provides an opportunity for illicit drug distribution. The Board would like to emphasize that Governments have an obligation to combat illicit drug trafficking in all its forms. …[89]

As argued by this author in a previous publication,[90] injection rooms may be an inevitable destination of the harm reduction continuum that starts with needle distribution. The reality is that 'clean' needles all too often become 'dirty' very quickly: there is nothing to stop the person abusing drugs from sharing the needle with others later on, defeating the entire purpose. Used needles can still be discarded in public spaces, causing public health risks.[91] Finally, the fact that a needle may be 'clean' does not prevent the person abusing drugs from overdosing with it. As noted above, the evidence suggests that needle distribution is effective in preventing HIV and other transmission, but there will always be a (relatively small) group of drug dependent persons who do not respond to the intervention.

Logically, therefore, it is not a long distance from the provision of sterile needles to the provision of a hygienic space to use those needles. This is not necessarily to argue against harm reduction in general—as noted above, such sweeping statements are of little value—or, on the opposite side, to argue that since needle distribution is legitimate, injection rooms should be recognised as such as well. It is merely to point out that the

[89] INCB, *Annual Report 2006* (Vienna, 2007) para 175. Of course, similar arguments could be made regarding needle exchange as well. See eg Ghodse (n 78) 277: 'The simplicity of this approach is appealing, but it has certain inbuilt disadvantages. There is a very real risk, for example, that the easy availability of sterile syringes and needles may make the transition to injecting easier and more acceptable and might encourage more young drug abusers to start injection and to do so sooner: equally there may be less incentive for others to give up injecting … Perhaps the best way forward is to judge each case on its merits, rather than to adopt a stereotyped response.'

[90] Saul Takahashi, 'Drug Control, Human Rights, and the Right to the Highest Attainable Standard of Health; By No Means Straightforward Issues' (2009) 31 *Human Rights Quarterly* 748.

[91] See eg 'Ottawa's needle-exchange policy too dangerous, shelter says', *Canadian Broadcasting Service*, 13 March 2008, which reports that residents of an area where a needle exchange programme was being implemented collected over 1,000 discarded needles in public spaces over a six-week period, prompting a review of the programme by the NGO running it. This review showed that, over a 25-day period, only 500 of over 2,000 needles distributed were returned to the outreach facility.

difference between the two measures is not as vast as might be suggested. This fact is not lost on advocates of drug liberalisation, some of whom have pointed out the conundrum. For example, the Beckley Foundation notes that 'if the INCB's claim is that *enabling users to take illegal drugs more safely* is inherently "contrary to the fundamental provisions of the international drug control treaties", then this applies as much to needle and syringe exchange as it does to [injection rooms].' (emphasis in original)[92]

Nevertheless, there appears to be some line that is crossed by the operation of injection rooms, at least according to INCB. What exactly this line is may be difficult to define, but it is submitted that INCB would be well advised to at least attempt to do so, if only to clarify the nature of obligations under the drug control conventions.

Conclusion on Harm Reduction

The general argument is that harm reduction is a practical way—the only way, so advocates of drug liberalisation would have one believe—to ensure the right to the highest attainable standard of health. There is of course merit in the argument that, in a general sense, measures aimed at mitigating drug abuse related harm may be necessary to ensure the right to health of persons who abuse drugs. It is clear that some harm reduction approaches are effective in providing some semblance of protection for the health of persons who abuse drugs. Obviously, it is far preferable that persons refrain from abusing drugs, and that persons who suffer from dependence undergo treatment for that aim. However, if that is not to happen immediately, then some services to at least mitigate the worst effects of drug abuse should be offered. Given that this would contribute to the highest attainable standard of health for the person concerned, at least in the immediate term, there are some grounds for stating that such measures are cognizant of human rights.

Nevertheless, there is little justification to argue that human rights law requires all of the above harm reduction measures, and any other which may be thought of in the future and included under the harm reduction umbrella. Which particular harm reduction approaches are appropriate would have to be decided upon by each community, with the actual impact on the community looked upon on an individual basis. For example, the Russian policy on methadone treatment is surely problematic, in that it is prohibiting large segments of its population from accessing treatment for drug addiction. However, one would be hard pressed to argue the same for injection rooms, which hardly qualify as treatment for drug addiction in and of themselves.

92 Beckley Foundation, 'Drug Consumption Rooms' (London, 2004) 3.

In any case, while human rights might justify harm reduction measures in a general sense, this in no way translates into an argument that human rights are opposed to the international drug control regime—as noted by UNODC, this is a false dichotomy.

Many advocates of drug liberalisation argue that penalties for drug abuse prevent persons who abuse drugs from coming forward and accessing health, including harm reduction, services. IHRA argues, for example, that '[p]unitive law enforcement in Europe has the same unfortunate consequences for health and rights as it does globally, exacerbating the HIV and HCV epidemics, increasing stigma, and resulting in human rights violations, fear of accessing health services …'.[93] This argument is connected with the notion that there is a 'human right to harm reduction'. Since ICESCR Article 12 requires states to ensure access to health care services without discrimination, any and all obstacles to harm reduction services must be removed. The argument appears to be that if only drug abuse were treated purely as a public health issue, then large numbers of persons dependent on drugs would be empowered to come to government supported injection rooms, where they would in turn access further social services.

This argument may have merit in some situations, but to present it as a universal fact seems simplistic—there is a wealth of reasons that many persons who abuse drugs do not willingly access public services. More to the point, this appears to be another instance of a foregone conclusion: there is a wide gap between the recognition that some persons who abuse drugs are dissuaded from accessing harm reduction services and the argument that, ergo, penalties for drug abuse must be removed in all instances.

As noted above, the benefits of some harm reduction approaches, such as needle exchange and methadone treatment, are well accepted, including by INCB. INCB also recognises harm reduction as a general concept, but as part of an overall government strategy aimed at combating drug abuse and trafficking. There does not seem to be much more to say on the matter, and arguments that a 'human right to harm reduction' should somehow trump all efforts against illicit drugs are without foundation.

As it became clear that the harm reduction argument on its own was not enough, advocates of drug liberalisation began to turn to more standard formulations of human rights to buttress their advocacy.

II. HUMAN RIGHTS AS A TOOL

Harm reduction is a somewhat technical concept that does not travel readily beyond drug policy circles—most people not directly affected by drug

93 IHRA (n 41) 63.

abuse do not know, and arguably do not really care, about it. In addition, the connotations of harm reduction remain controversial—some governments, in particular the US, have historically been opposed to it, and argue against recognition of the concept in international policy fora (though to say one is 'against harm reduction' in a sweeping sense is, as has been shown, not altogether meaningful). Therefore, while continuing to argue for harm reduction, and using it in their advocacy, advocates of drug liberalisation required a new marketing framework—a language that had more universal value, that would appeal to the public in a more effective manner. This language also had to be something that persons could not so easily oppose, at least not in a general sense. With this in mind, advocates of drug liberalisation started to turn to human rights, as a tool to advance their goals.

Several arguments have been advanced by advocates of drug liberalisation, using human rights standards in an attempt to show how persons who abuse drugs are subject to a wide range of human rights violations. As noted above, those advocates had already been citing the right to the highest attainable standard of health in arguing for harm reduction. However, the fact that the right to health is enumerated in ICESCR inevitably causes difficulties, because economic, social and cultural rights remain controversial in many arenas outside of human rights circles. In particular in the US, the notion that states should intervene in the free market and ensure that residents have access to health care is not universally accepted, meaning that the right to health argument is somewhat of a weak tool.

On the other hand, international standards regarding 'traditional' rights, such as the right to be free from torture or arbitrary detention, do not suffer from this constraint, and are arguably more readily acceptable to the public in many countries as 'real' human rights. Advocates of drug liberalisation, therefore, started to utilise standards of civil and political rights, such as the ICCPR and the Convention against Torture (CAT), to highlight how, in various different countries and contexts, persons who abuse drugs have been subject to violations of these standards. These include, for example, excessive use of force by law enforcement officials, even to the extent that extrajudicial executions have taken place (though this is much more rare). In some countries, persons who abuse drugs are also victimised by arbitrary detention practices. Finally, the death penalty for drug-related offences has also been raised, though the number of countries where this takes place is also not large.

As shall be explored below, all of these human rights arguments are correct, in narrowly defined technical terms. Research by numerous actors (mainly human rights NGOs) indicate that problematic practices violating human rights indeed take place, and the lack of compatibility of those practices with human rights standards is not in question. However, as shall be shown, most of the situations are in fact not unique to persons who abuse drugs—persons who for whatever reason fall foul of law enforcement in the countries concerned are generally vulnerable to similar treatment. In any case, contrary to what advocates of drug liberalisation attempt to argue, none of those situations can stand as justification to dismantle the international drug control regime as a whole. The notion that prohibiting drug abuse in general, and the international drug control conventions in particular, require, or even inevitably result in, the violations outlined by drug liberalisation advocates is disingenuous. It is also easily refuted by the fact that such violations in fact do not take place in the vast majority of countries where drug abuse remains prohibited. The human rights arguments are, in fact, not as strong as they first appear.

Death Penalty

The first issue to be taken up by advocates of drug liberalisation, and perhaps one of the easiest to promote, is that of the death penalty for drug-related offences. Advocates of drug liberalisation have engaged in considerable advocacy regarding the fact that some countries provide for the death penalty for non-violent drug-related offences. Nevertheless, though comprehensive data is difficult to obtain, all observers agree that the number of countries that provide for the death penalty for drug related offences is small, and appears to be decreasing. For example, Harm Reduction International and the World Collation against the Death Penalty admit that:

> [The] consensus among human rights and international drug control bodies [that the death penalty should not be applied to drug offences] is reflected in state practice. A very small number of governments actually execute drug offenders. Fewer than 10 per cent of the world's countries retain the death penalty for drug offences in both law and practice. In addition, despite the rise in countries applying the death penalty for drugs during the 1980s and 1990s, there has been a drop over the past 15 years.[94]

This is a significant drop, given that the UN Secretary General stated in a report in 2001 that, at the end of 2000, at least 35 countries provided for the death penalty for such offences.[95] The assessment of IHRA is even smaller. They state that 'only between 5 and 7 per cent'[96] of states retain the death penalty for drug-related offences—though this figure was published in 2012. Amnesty International (AI) lists only seven countries (China, Indonesia, Malaysia, Singapore, Sri Lanka, Thailand and

[94] Harm Reduction International and the World Coalition against the Death Penalty, 'Submission: Impact of the world drug problem on the enjoyment of human rights' (London, 15 May 2015) 2.

[95] United Nations Secretary General, 'Capital punishment and implementation of the safeguards guaranteeing protection of the rights of those facing the death penalty, Report of the Secretary-General' (Vienna, E/CN.15/2001/10, 29 March 2001).

[96] IHRA, 'The Death Penalty for Drug Offences: Global Overview 2012' (London, 2012) 5.

Vietnam) as having sentenced drug-related offenders to death in 2014, and four for having conducted executions—China, Malaysia, Singapore and Vietnam.[97]

Despite the above decreasing trend, in 2015, Harm Reduction International and the World Coalition against the Death Penalty refer to the aforementioned 2001 UN report in stating that there was 'a more than 50% increase in the number of countries prescribing the death penalty for drugs into domestic law between 1985 and 2000.'[98] An increase from 22 to 35 would indeed be an increase of over 50 percent—but without the numbers, this figure comes across as somewhat sensationalist (which arguably may be the intent). The two organisations then go on to make the unsubstantiated claim that this increase was a direct result of the 1988 Convention and the international drug control regime in general, arguing that:

> This window of time coincides remarkably closely with the period of the drafting, adoption and State ratification of the [1988 Convention], the third UN drug treaty that established State obligations in international law to enact harsh penal provisions for drug offences at domestic level, suggesting a link between international drug control law and domestic human rights violations.[99]

The two organisations then state that '[t]oday, the criminalization of drugs is now driving the imposition of capital punishment in many parts of the world',[100] implying that the two are intrinsically intertwined, and that the only way to solve the problem is to stop criminalising drugs altogether despite the fact that the current trend is in the opposite direction, and that this is also explicitly noted elsewhere in the same paper.

Nevertheless, though the number of the countries that do execute persons for drug-related offences is small, some of those countries—mainly China, Iran, and Saudi Arabia—execute a disproportionately large number of people in general, with the corresponding result that the number of persons worldwide executed for drug-related offences is presumably significant.

International human rights law does not prohibit the death penalty outright, but there is arguably a bias towards abolition, and most human rights organisations, including OHCHR, AI, and HRW, advocate for abolition. ICCPR Article 6(2) states that '[i]n countries which have not abolished the death penalty, sentence of death may be imposed only for the most serious crimes'. The Human Rights Committee (HRC) has noted in its General Comment on Article 6 that 'the article … strongly [suggests]

[97] AI, 'Death Sentences and Executions 2014' (London, 2015) 3.
[98] Harm Reduction International (n 94) 3.
[99] Ibid.
[100] Harm Reduction International (n 94) 2.

that abolition is desirable' and that the term 'most serious crimes' indicates that 'the death penalty should be a quite exceptional measure.'[101]

The jurisprudence of HRC indicates that the 'most serious' criterion is meant to indicate only crimes that result directly in death. As pointed out rightly by Nowak, 'in no event was the death penalty to be provided for crimes of property, economic crimes, political crimes or in general for offences not involving the use of force.'[102] HRC has stated explicitly on several occasions that drug-related offences do not fulfill the 'most serious crime' criterion: for example, in reviewing the state report of Kuwait in 2000, HRC expressed 'serious concern over the large number of offences for which the death penalty can be imposed, including … drug related offences.'[103] In 2005, reviewing the initial report of Thailand, HRC:

> … [noted] with concern that the death penalty is not restricted to the 'most serious crimes' … and is applicable to drug trafficking. [Thailand] should review the imposition of the death penalty for offences related to drug trafficking in order to reduce the categories of crime punishable by death.[104]

In July 2015, the HRC commenced discussion on a further General Comment on Article 6. Though the new General Comment has yet to be adopted, a draft published by the HRC after the first general discussion states that '[c]rimes not resulting directly and intentionally in death, such as drug offences … although serious in nature, do not manifest the extraordinary high levels of violence, utter disregard for human life, blatant anti-social attitude and irreversible consequences that could conceivably justify the imposition of the death penalty as a form of legal retribution.'[105] It is worthy to note that, while stating that it does not warrant the death penalty, the HRC qualifies drug-related offences as 'serious'.

ICCPR's Second Optional Protocol (titled aptly 'Aiming at the Abolition of the Death Penalty') does require the abolition of executions, though even that is not complete, with an exception allowed for 'most serious crime[s] of a military nature committed during wartime'. The number of state parties to this Optional Protocol is still relatively small, standing at 81 as of 30 September 2015. Of course, states are free to abolish the death penalty without becoming state party to this instrument.

[101] HRC, 'General comment No. 6: Article 6 (Right to life)' (Geneva, 1982) paras 6, 7.

[102] Manfred Nowak, *UN Covenant on Civil and Political Rights; CCPR Commentary*, 2nd revised edition (Kehl, NP Engel, 2005) 141.

[103] HRC, 'Concluding observations of the Human Rights Committee: Kuwait' (Geneva, UN index CCPR/CO/63/KWT, 27 July 2000) para 8.

[104] HRC, 'Concluding observations of the Human Rights Committee: Thailand' (Geneva, UN index CCPR/CO/84/THA, 08 July 2005) para 14.

[105] HRC, 'Draft general comment No. 36, Article 6: Right to life, Draft prepared by Yuval Shany and Nigel Rodley, Rapporteurs' (Geneva, UN index CCPR/C/GC/R.36/Rev.2, 2 September 2015) para 37.

Perhaps more significantly, the UN General Assembly has called on all states retaining the death penalty to implement a moratorium on executions. Starting in 2007,[106] the General Assembly has adopted resolutions on five occasions calling for a moratorium to all executions. In the most recent resolution, in 2014, the General Assembly:

> ... [r]eaffirming the Universal Declaration of Human Rights, the [ICCPR] and the Convention on the Rights of the Child,[107] ... convinced that a moratorium on the use of the death penalty contributes to respect for human dignity and to the enhancement and progressive development of human rights, and considering that there is no conclusive evidence of the deterrent value of the death penalty,[108] ... expresses its deep concern about the continued application of the death penalty;[109] ... [c]alls upon all States ... [t]o progressively restrict the use of the death penalty and[110] ... reduce the number of offences for which it may be imposed;[111] [t]o establish a moratorium on executions with a view to abolishing the death penalty.[112]

When the first resolution was adopted in 2007, AI called it a 'landmark victory' in human rights.[113] OHCHR reports that more than 160 states have abolished the death penalty either in law or in practice.[114]

It is, therefore, clear that, aside from the question of the general legality of the death penalty in international human rights law, it is not lawful under international human rights law to execute an individual for drug-related offences. Nevertheless, as noted above, some countries still maintain the death penalty for drug-related offences, and executions take place.

China is by far the worst offender with regard to the death penalty generally. According to Amnesty International, at least 22 states executed persons in 2014, the same figure as in 2013.[115] Four states, China, Iran (at least 289), Saudi Arabia (at least 90), and Iraq (at least 61) account for the largest number of executions.[116] The number of people executed in China is a state secret, and AI stopped its attempts at calculating figures in 2009.[117] Nevertheless, the organisation has estimated previously that the

[106] UN General Assembly, '69/186 Moratorium on the use of the death penalty' (New York, UN index A/RES/69/186, adopted 18 December 2014).
[107] UN General Assembly, '69/186 Moratorium' (n 106) preamble para 2.
[108] UN General Assembly (n 106) preamble para 6.
[109] UN General Assembly (n 106) para 1.
[110] UN General Assembly (n 106) para 5(d).
[111] UN General Assembly (n 106) para 5(e).
[112] UN General Assembly (n 106) para 5(f).
[113] AI, 'UN calls for halt to execution' (London, 18 December 2007).
[114] OHCHR, 'Death Penalty', www.ohchr.org/EN/Issues/DeathPenalty/Pages/DPIndex.aspx.
[115] AI (n 97) 3.
[116] AI (n 97) 3.
[117] AI (n 97) 2.

country executes more than the rest of the world combined.[118] Estimates regarding the number of persons executed vary widely; for example, estimates for the year 2007 range from 2,000 to as high as 15,000.[119] Included amongst the large number of persons executed are many persons convicted of drug-related offences, though exactly how many people is not clear. Since 2007, all death penalty sentences have been reviewed by the Chinese Supreme Court. The government has stated that this has led to a drop in executions,[120] but since the actual numbers remain secret, it is impossible to judge the effects of this new policy. Between 2009 and 2011, the government reportedly abolished the death penalty for 13 types of 'economic and non violent crimes',[121] and IHRA states that the government has at least considered abolition for drug-related crimes.[122] However, with so little information made public, it is impossible to determine what, if any, effect there has been.

China has always had a harsh stance towards illicit drug trafficking, and the country has for a number of years held large scale public sentencing and executions of 'convicted' drug traffickers on 26 June, the International Day against Drug Abuse and Illicit Drug Trafficking. The drug abuse problem in the country remains serious, with UNODC assessing that the country 'accounts for around 16% of the world's heroin users. Consuming between 46 and 60 tons of heroin per year … [the country constitutes] what is probably the single largest injecting drug user population in the world.'[123] China signed the ICCPR in 1998, committing itself to refrain from actions that would violate the object and purpose of the convention;[124] however, it has not ratified the convention and is, therefore, not legally bound by the convention's provisions. There have been occasional announcements by the government suggesting it was taking steps towards ratifying the ICCPR, but it is difficult to gauge what, if any, progress has actually been made.[125]

In any case, though the number of persons executed for drug-related offences is unknown, commentators all agree that it is significant.[126]

[118] AI, 'Death Sentences and Executions 2012' (London, 2013) 2.

[119] IHRA, 'The Death Penalty for Drug Offences: Global Overview 2010' (London, 2010) 20.

[120] See Yingxi Bi, 'On the Death Penalty for Drug-Related Crime in China' (2012), in 2 *Human Rights and Drugs* 33.

[121] 'China gov't announces plans to ratify 1998 ICCPR treaty', *The China Post*, 20 July 2011.

[122] IHRA (n 96) 8.

[123] UNODC, 'Transnational Crime in East Asia and the Pacific: a Threat Assessment' (Vienna, 2013) 51.

[124] Vienna Convention on the Law of Treaties, Article 18.

[125] See eg US Congressional-Executive Commission on China, 'China Announces Formation of "Working Group" on Ratification of the ICCPR' (Washington DC, 20 December 2004); 'China amends laws for ratification of ICCPR', *China Daily*, 14 July 2011.

[126] See eg International Harm Reduction Association (n 96).

At the same time, it should also be stressed that it is not only drug-related offences that are subject to execution in China: Chinese law provides for the death penalty for a wide range of crimes that would not fulfil the HRC's 'most serious crime' criterion.[127] The US Department of State notes that the criminal code includes '55 capital offenses, including nonviolent financial crimes such as embezzlement and corruption.'[128]

Adding to the problem is the fact that the criminal justice procedure in China is rife with inadequacies, with little protection of the right to a fair trial. What few safeguards that do exist on paper are often simply ignored in practice. The human rights shortcomings are widespread; just to provide a glimpse, the US Department of State notes that:

> [Chinese] law grants police broad administrative detention powers and the ability to detain individuals for extended periods without formal arrest or criminal charges … [H]uman rights activists, journalists, religious leaders, and former political prisoners and their family members [continue] to be among those targeted for arbitrary detention or arrest … In many politically sensitive trials, courts handed down guilty verdicts immediately following proceedings with little time for deliberation. Courts often punished defendants who refused to acknowledge guilt with harsher sentences than those who confessed … Human rights lawyers reported that authorities did not permit them to defend certain clients or threatened them with punishment if they chose to do so. The government suspended or revoked the licenses of lawyers or their firms to stop them from taking sensitive cases.[129]

In July 2015, the government engaged in an arrest campaign of human rights lawyers and activists, arresting arbitrarily more than 50 persons.[130]

Cohen has summarised the situation in China succinctly:

> The police still have enormous, virtually unfettered discretion in dealing with what they deem to be anti-social elements of all types. Some of the measures they impose are totally without legal foundation and often violate constitutional and legislative norms. Human rights activists, dissidents, protesters, petitioners, and their lawyers and families are frequent targets of illegal intimidation, threats, house arrest, kidnapping, beating, 'black jails' and temporary internal exile.[131]

[127] See eg Amnesty International (n 97) at 9.

[128] US Department of State, *Country Reports on Human Rights Practices for 2014*, China entry (Washington DC, 2015) at www.state.gov/j/drl/rls/hrrpt/humanrightsreport.

[129] Ibid.

[130] AI, 'China: Dozens of human rights lawyers targeted in nationwide crackdown' (London, 11 July 2015).

[131] Jerome A Cohen, 'Criminal Justice in China: From the Gang of Four to Bo Xilai' (New York, Human Rights Watch, July 2013), at www.hrw.org/news/2013/07/25/criminal-justice-china-gang-four-bo-xilai.

In addition, the Chinese judiciary is not independent. Judges:

> … regularly [receive] political guidance on pending cases, including instructions on how to rule, from both the government and the [Communist Party], particularly in politically sensitive cases. The [Party] Law and Politics Committee has the authority to review and influence court operations at all levels of the judiciary.[132]

None of this is to argue that China is in any way justified in executing persons convicted of drug-related offences, but simply to point the obvious: the issue goes far beyond China's policies towards drug abuse.

Similar problems in criminal justice procedure exist in the other large scale executing countries. In Iran:

> Authorities often [violate] [the established] procedures by holding some detainees, at times incommunicado, for weeks or months without charge or trial, frequently denying contact with family or timely access to legal representation. The law obligates the state to provide indigent defendants with attorneys only for certain types of crimes. …Pretrial detention was often arbitrarily lengthy, particularly in cases involving alleged violations of national security laws. … pretrial detention often [lasts] for months.[133]

Torture is widespread, and the judiciary in Iran is subject to political interference, with judges appointed on 'religious criteria'.[134] The above notwithstanding, an increase in drug abuse is apparently at least partially behind an increase in executions in Iran. The Special Rapporteur on the situation of human rights in Iran reports that:

> [a]t least 69 per cent of executions during the first six months of 2015 were reportedly for drug-related offences. The Government holds the view that the implications posed by drug-trafficking to the health and security of the Iranian people render drug-related offences 'most serious' crimes and, therefore, they deserve to be considered capital offences.[135]

In any case, there is a general consensus regarding the death penalty issue amongst actors in the drug control field. Though INCB's position on this was somewhat vague—the body noted in its Annual Report 2003 merely that '[s]tates are encouraged to avoid using the death penalty'—in 2014, the body issued a statement noting that it 'encourages those State Parties that still provide for the death penalty for drug-related offences … to consider

[132] United States Department of State (n 128).

[133] US Department of State, *Country Reports on Human Rights Practices for 2014*, Iran entry (Washington DC, 2015) at www.state.gov/j/drl/rls/hrrpt/humanrightsreport.

[134] Ibid.

[135] Ahmed Shaheed, 'Report of the Special Rapporteur on the situation of human rights in the Islamic Republic of Iran to the seventieth session of the General Assembly' (New York, UN index A/70/411, 6 October 2015) para 12.

the abolition of the death penalty for drug-related offences.'[136] Still, the somewhat optional language used appears to allow leeway to retain the death penalty, and it is not clear why INCB did not take a stronger stance. Many advocates of drug liberalisation have criticised INCB for not speaking out when countries execute drug-related offenders.[137]

As noted above, UNODC has publicly stated several times that it discourages states from executing drug-related offenders, including in the address of the Executive Director to the CND in 2008. In a policy paper published in 2012, UNODC even indicates that it might be suspend capacity building and other support for countries that retain the death penalty for drug related offences—a bold move for an organisation so dependent on voluntary contributions. After outlining international human rights standards on the death penalty, UNODC states that:

> Even training of border guards who are responsible for arrest of drug traffickers ultimately sentenced to death may be considered sufficiently proximate to the violation … If, following request for guarantees and high-level political intervention, executions for drug related offences continue, UNODC might have no choice but to employ a temporary freeze or withdrawal of support.[138]

Given this consensus, there is little room for advocates of drug liberalisation to criticise the international drug control regime. The conventions clearly neither require nor encourage the execution of drug offenders, and actors charged with monitoring the regime urge states to refrain from this as well—UNODC more than INCB.

It is also important to reiterate that the countries that do execute drug offenders also execute a large number of other people whose offence does not fulfil the 'serious crime' criterion enumerated in ICCPR. The notion that persons who abuse drugs are being targeted and singled out for execution in many countries, in particular China, is without foundation—that they are being subject to execution is clearly a human rights problem, but it is no more so than the fact that other persons are being executed as well. The problem is one of the death penalty, and its general compatibility with international human rights standards in those countries in general—not one of drug control as such.

[136] INCB, 'INCB encourages States to consider the abolition of the death penalty for drug-related offences' (Vienna, 5 March 2014).

[137] See eg International Drug Policy Consortium, 'The International Narcotics Control Board: Current Tensions and Options for Reform' (London, 2008) 15.

[138] UNODC, 'UNODC and the Protection and Promotion of Human Rights' (Vienna, 2012) 9.

Nevertheless, advocates of drug liberalisation attempt to present the death penalty issue as one showing a fundamental flaw in international drug control as a whole. For example, IHRA states that:

> The death penalty for drug offences ... violates international human rights law and dehumanises, in the most final and irreversible of ways, those convicted of drug offences. It is in many ways the ultimate example of the absence of human rights considerations in the push to 'get tough' on drugs. ... Just as the gradual abolition of the death penalty over time became a yardstick by which to measure the growing respect for human rights around the world, so too may the gradual abolition of the death penalty for drug offences serve as a measure for the increased respect for human rights in drug control.[139]

The Transform Drug Policy Foundation condemns efforts against drugs by governments as a 'smokescreen for various forms of illegal government action, including torture and the use of the death penalty ...'[140]

These arguments would seem to be easily refutable. As noted above, it is clearly a human rights issue that persons are being executed despite not having committed serious crimes. However, advocates of drug liberalisation present the issue as if it is unique to persons who abuse drugs, showing, in their eyes, fundamental flaws in the international community's approach towards drugs. This is inaccurate, and clearly misleading.

Law Enforcement and the Excessive Use of Force

Since human rights standards have evolved as a way of checking state power, they understandably have a strong focus on preventing arbitrary actions by law enforcement officials. Article 7 of ICCPR prohibits torture, stating that '[n]o one shall be subjected to torture or to cruel, inhuman or degrading treatment or punishment.' Indeed, there is an entire separate convention, the Convention against Torture and Other Cruel, Inhuman or Degrading Treatment or Punishment, dedicated to this subject. Human rights law also contain provisions against arbitrary detention (eg Article 9 of ICCPR, which states, *inter alia*, 'No one shall be subjected to arbitrary arrest or detention. No one shall be deprived of his liberty except on such grounds and in accordance with such procedure as are established by law' and stipulations of fair trial rights that all individuals should be afforded (Article 14 of the ICCPR outlines some detailed provisions in this regard). Other standards exist, including the Basic Principles on the Use of Force and Firearms by Law Enforcement Officials, the Body of Principles for the

139 IHRA (n 119) 50.

140 Transform Drug Policy Foundation, 'The Alternative World Drug Report' (London, 2012) 10, 11.

Protection of All Persons under Any Form of Detention or Imprisonment, and others. There is a large body of jurisprudence, including human rights treaty body jurisprudence, regarding the rights of persons detained by law enforcement officials, including criminal suspects and convicted persons.

A common theme in the arguments of advocates of drug liberalisation is that persons who abuse drugs are subject to widespread violations of the above standards at the hands of police and other law enforcement officials. As noted above, HRW has stated that:

> In countries around the world, state enforcement of criminal drug laws has resulted, directly or indirectly, in serious and sometimes widespread and systematic human rights violations. Military and police forces engage in extrajudicial killings, enforced disappearances, torture and ill-treatment, and arbitrary detention … In Canada, Kazakhstan, Bangladesh, and Ukraine, police have violently mistreated people who use drugs. In Tanzania, police and quasi-official vigilante groups have brutally beaten people who inject drugs …[141]

Likewise, Count the Costs argues that:

> People who use drugs, or who are arrested or suspected of drug offences, are frequently subject to various forms of cruel and unusual punishment. This includes abuses such as death threats and beatings to extract information; extortion of money or confessions through forced withdrawal without medical assistance; judicially sanctioned corporal punishment for drug use; and various forms of cruel, inhuman and degrading treatment in the name of 'rehabilitation', including denial of meals, beatings, sexual abuse and threats of rape, isolation, and forced labour.[142]

The Beckley Foundation, in a joint paper with the IHRA, HRW, and the Canadian HIV/AIDS Legal Network, makes similar observations, stating that:

> People who use drugs make especially easy targets for arrest or ill-treatment by police needing to fulfill arrest quotas, as Human Rights Watch has documented in reports on Russia, Kazakhstan, and Ukraine … Police also use drug addiction as a tool to coerce incriminating testimony from drug users. A former senior detective specializing in drug enforcement cases, and attorneys and social workers to drug users in Ukraine have reported, for example, that police intentionally use withdrawal as an investigative tool to coerce incriminating testimony from drug users, extort money from drug users by threatening to detain them, forcing them to suffer withdrawal and deny medical assistance to drug users …[143]

As with the death penalty, the suggestion is that the 'criminalization of drugs' imposed upon states by the international drug control regime is

[141] HRW (n 35) 2.

[142] Count the Costs, 'The War on Drugs: Undermining Human Rights' (London, 2015) 5.

[143] Beckley Foundation Drug Policy Programme, 'Recalibrating the Regime: The Need for a Human Rights-Based regime to International Drug Policy' (London, 2008) 26.

responsible for these abuses. It is the 'war on drugs', based on the drug control conventions, that is to blame:

> In every region of the world the war on drugs is severely undermining human rights. It has led to a litany of abuse, neglect and political scapegoating through the erosion of civil liberties and fair trial standards; the denial of economic and social rights; the demonizing of individuals and groups; and the imposition of abusive and inhuman punishments. Too often these human rights violations are considered in isolation … But they are not isolated. They are all a direct consequence of the war on drugs. Like the war on terror, the war on drugs is framed as a response to an exceptional, existential threat to our health, our security, and indeed the very fabric of society. The 'Addiction to narcotic drugs' is portrayed as an 'evil' the international community has a moral duty to 'combat'. This is not an exaggeration of the political rhetoric. These words are enshrined in international law, including the 1961, 1971 and 1988 UN drug conventions. This crusading language has created a political climate in which drug war policy and enforcement are not required to meet human rights norms. In fact, despite being one of the three pillars of the UN's work (along with development and security), these international agreements lack any obligation to ensure compliance with human rights. … Through production, transit, sales and use, the responses to every stage in the supply chain of illicit drugs are characterised by extensive human rights violations, committed in the name of supply and demand reduction.'[144]

As with the death penalty, the above are all serious human rights concerns that need to be addressed. Nevertheless, advocates of drug liberalisation neglect to mention that police excesses tend to be widespread in the countries they cite, affecting not only persons who abuse drugs but any person suspected of committing an offence. Just to take the oft-cited example of Ukraine, AI notes that '[v]iolations by police, including torture and other ill-treatment as well as abusive use of force during demonstrations, [continue] with near-total impunity for the perpetrators, while investigations into such incidents [remain] ineffective.[145] Police abuses are widespread, and the problem is longstanding:

> Based on the numerous incidents reported in the media, social surveys, and complaints received by human rights NGOs, it is estimated that thousands of Ukrainians are subjected to torture and other ill-treatment by police and other law enforcement officials every year, without redress. Police impunity is a longstanding concern of Amnesty International, and over the past year there has been growing public outrage and frustration at lack of progress in tackling the problem.[146]

[144] Count the Costs (n 142) 1, 2.

[145] AI, *Amnesty International Report 2014/15* (London, 2015) 382.

[146] AI, 'Ukraine: Sorry is not Enough! Police Impunity Must End' (London, 11 February 2014) 2.

Similar issues can be noted in Russia ('Allegations of torture and other ill-treatment continued to be reported across the country, while many of those who sought redress faced pressure to withdraw their complaints. Investigations into such allegations were almost invariably ineffective. Confessions extracted under torture were used as evidence in court.'),[147] Kazakhstan ('There was no improvement in investigating reports of human rights violations by law enforcement and security services and holding alleged perpetrators to account. Bureaucratic obstacles and opaque internal ministerial regulations prevented victims of torture and their relatives from obtaining justice. Similar obstacles continued to hinder effective independent monitoring of places of detention.'),[148] and the other countries named by advocates of drug liberalisation. In other words, it is hardly just persons who abuse drugs who are vulnerable to abuse in those countries—it is a far more widespread problem. Yet, in an attempt to show how drug control violates human rights, advocates of drug liberalisation present the abuses as if they only affect persons who abuse drugs. This is misleading and disingenuous.

An oft cited example, and a very extreme one, is the anti-drug trafficking campaign conducted in Thailand in early 2003. The country had the world's highest abuse rate of methamphetamine, with 5.9 percent of the population over 15 years of age having abused illicit tablets containing the substance. According to information provided by the Thai Government to UNODC, the number of people in treatment for methamphetamine abuse increased fourfold from 1996 to 2000.[149] In early 2003, the government announced a nationwide campaign against methamphetamine abuse, with the goal of eradicating the country of illicit drugs over a three-month period. Reports indicate that 'blacklists' containing a total of over 46,000 'known' drug traffickers were created, with numerical targets for 'elimination'. Amnesty International notes that there was 'widespread concern about the methodology used to draw up these blacklists, and it appears that authorities have no obligation to notify suspects that their names are on the blacklist. In addition, … there is no judicial mechanism for appeals to be made to challenge inclusion in the blacklist.'[150] Provincial officials were threatened with termination if they did not achieve the targets for 'elimination'.

147 AI (n 145) 308.
148 AI (n 145) 209.
149 UNODC, *World Drug Report 2004* (Vienna, 2005).
150 AI, 'Thailand: Grave developments; killings and other abuses' (London, November 2003) 7.

Predictably, the ensuing campaign was characterised by widespread suspicious killings. Both AI and HRW documented numerous cases of suspected extra-judicial executions. AI stated its concern that the:

> … stated policy of the Royal Thai Government has allowed the killing of over 2,000 people by unknown assailants with impunity. Some of these killings may have been extrajudicial executions by the police or other members of the security forces. Relatives and associates of those who have been murdered are often too terrified for their own lives to seek an investigation from the authorities.[151]

The Special Rapporteur on Extra-judicial Executions expressed her 'deep concern' at the situation, and urged the Thai government to ensure that law enforcement officers comply with international standards limiting the lethal use of force.[152] At the end of the three-month period, over 2,800 people had been killed.[153] HRW stated 'the government crackdown has resulted in the unexplained killing of more than 2,000 persons, the arbitrary arrest or blacklisting of several thousand more, and the endorsement of extreme violence by government officials at the highest levels.'[154] A government committee later found that over half of those killed had no links with the illicit drug trade. However, other than an apparently isolated case reported in 2009 by HRW of eight police officers being convicted for assault and other related charges, and notwithstanding government assurances to INCB (see below), it does not appear that any official has been held accountable for the abuses.[155] In its second periodic report to the HRC, which was due in 2009 but was not submitted until 2015, Thailand stated merely that there might have been 'mistakes', which needed to 'be further studied and examined to find out facts and develop measures to prevent such mistakes in the implementation of the policy from happening again.'[156]

INCB visited Thailand in 2004. As with all other missions to countries, the report of this mission, and the subsequent recommendations that would have been communicated to the government by INCB, are not

[151] See AI, 'Thailand: Grave developments' (n 150) 7; also HRW, 'Thailand: Not enough graves: the war on drugs, HIV/AIDS, and violations of human rights' (New York, June 2004).

[152] OHCHR, 'UN expert on extra judicial executions expresses concern over recent killings in Thailand' (Geneva, 24 February 2003).

[153] The independent committee appointed by the interim Thai government to investigate the killings reported that there were '2,559 cases with 2,819 deaths': Independent Commission For Examination, Study and Analysis of the Formation And Implementation of the Drug Suppression Policy, 'Official Report' (Bangkok, 2008) 1.

[154] HRW (n 151) 2.

[155] See HRW, 'Thailand: Convictions of Police in Drug Campaign Abuse a "First Step"' (New York, 14 December 2009).

[156] Government of Thailand, 'Second periodic report under Article 40 of the International Covenant on Civil and Political Rights of the Government of Thailand' (Geneva, UN index CCPR/C/THA/2, 19 March 2015) para 23.

public, making it difficult to assess what was discussed during the mission. Nevertheless, judging from the text referring to this mission in INCB Annual Report, it does appear that INCB raised concerns with the Thai government regarding the anti-drug campaign, and pressed for an explanation regarding measures to ensure accountability for any violations.

Though buried deep in the Report, INCB states:

> The Board sent a mission to Thailand in May 2004, mainly to assess the efforts of the Government during the 'war on drugs', an ongoing nationwide campaign against drug trafficking and abuse. In particular, the Board had noted reports that killings had taken place during the 'war on drugs' and it wished to gather comprehensive information regarding the campaign and the measures and action that had subsequently been taken. The mission received detailed information from the Government regarding special committees established to investigate those cases and was informed that certain cases had already been the subject of judicial procedures. In addition, the mission was informed that criminal proceedings had been initiated against a significant number of government officials accused of corruption. The Board appreciates those efforts and trusts that the Government will continue to provide information to it regarding the progress of those investigations.[157]

INCB then puts a somewhat more positive spin on the situation, stating that:

> The Board was also informed that, subsequent to the 'war on drugs', the problem of methamphetamine abuse had been reduced. The Board received detailed information on the treatment of drug addicts in Thailand. The Board notes the efforts of the Government and urges it to undertake sustainable measures to address the drug abuse problem in Thailand.[158]

In 2007, in what is a normal procedure, INCB contacted the Thai Government requesting information on its implementation of the INCB's recommendations after the 2004 mission. Though, once again, the correspondence is not public, the relevant text in the Annual Report at this time is arguably somewhat stronger than in 2004, noting that 'The "war on drugs" resulted in a large number of killings, many in what could only be described as suspicious circumstances.'[159] INCB then notes with some satisfaction that:

> … according to information recently received from the [Thai Government], a total of 55 law enforcement officers are to be prosecuted for possible involvement in killings during the 'war on drugs'. The Government has also informed the Board that it does not intend to recommence the 'war on drugs' and that any

[157] INCB, *Annual Report 2004* (Vienna, 2005) para 388.
[158] Ibid para 389.
[159] INCB, *Annual Report 2008* (Vienna, 2009) para 212.

> measure taken by the Government against drug trafficking will be in accordance with human rights principles. The Board notes that current efforts of the Government to counter drug trafficking and abuse are aimed at, among other things, increasing community involvement in combating drug problems, at least partially to monitor Government measures and ensure that legal bounds are respected.[160]

Advocates of drug liberalisation continue to cite the campaign in Thailand as a prime example of how governments, crazed with their zeal to stamp out drugs, trample on human rights in the process. In its 2015 submission to OHCHR, for example, HRW puts forward the 2003 campaign as an example of 'human rights abuses … in connection with state enforcement of drug policies'.[161] Advocates of drug liberalisation also criticise INCB for not having taken a stronger stance vis-à-vis the Thai government. Canadian HIV/AIDS Legal Aid Network and Open Society Institute (OSI),[162] for example, suggest that INCB's comments are an example of how the body 'has demonstrated little sensitivity to overly harsh policing, and has failed to recognize that illicit drug use should not be synonymous with forfeiture of due process or human rights protections.'[163]

It is clear that wide scale violations of human rights took place during the Thai campaign. It is also certainly arguable that INCB should have taken a stronger position condemning the abuses, perhaps even during the Thai campaign (as opposed to over a year afterwards). Though INCB is obviously not a human rights body as such, given that the violations were taking place in the name of drug control, it is submitted that it would have been desirable for INCB to have taken a stronger, and more public, stand earlier.

Nevertheless, the extrapolation of advocates of drug liberalisation, that the violations in Thailand were somehow an inevitable result of global efforts against drugs, is without foundation. Extra-judicial killings and a lack of accountability are long-standing human rights issues in Thailand, issues that far predate the anti-drug campaign. In 2002, for example, the US Department of State reported that '[r]outine exoneration of police officers contributed to a climate of impunity that was a significant factor in preventing any major change in police behavior. It also discouraged relatives of victims from pressing for prosecution.'[164] There is little question

[160] Ibid para 214.

[161] HRW (n 35) 3.

[162] The Open Society Foundation was called the Open Society Institute until 2010. See H Edward Schrier, *The Battle of the Three Wills: as it Relates to Good and Evil* (Bloomington, Authorhouse, 2013) at 337.

[163] Canadian HIV/AIDS Legal Aid Network (n 76) 14. See also eg International Drug Policy Consortium (n 137) 15.

[164] US Department of State, *Country Report on Human Rights Practices 2002*, Thailand entry (Washington DC, 2003) at www.state.gov/j/drl/rls/hrrpt/2002/18265.htm.

that the situation was exacerbated during the campaign, but first and foremost the problem is one of law enforcement (or lawlessness) in general, not one of drug control as such.

What is needed in the Thai context is the rule of law in general, not less enforcement of particular, arbitrarily selected categories of laws (ie drug laws). As noted by this author in a previous publication, if similar violations took place in a campaign against traffic violations, for example, it is difficult to imagine that there would be calls for a human rights framework in traffic control.[165]

Flacks believes otherwise, arguing that this author's opinion:

> detaches the violence of the penalty from the identity, beliefs, or actions of the accused. If one were to separate the issue of a person's sexual orientation in Iran, for example, from the subsequent death penalty imposed, the effect would be to both minimize and marginalize the issue of homophobia, both nationally and internationally, to a mere procedural criminal justice matter. This approach neglects and diminishes societal discrimination towards vulnerable groups and marginalizes the harm suffered by thousands of drug users in the name of drug control. Can the fact that, as Damon Barrett and Manfred Nowak document, China uses the UN Day against Drug Abuse and Illicit Trafficking to conduct public executions really be disassociated from the issue of drug control?[166]

Flacks' question is of course rhetorical, but the answer is yes, of course it can be. In examining a state's criminal justice system, human rights activists of course look at not only procedural issues but also the reasons for criminal sanctions, and whether those reasons are, in light of that state's international obligations, legitimate. However, the two are not one and the same. A state can have perfectly legitimate reasons for imposing criminal sanctions on a particular action, and yet still fall foul of its human rights obligations because of the manner in which the enforcement is conducted. For example, a state could commit widespread violations in a campaign against murder suspects. While human rights activists should condemn those violations, this would surely not lead to a discussion regarding whether murder should be a crime or not. It would certainly not lead to a discussion about murder suspects as a 'particularly vulnerable group' that requires special protection, which is essentially what Flacks intends to argue by comparing persons who abuse drugs with persons at risk of persecution in Iran for their sexual orientation (more on the question of persons abusing drugs as a 'vulnerable group' below).

This is not to compare persons who abuse drugs with murder suspects, but simply to make the point: violations in criminal justice procedure do

[165] Takahashi (n 90) 757.

[166] Simon Flacks, 'Drug Control, Human Rights, and the Right to the Highest Attainable Standard of Health: A Reply to Saul Takahashi' (2011) 33 *Human Rights Quarterly* 859.

not necessarily call into question the legitimacy of the offence itself. Flacks, and other advocates of drug liberalisation, fail to address this, presumably because they have already come to their conclusion: that any criminalisation of drug abuse is wrong and a violation of human rights.

Arbitrary Detention, Ill-Treatment and Forced Labour

Another human rights issue connected to law enforcement that has been highlighted is that of the detention of persons who abuse drugs, within the context of mandated (ie forced) treatment. Advocates of drug liberalisation have reported that in some countries, persons who abuse drugs (or even persons merely suspected of having abused drugs) are arrested, sometimes in mass roundups. They are committed to closed 'treatment centres' without any semblance of due process. These 'treatment centres' rarely offer any sort of treatment for drug dependency, being either military-style boot camps or forced labour camps, and detainees are also often subject to ill-treatment. The abuses associated with these practices are systemic. Yet another example of the 'war on drugs' run amok, so the argument goes, with persons who abuse drugs targeted for human rights abuses.

Cambodia has received sustained attention from HRW, with two reports, in 2010 and 2013. The treatment of detainees in the centres in that country is deplorable. HRW notes that '[m]any detainees are subjected to sadistic violence, including being shocked with electric batons and whipped with twisted electrical wire. Arduous physical exercises and labor are the mainstays of supposed drug "treatment". Some detainees are forced to donate their blood.'[167] HRW's reporting is full of harrowing testimony from former detainees about widespread abuse, and on the basis of its research, HRW recommends that the centres should be closed and detainees released. HRW continues to demand that:

> To respect, protect, and fulfill the right to health of people with drug dependency, the government should expand access to voluntary, community-based drug treatment through the Ministry of Health with the involvement of competent nongovernmental organizations (NGOs). This expansion of voluntary treatment services should not be a precondition for closing the centers.[168]

[167] HRW, 'Skin on the Cable: the illegal arrest, arbitrary detention, and torture of people who use drugs in Cambodia' (New York, 2010) 3.

[168] HRW, '"They Treat Us Like Animals": mistreatment of drug users and "undesirables" in Cambodia's drug detention centers' (New York, 2013) 5.

The UN agencies in Cambodia have also pronounced themselves on the issue, though they do not go so far as to specifically demand closure of the centres. Rather, the UN agencies state that:

> Drug dependence treatment services must comply with the State's human rights obligations and recognize the inherent dignity of all individuals. This includes respecting, protecting and fulfilling the right to the highest attainable standard of mental and physical health ... All drug dependence interventions (including detoxification, treatment, rehabilitation and reintegration) must comply with Cambodia's international human rights obligations.[169]

'Treatment centres' in Laos and Vietnam have similar problems, as do ones in China. HRW shows that centres in Vietnam act mainly as forced labour camps, with no due process for persons being confined to the centres:

> Refusing to work, or violating any one of a number of center rules, results in beatings or confinement in disciplinary rooms ... Staff beat detainees with wooden truncheons or shock them with electrical batons, sometimes causing them to faint. In disciplinary rooms— either crowded punishment rooms or solitary confinement cells—physical deprivation is used as an additional form of punishment: food and/or drinking water rations are often reduced, access to bathing is restricted, and family visits are prohibited. People held in disciplinary rooms often have to work longer hours or conduct more strenuous work than usual ...[170]

At the one centre that the organisation examined in Laos:

> ... detainees live in a punitive and heavily controlled environment. Those who try to escape may be brutally beaten by "room captains"—trusted detainees whom staff designate to play a central role in the daily control of other detainees, including serving the center's police as guards and punishing detainees who infringe center rules.'[171]

As for China:

> Former detainees ... told Human Rights Watch that while in drug detention centers they were beaten and made to work up to 18 hours daily in wretched conditions without pay. Multiple sources told Human Rights Watch that detainees are consistently denied access to basic medical care. Former detainees in Yunnan report that TB is common, and untreated, among detainees ... Far from protecting the health of detainees, the policies and practices of these

[169] UN in Cambodia, 'Support to the Royal Government of Cambodia to deliver evidence-based drug dependence detoxification, treatment and aftercare for people who use drugs' (Phnom Penh, May 2010) 1.

[170] HRW, 'The Rehab Archipelago: forced labour and other abuses in drug detention centers in southern Vietnam' (New York, 2011) 4.

[171] HRW, 'Somsanga's Secrets Arbitrary Detention, Physical Abuse, and Suicide inside a Lao Drug Detention Center' (New York, 2011) at 7.

> 'treatment' and 'rehabilitation' centers systematically endanger their health and well-being.[172]

Rights violations in these centres are clearly systemic. It is worth noting, however, that these practices exist only in a handful of countries. As noted above, HRW has reported on China and several countries in South East Asia. OSF has also reported on instances of abuse in drug treatment centres in Mexico and Russia, in a paper which also features HRW's reporting on China and Cambodia.[173] Nevertheless, though OSF seems to suggest that the four country situations are essentially the same, as a legal matter they are fundamentally different: the abuses reported in Mexico and Russia appear to be at the hands of private actors, rather than in centres to which persons are confined by the state (as is the case with China and Cambodia). The issue, therefore, in Mexico and Russia, is one of inadequate government regulation and oversight, not official compulsion.

The above is not to say that the violations in any of these states do not deserve attention, and condemnation—they do. However, extrapolating a global statement regarding international efforts against drugs from just these few countries, as advocates of drug liberalisation attempt to do, is unwarranted.

In addition, it is clear from HRW's own reporting that, in particular in Cambodia, it is not only persons who abuse drugs who are subject to arbitrary arrest and detention in the centres—many other groups of people such as street children, homeless, and sex workers also are at risk of this fate. The 2010 Cambodia report states clearly that at least one of the centres 'regularly detains people who use drugs (as well as other groups of "undesirables" such as homeless people, beggars, street children, sex workers, mentally ill people and so on)[174] … the motivation for detaining these people is to keep the streets clear of "undesirables"…'[175] The cases in the report include a multitude of people whose detention does not appear to have any connection with drug abuse, or even suspected drug abuse. For example, Teap, a 14-year old, states 'I was sleeping inside the pagoda compound in the open air … The police asked me, "Did you steal someone's car mirror?" I said, "No, I didn't". Then they arrested me and beat me.'[176] Chrolong reports 'I was walking at night and I came out from a dancing club. I was sitting with my girlfriend … There was no reason given for our arrest. They said "You stroll in the night; strolling at night is

[172] HRW, 'Where Darkness Knows No Limits: incarceration, ill-treatment, and forced labor as drug rehabilitation in China' (New York, 2010) 4.

[173] OSF, 'Treated with Cruelty: Abuses in the Name of Drug Rehabilitation' (New York, 2011).

[174] HRW (n 167) 18.

[175] HRW (n 167) 34.

[176] HRW (n 167) 26.

not good."'[177] If there is any putative connection with the fact that these people were detained and any suspicion that they were abusing drugs, it is not made clear in the report.

The report also goes on to quote one person that '[t]hey arrested even crazy people … They were just arrested and thrown in the truck. There were about four [mentally ill] people in the center … They do the work like cleaning the grass and carrying water and watering vegetables.'[178] The 2013 report has many similar cases, such as one homeless man who was arrested when he was drinking wine.[179] HRW says in 2013:

> People who use drugs in Cambodia are not the only people considered 'undesirable' by authorities. In early 2012, local media quoted an official at Phnom Penh's Social Affairs department explaining that beggars and sex workers make the city 'messy' and that rounding them up was necessary to 'keep public order and make the city beautiful for ASEAN.' He said, 'We've taken them for training.' In fact, homeless people, beggars, street children, sex workers, and people with actual or perceived disabilities are routinely held in drug detention centers.[180]

In other words, the text of the report makes clear that though the facilities are called 'drug treatment detention centres', they are in fact used by the authorities as a method of social control, a catch all way to arbitrarily detain any person deemed as 'undesirable'. They do not appear to be targeted solely, or perhaps even predominantly, at persons who abuse drugs. Nevertheless, as the title of the 2010 report ('Skin on the Cable: the illegal arrest, arbitrary detention, and torture of people who use drugs in Cambodia') suggests, HRW's focus is only that one group—it is persons who abuse drugs who are held to be 'vulnerable', and needing special protection against human rights violations. It is certainly legitimate to question why the rights of this one group appears to be so important, when the rights of many others are being violated in a similar fashion.

HRW's reporting also lists several issues that are common, and longstanding, to criminal justice in Cambodia as a whole:

> From first contact with police to detention in the police station, severe beatings and other forms of violence are common. According to former detainees, police use forms of physical torture, such as the administration of electric shocks or beatings with gun butts, to force people to confess or reveal information. Police regularly extort money from people after arrest. People are frequently arrested without a warrant or reasonable cause, without being informed of the reasons for their arrest, or are lied to about the reasons for their arrest. They have no

[177] HRW (n 167) 27.
[178] HRW (n 167) 79.
[179] HRW (n 168) 26.
[180] HRW (n 168) 25.

> access to a lawyer during their period in police custody or during the subsequent period of detention in the centers.[181]

These are human rights violations, and rightly condemned—however, it is disingenuous to suggest that they take place only when persons are arrested for suspected drug abuse. The US Department of State reports that:

> Kicking, punching, and pistol whipping were the most common methods of reported physical abuse [in police custody], but authorities also used electric shock, suffocation, caning, and whipping with wires. NGOs reported it was not uncommon for police to abuse detained suspects until they confessed to a crime. Courts used forced confessions as evidence during trials despite legal prohibitions against the admissibility of such confessions … Police officials committed abuses with impunity and in most cases the government took little or no action.[182]

The longstanding problem of police abuse in Cambodia cannot possibly be reduced to an issue affecting only persons who abuse drugs.

On the other hand, there is no indication that persons besides suspected drug abusers are detained in the 'treatment centres' in China, and the number of people incarcerated in the centres is huge—a 2009 UNAIDS estimate of half a million is cited,[183] though, in 2015, OHCHR cites a figure from the UN Development Programme that is considerably lower.[184] This makes the situation somewhat different from South East Asia, where drug detention centres act as centres for arbitrary roundups of 'undesirables' of all sorts. In addition, in China, persons who abuse drugs are reportedly arrested while attempting to access wholly legal harm reduction services,[185] and the fact that they were once detained for drug abuse is printed on their identity cards, making it extremely difficult for the person to reintegrate into society after release.[186] These are all specific to persons who abuse drugs, and, as such, need to be addressed with the rights of those persons in mind. Nevertheless, the issues are specific to China, and hardly suggest fundamental problems with the international drug control regime as a whole.

HRW also makes the somewhat bold claim that the lack of adequate treatment in Chinese drug detention centres amounts to torture. Jumbling

[181] HRW (n 168) 25.

[182] US Department of State, *Country Reports on Human Rights Practices*, Cambodia entry (Washington, March 2015) at http://www.state.gov/j/drl/rls/hrrpt/humanrightsreport.

[183] HRW (n 172) 11.

[184] OHCHR gives the figure of 235,000 for all compulsory drug detention centres in East and South East Asia: OHCHR, 'Study on the impact of the world drug problem on the enjoyment of human rights' (Geneva, UH index A/HRC/30/65, 4 September 2015) para 49.

[185] HRW (n 172) 20.

[186] HRW (n 172) 20.

together citations on different subjects from a number of differed sources, HRW argues that:

> ... failure to provide adequate health care or medical treatment to a detainee in prison may contribute to conditions amounting to 'inhuman or degrading treatment.' Beyond being ill-treatment, China's denial of proper medical treatment to detained drug users that causes severe pain or suffering might amount to torture ... The Committee against Torture, commenting on protection for individuals and groups made vulnerable by discrimination or marginalization, 'emphasises that the discriminatory use of mental or physical violence or abuse is an important factor in determining whether an act constitutes torture.' ... The UN Special Rapporteur on torture and other cruel, inhuman or degrading treatment or punishment, Manfred Nowak, states that ... 'if withdrawal symptoms are used for any of the purposes cited in the definition of torture enshrined in article 1 of the Convention against Torture, this might amount to torture.'[187]

HRW is clearly correct to argue that the lack of appropriate treatment within Chinese drug detention centres is a violation of the right to health[188] (and that it brings into question the entire goal of the centres, which ostensibly is to protect the health of the detainees). However, the claim that it also amounts to torture seems somewhat questionable. As Nowak rightly points out (and as mentioned earlier in this study), the intentional withholding of particular treatment in an effort to, for example, make a suspect confess to a crime, would surely amount to torture. However, the general lack of treatment as a whole in Chinese drug detention centres does not necessarily make them mass torture centres, as HRW seems to be suggesting. The problem—above and beyond the fact that people are incarcerated in the centres in a wholly arbitrary manner—is that there is no appropriate treatment whatsoever, not that it is being withheld from particular individuals for particular reasons. Using the language of torture may be successful in grabbing the attention of the general public, but it is somewhat questionable as a matter of law.

Above and beyond the issue of the conditions within these centres, and the arbitrary manner in which persons are committed to the facilities, the question remains as to whether closed centres for drug dependence treatment, ie facilities where persons committed to treatment are not allowed to leave freely, are legitimate under any circumstances. Unsurprisingly, advocates of drug liberalisation answer in the negative. HRW, for example, extrapolates from the situation in the above countries to make a universal statement regarding treatment in closed centres in general, stating that it is without exception unlawful. They argue that:

> ... [such] facilities may differ greatly by, and even within, a country. However, regardless of their name, centers that hold people against their will for drug

[187] HRW (n 172) 16.
[188] HRW (n 172) 16.

> dependency treatment should be considered 'drug detention centers' operating outside international law … Even when such centers are enabled by national legislation (and where that legal framework is fully respected in practice), detention in such centers is arbitrary, and violates international law because it is a medically and scientifically inappropriate response to any actual clinical need for treatment of drug dependence. The various restrictions on individual rights resulting from detention in such centers are not strictly necessary, nor the least restrictive means, to achieve the purpose of drug treatment.[189]

In one fell swoop, therefore, HRW has created a new category of arbitrary detention facilities, known as 'drug detention centres', which are always and under any circumstances violative of international human rights law.

Most relevant UN agencies would seem to agree with this position. In a joint statement issued in 2012, OHCHR and UNODC were joined by ten other UN agencies in calling on governments to 'close compulsory drug detention and rehabilitation centres and implement voluntary, evidence-informed and rights-based health and social services in the community.'[190] The views elaborated in the joint statement appear to be heavily influenced by some of the generalisations advanced by advocates of drug liberalisation. The agencies state that:

> The continued existence of compulsory drug detention and rehabilitation centres, where people who are suspected of using drugs or being dependent on drugs, people who have engaged in sex work, or children who have been victims of sexual exploitation are detained without due process in the name of 'treatment' or 'rehabilitation', is a serious concern. Compulsory drug detention and rehabilitation centres raise human rights issues and threaten the health of detainees, including through increased vulnerability to HIV and tuberculosis (TB) infection. Criteria for detention of individuals in these centres vary within and among countries. However, such detention often takes place without the benefit of sufficient due process, legal safeguards or judicial review. The deprivation of liberty without due process is an unacceptable violation of internationally recognized human rights standards. Furthermore, detention in these centres has been reported to involve physical and sexual violence, forced labour, sub-standard conditions, denial of health care, and other measures that violate human rights.[191]

There are no specific country situations mentioned in the statement, and no real effort made to define the terminology used, with the last sentence

[189] HRW (n 168) 14.

[190] International Labour Office, Office of the High Commissioner for Human Rights, United Nations Development Programme, United Nations Education, Science and Culture Organisation, United Nations Fund for Population Assistance, United Nations High Commissioner for Refugees, United Nations International Children's Fund, United Nations Office on Drugs and Crime, UN Women, World Food Programme, World Health Organisation, and UNAIDS, 'Joint statement on compulsory drug detention and rehabilitation centres' (Geneva, 2012).

[191] Ibid.

of the statement noting simply that '[v]arious terms are used for these centres.'[192] While the violations that have been reported on are very real, it is unfortunate that this group of UN organisations would issue a position containing such vague generalisations.

UN agencies have also published reports on other occasions that seem to accept the sweeping statements of advocates of drug liberalisation without scrutiny. For example, OHCHR's 2015 study for the Human Rights Council states that the 'Working Group on Arbitrary detention has found that people who use drugs are particularly at risk of arbitrary detention',[193] leading the reader to believe that persons who abuse drugs are vulnerable globally. However, the report cited focuses on a country visit to China in 1998, and states merely that the Chinese system of re-education through labour (which, as it was applied in China, was by definition arbitrary) 'only concerns the perpetrators of offences classified as minor which do not seriously disturb public order (consumption of drugs, prostitution, petty larceny, etc.)'[194] making clear that large categories of persons are targeted. It is extremely unfortunate, not to mention sloppy, that OHCHR would not even check the citation of a Special Procedures report to ensure it was not being used out of context, as is the case here. In addition, any discussion of re-education through labour in China would also obviously be incomplete without noting that it was widely used to detain without trial political opponents of the regime.[195]

Another country that is often highlighted with regard to the detention of persons who abuse drugs is the US. Besides the ongoing issue of excessive use of force by police officers, the statistics related to the numbers of persons incarcerated in the country for drug-related offences (mainly simple possession) are simply staggering, amounting to 50 percent of inmates in federal prison, a total of 95,800 persons.[196] The proportion is lower in state prisons at 16 percent, but that still amounts to 208,000 persons,[197] meaning that a total of over 300,000 persons—almost one in a thousand of the total population of the country—are behind bars in the US for possession of drugs.

[192] Ibid.

[193] OHCHR (n 184) para 36.

[194] Working Group on Arbitrary Detention 'Visit to the People's Republic of China' (Geneva, UN index E/CN.4/1998/44/Add.2, 22 December 1997) para 81.

[195] Re-education through labour has now been abolished in China, but systemic arbitrary detention of political opponents still takes place. See eg Amnesty International, '"Changing the Soup but Not the Medicine?": Abolishing Re-education through Labour In China' (London, 2013).

[196] US Bureau of Justice Statistics, 'Prisoners in 2014' (Washington, 2015) 17.

[197] Ibid.

There are stark elements of racial discrimination in these statistics. The American Civil Liberties Union notes that:

> Racial disparities in sentencing are consistent with a larger pattern of racial disparities that plague the U.S. criminal justice system from arrest through incarceration … These racial disparities are particularly pronounced in arrests and incarceration for drug offenses. Despite similar rates of drug use, Blacks are incarcerated on drug charges at a rate ten times greater than Whites. Blacks represent 12 per cent of drug users, but 38 per cent of those arrested for drug offenses, and 59 per cent of those in state prison for drug offenses. Although Blacks and Whites use [cannabis] at comparable rates, Blacks are 3.73 times more likely to be arrested for [cannabis] possession. In some counties, Blacks are 10, 15, even 30 times more likely to be arrested.[198]

The international definition of racial discrimination, as enumerated in ICERD, is 'any distinction, exclusion, restriction or preference based on race, colour, descent, or national or ethnic origin which has the purpose or effect of nullifying or impairing the recognition, enjoyment or exercise, on an equal footing, of human rights and fundamental freedoms'. Vital is the language 'purpose or effect'—a state may be violating its international obligations if a policy brings about a discriminatory result, even if unintended. ICERD has stressed the importance of this language, stating in its General Recommendation 14 that:

> A distinction is contrary to the Convention if it has either the purpose or the effect of impairing particular rights and freedoms … In seeking to determine whether an action has an effect contrary to the Convention, it will look to see whether that action has an unjustifiable disparate impact upon a group distinguished by race, colour, descent, or national or ethnic origin.[199]

Whether intended or not, it seems clear that drug law enforcement in the United States has a disproportionate effect on African Americans, therefore, falling foul of this provision. The situation must be rectified, so that the country abides by its international human rights obligations. This point has been made on several occasions by UN human rights bodies; for example, in its review of the US in 2014, ICERD reiterated its concern that:

> … members of racial and ethnic minorities, particularly African Americans, continue to be disproportionately arrested, incarcerated and subjected to harsher sentences … [and that] the overrepresentation of racial and ethnic

[198] American Civil Liberties Union, 'United States' Compliance with the International Convention on the Elimination of All Forms of Racial Discrimination: Shadow Report to the 7–9th Periodic Reports of the United States' (New York, 9 July 2014) 18.

[199] Committee on the Elimination of Racial Discrimination, 'General recommendation XIV on article 1, paragraph 1, of the Convention' (Geneva, 1993) paras 1, 2.

> minorities in the criminal justice system is exacerbated by the use of prosecutorial discretion, the application of mandatory minimum drug-offence sentencing policies.[200]

Nevertheless, it would be incomplete to present this as only a question of drug law enforcement. As noted by the American Civil Liberties Union in the aforementioned paper, and has been highlighted throughout the years by numerous advocates, racial discrimination, in particular against persons of African American descent, is a prominent feature of law enforcement in the Untied States in general. In other words, practically all areas of law enforcement in the United States appear plagued by racial discrimination—not just drug law enforcement.

An in-depth examination of the relevant social context would be out of the scope of this study. The point is that the issues of mass incarceration and the extent to which racial discrimination features as an element in criminal justice are very specific to the United States, and do not lend themselves to the kind of extrapolation that opponents of drug control attempt. The vast majority of countries provide for some sort of criminal penalty for drug possession, but do not exhibit the same kind of issues that are so problematic in the United States. One can debate the effectiveness of such measures, but the point is that the situation in the United States is a result of numerous factors that are very country specific, and that, at their core, have little to do with drug control as such. The problem of mass incarceration and racial discrimination in the United States certainly does not prove in any way that efforts against drugs are by definition misguided or that they result in similar problems—they are essentially unique.

Arbitrary Detention and the International Drug Control Conventions

As with the other arguments of the advocates of drug liberalisation, the case of arbitrary detention is indicative. These advocates are not truly promoting human rights—at least not for universal human rights. Rather, they are arguing for better treatment only for persons who abuse drugs, and, by extension, the abandonment of the international drug control regime. Human rights language is but a tool to market their ideas, not a true guiding principle.

Even a simple reading of the international drug control conventions shows that the kind of violations described by advocates of drug

[200] Committee on the Elimination of Racial Discrimination, 'Review of the United States of America' (Geneva, UN index CERD/C/USA/CO/7-9, 25 September 2014) para 20.

liberalisation are neither required nor encouraged. The issue is one of non-compliance with human rights standards by a limited number of governments, not any fundamental problem with the international drug control conventions. Advocates of drug liberalisation are unable to point to a single example where INCB or UNODC promoted incarceration for drug abuse, for the simple reason that these bodies have never done so (though it may be the case that they could have been more vocal when such abuses have taken place).

Some advocates of drug liberalisation do admit that the international drug control conventions do not require that persons be imprisoned for simply using drugs.[201] However, this is then turned on its head, to say that this flexibility on the part of the conventions must be exploited to its fullest pending a complete discarding of what are fundamentally outdated treaties. Barrett and Nowak state, for example, that:

> There is no requirement of imprisonment for possession, or, indeed, other such penalties. There is therefore flexibility within the drug conventions for the de facto decriminalisation of personal use through the use of nominal penalties for possession, what may be referred to as 'prosecutory tolerance'.[202]

The suggestion is that states have a mistaken idea regarding the international drug control conventions. They think that the provisions of the conventions require incarceration and prohibit a more 'pragmatic' approach, but they are mistaken. Advocates of drug liberalisation, therefore, assume the role of advisor, showing states that there is in fact more flexibility within the international conventions, and encourage states to use this flexibility. Ironically, however, by doing so, these advocates assume the position of promoting the international conventions, as opposed to arguing against the conventions in their entirety.

Mindful of this conundrum, advocates of drug liberalisation are quick to stress that they would prefer that the conventions were revised comprehensively already at this point, and that their promotion of flexibility is merely a strategic tool.[203] The idea appears to be that 'exploiting' this flexibility will result in a slow but sure domino effect, eventually bringing an end to the international drug control regime. Whether this is the case remains to be seen, but there appears to be an inherent dilemma in the logic of these advocates.

[201] See eg Barrett and Nowak (n 23) 463.

[202] Ibid.

[203] See eg Martin Jelsma, 'UNGASS 2016: Prospects for Treaty Reform and UN System-Wide Coherence on Drug Policy' (Washington, Brookings Institution, 2015).

III. PERSONS WHO ABUSE DRUGS AS A 'VULNERABLE GROUP'

A point closely related to the law enforcement arguments is the notion that persons who abuse drugs are a 'vulnerable group', or a 'socially marginalised group', that is they make up a distinctive social group with particular traits that make them particularly vulnerable to abuses at the hands of the authorities. This notion is a common thread throughout the arguments of advocates of drug liberalisation, with many of them making such statements without any attempt at explanation, as if the issue was self-evident. For example, OSF refers in passing to 'patients from socially marginalised groups—people living with HIV, gays and lesbians, transgender persons, people who use drugs, and people with intellectual disabilities or mental health problems.'[204]

Mendez, who states that '[p]eople who use drugs are a highly stigmatised and criminalised population whose experience of health-care is often one of humiliation, punishment and cruelty',[205] does attempt to give examples to justify his argument. Nevertheless, they are somewhat isolated, and hardly justify the notion that persons who abuse drugs as a whole constitute a vulnerable group:

> Drug users living with HIV are often denied emergency medical treatment. In some cases the laws specifically single out the status of a drug user as a standalone basis for depriving someone of custody or other parental rights. Use of drug registries—where people who use drugs are identified and listed by police and health-care workers, and their civil rights curtailed—are violations of patient confidentiality that lead to further ill-treatment by health providers.[206]

In his section titled 'Discrimination and stigma', Grover also cites a small number of somewhat extreme examples, some of which he admits even contravene the national policy of the countries concerned, such as reports in the United Kingdom that 'past or current users of drugs have been denied treatment for the hepatitis C virus, contrary to official guidance, on the basis that they would not adhere to treatment.'[207]

Barrett and Nowak are more extreme, stating that:

> Unlike human rights law, which focuses to a large extent on the protection of the most vulnerable, the drug conventions criminalise specifically vulnerable

[204] OSF: 'Treatment or Torture? Applying international human rights standards to drug detention centers' (New York, 2011) 1.

[205] Juan Mendez, 'Report of the Special Rapporteur on torture and other cruel, inhuman or degrading treatment or punishment' (Geneva, UN index A/HRC/22/53, 1 February 2013) para 72.

[206] Ibid.

[207] Anand Grover, 'Right of everyone to the enjoyment of the highest attainable standard of physical and mental health' (Geneva, UN index A/65/255, 6 August 2010) para 23.

> groups. They criminalise people who use drugs, known to be vulnerable to HIV, homelessness, discrimination, violence, and premature death; and they criminalise farmers involved in the cultivation of crops made illicit by the conventions, despite generations of traditional use and existing vulnerability to poverty.[208]

They descend into polemic in their attempts at demonising drug control as a whole, stating that:

> Alongside war criminals, mass murderers, human traffickers, torturers and terrorists, drug users and farmers are deemed worthy of criminal sanction in international law in order to address what is seen as an 'evil' and a danger of 'incalculable gravity' and which poses 'a serious threat to the health and welfare of human beings'.[209]

Seemingly preaching to the converted, Barrett and Nowak then go on to state disparagingly that '[t]his is the international legal environment within which national decisions on drugs have been made, laws enacted, policies developed and practices shaped.'[210]

Pillay has also made statements as the UN High Commissioner for Human Rights suggesting that persons who abuse drugs are often subject to 'discrimination' and 'marginalization' by 'approaches which overemphasize criminalization and punishment'.[211]

The issue is an important one, in many ways going to the heart of the arguments of advocates of drug liberalisation. Human rights are by definition universal, stipulating rights that individuals and communities have, in principle, under any circumstances. At the same time, there is a strong focus on the protection of 'vulnerable groups'—that is, groups of persons who, because of a particular trait, or because of the situation they may find themselves in at a particular point in time, are particularly vulnerable to abuse. Human rights does this because blanket assertions of rights are often not meaningful without special attention to the power structures that underlie rights violations. Groups that are at particular risk, therefore, are understood to require special attention, to ensure that they are able to exercise the rights recognised for all.

Despite this recognition, the concept of vulnerability is not clearly defined in international human rights law. The Brasilia Regulations regarding Access to Justice for Vulnerable People, which were adopted by the Ibero-American Judicial Summit in 2008, make an attempt at defining the concept as follows:

> Vulnerable people are defined … as those who, due to reasons of age, gender, physical or mental state, or due to social, economic, ethnic and/or cultural

208 Barrett and Nowak (n 23) 456.

209 Ibid.

210 Ibid.

211 OHCHR, 'High Commissioner calls for focus on human rights and harm reduction in international drug policy' (Geneva, 2009).

> circumstances, find it especially difficult to fully exercise their rights before the justice system as recognised to them by law. The following may constitute causes of vulnerability: age, disability, belonging to indigenous communities or minorities, victimization, migration and internal displacement, poverty, gender and deprivation of liberty.[212]

Vulnerable groups, therefore, are generally understood to mean specific groups of people who face particular difficulties in exercising their rights, either due to a characteristic that is a priori or inherent to their identity; or due to their particular situation at a given time.

Persons who are vulnerable due to their race, ethnic group, sex, or age could be said to be vulnerable due to an a priori characteristic, ie a trait that they were born with and/or cannot change. For example, a person's race cannot be changed, nor, without expensive surgery, can one's sex: these are prime examples of a priori characteristics which often result in special vulnerability to abuse of rights.

In addition, persons are also often vulnerable due to characteristics such as their political opinion or religion. These are not characteristics that an individual are born with, and often can be, and are, changed by the individual concerned. However, these traits of course involve the exercise of fundamental rights, and it is understood that they are so fundamental to one's identity that individuals should not be compelled to change them, ie they have the human right, recognised under international law, to freely choose and hold these views or faiths without any kind of penalty or discrimination.

Separately from persons vulnerable due to those above traits are persons who are situationally vulnerable, ie they are vulnerable not because of any a priori trait or because of the exercise of any fundamental right, but merely as a result of the situation that they find themselves in at a particular time. For example, prisoners are vulnerable because they are in the custody of the authorities, and are known to be often subject to human rights abuses. Being a prisoner is not an a priori characteristic; it is (usually) transient and subject to change. The individual is vulnerable, and requires special attention, only during that period of time in which he is in that particular situation.

Nor, in the case of the prisoner, is the situation necessarily the result of the exercise of any fundamental right on the individual's part. The person may very well be in the custody of the police because of having committed a crime. In other words, the designation of a particular individual as vulnerable is independent of any legal or moral judgment regarding any actions that individual may have taken. Public debate regarding the rights

[212] Ibero-American Judicial Summit, 'Brasilia Regulations regarding Access to Justice for Vulnerable People' (Brasilia 2008) 5.

of prisoners is often shrouded by the notion that persons who have broken the law have somehow forfeited their rights, and are not entitled to the same protection as other persons. This is, of course, false. A person does not somehow discard their human rights, no matter what sort of action they may have taken until that point.

The question is whether persons who abuse drugs can be said to fall into one of the above categories. It is manifest that drug abuse is not an a priori characteristic. Though there may or may not be genetic predispositions to substance abuse, it is obvious that drug abuse is not something one is born with. It strains credibility to suggest that there may be some strand of DNA that inevitably results in an individual abusing drugs.

Drug abuse is, clearly, a choice, at least at the outset. If a person becomes drug dependent, then that dependency is a medical condition that, arguably, suspends that element of choice, to varying extents. However, until and unless the individual reaches the point of dependency (and the majority of course do not), abusing drugs is always the result of a free choice. This is not to make a moral judgment of that choice, but to state the obvious: though many social and other factors surely make drug abuse more likely for particular people, it is never inevitable in the way that one's race or sex is.

Nor can it possibly be argued that drug abuse is a fundamental element of one's identity. To suggest that it is would be to elevate drug abuse to the level of political opinion or religion, as if persons 'at risk' of human rights violations because of their drug use were comparable to apostates in Iran or political opponents of the Chinese regime. This is clearly ludicrous, and is an insult to the millions of people globally who are in fact subject to human rights abuses because of the exercise of their fundamental rights. Though advocates of drug liberalisation keep this issue somewhat vague, that is essentially the logical conclusion of their arguments, which rely on the notion that drug abuse is, or should be recognised as, a human right—something that no individual should be asked to change.

Even worse, some advocates of drug liberalisation have argued that persons who abuse drugs are similar in this manner to sexual minorities who face discrimination because of their sexual orientation. This comparison is surprisingly common. For example, Flacks states:

> The analogy with sexual orientation is a pertinent one because relations between people of the same sex have also historically attracted social condemnation and criminal sanction, and still do in many countries … Indeed, in many countries, members of the LGBT community are considered threats to public health and public safety, an assumption also made about drug users.[213]

[213] Flacks (n 166) 859, 860.

Flacks goes on:

> Some argue, either implicitly or explicitly, that drug users 'choose' their fate in a way that, for example, those of varying sexual persuasions and identities do not, thus presuming fault on the part of the drug user. The emphasis on choice, however, is misplaced in regard to both drug use and sexual orientation. Societal discrimination towards those who are different should not be tolerated and rights should not be interfered with unless the furtherance of such rights impacts negatively on the rights of others or the wellbeing of the public at large, the legal basis for which is discussed further below. In this respect, whether one chooses their sexual orientation is of no import and the concern for gay 'innocence' should be of scientific interest only, with resources directed instead toward addressing those attitudes that lead to judgmental and discriminatory behavior. So it is with drug use. The apportionment of blame or responsibility, however conceived, can never amount to justification for interferences with human rights.'[214]

HRW also advances similar arguments, making the problematic assertion that the prohibition of drugs is analogous to bans of LGBT conduct in that they are based on public morality. Since 'human rights jurisprudence leaves no doubt today that majority public morality, if so inclined, cannot justify criminalization of private homosexual conduct by consenting adults',[215] they argue, such must also be the case for drug abuse.

However, the comparison with sexual orientation is particularly inappropriate, and potentially extremely dangerous for LGBT rights. Discrimination based on sexual orientation is an issue that has only recently received the international attention it warrants, with a resolution of the Human Rights Council in 2011 being the first time a UN body pronounced itself on the issue. In this resolution, the Council '[expressed] grave concern at acts of violence and discrimination, in all regions of the world, committed against individuals because of their sexual orientation and gender identity'[216] and noted that this was a 'priority issue'.[217] As Flack notes, groups against LGBT rights often state that sexual orientation is a free but benighted choice, one that can and should be reversed through individual instruction (and punishment). As noted by advocates of drug liberalisation, on a superficial level at least, these arguments are similar to what some (though certainly not all) proponents of drug control advance, and the condescending morality with which such ideas are often expressed make such statements an easy target for advocates of drug liberalisation.

214 Flacks (n 166) 860.

215 HRW (n 35) 6.

216 HRC, '17/19: Human rights, sexual orientation and gender identity' (Geneva, UN index A/HRC/RES/17/19, adopted 17 June 2011) preamble para 4.

217 Ibid at para 4.

Nanny state attitudes about persons private lives are wrong, so the argument goes—such attitudes are wrong about LGBT persons, and they are wrong about persons' who abuse drugs.

Nevertheless, the comparison of drug abuse with sexual orientation cheapens the entire idea of such orientation as an a priori trait and a fundamental pillar of one's identity. As is clear from the citation above, the arguments of HRW and the others are based on a simplistic notion that persons who abuse drugs, as LGBT persons, are simply 'different', and should not be discriminated against because of their difference from the mainstream. This either elevates drug abuse to the existential plane that sexual orientation is on, which, as noted above, clearly has little foundation in reality—or it lowers sexual orientation to a mere lifestyle choice.

In addition, in their efforts to show that drugs are less harmful than substances such as alcohol and tobacco, advocates of drug liberalisation often stress that the majority of drug abuse is not problematic, and does not result in addiction. The harmless nature of 'recreational use' is a recurring theme throughout their statements.[218] This hardly sits well with their comparison of drug abuse to sexual orientation, the latter being a fundamental pillar of an individual's identity, not a mere recreational whim.

Of course, persons who abuse drugs may, at times, be situationally vulnerable, for example, they are vulnerable to ill-treatment at the hands of law enforcement officers. However, this is generally only to the extent that all persons are vulnerable in such situations. In other words, their drug abuse does not necessarily make them any more vulnerable than any other individual would be. Persons who abuse drugs are merely subject to the same potential violations that other criminal suspects are, or at least other persons who are often deemed 'undesirable' by official actors (such as homeless persons, sex workers, and others).

Naturally, persons who abuse drugs, or at least persons who are dependent on drugs, are in need of particular health care, and run the risk of not receiving appropriate treatment while they are in custody. Again, though, this could be said of persons with other health conditions. Though advocates of drug liberalisation cite examples of police officers depriving persons of drugs to force confessions, these are tactics that law enforcement officials have been known to use against any suspect with health conditions. Those tactics are certainly abusive and should be condemned, but one could just as easily say that persons with diabetes constitute a 'vulnerable group', because police officers have been known to withhold medication in an effort to have them confess.

[218] See eg Damon Barrett and Philp E Veerman, *A Commentary on the United Nations Convention on the Rights of the Child: Article 33: Protection from Narcotic Drugs and Psychotropic Substances* (Leiden, Martinus Nijhoff, 2012) 35.

The argument that persons who abuse drugs constitute a vulnerable group in and of themselves, therefore, would generally not seem to be meaningful. There are some situational vulnerabilities, in particular if one is dependent on drugs (and it is the advocates of drug liberalisation who are quick to point out only a small proportion of persons who abuse drugs advance to a state of dependency). However, that is not what the advocates of drug liberalisation are suggesting: they argue that persons who abuse drugs are inherently vulnerable to human rights violations and require special protection in all circumstances, akin to ethnic or religious minorities. This argument can only be sustained, of course, if one accepts the premise that abusing drugs is a human right, somehow at the same level as freedom of expression or religion. It is submitted that this is clearly preposterous, and cannot be accepted.

IV. MILITARISATION OF DRUG LAW ENFORCEMENT

Yet another argument advanced by advocate of drug liberalisation is that an overly strong emphasis on law enforcement in drug control has led to a militarisation of anti-drug efforts, with countries turning over enforcement of drug laws from civilian police forces to the military. This, in turn, has lead to widespread and systematic human rights violations by the military. For example, Count the Costs cites several horrendous abuses:

> Complaints relating to military and police abuses made to national human rights commissions have increased by 900% since the beginning of the militarised 'war on drugs' in 2006. Attacks on journalists, human rights defenders and migrants by criminal groups and security forces have gone uninvestigated … Children and entire families have been killed at drug war military checkpoints.'[219]

As with the other law enforcement related violations, these are presented as being inevitable consequences of efforts against drugs: a necessary destination of the continuum of the 'war on drugs'.

Nevertheless, though these situations are presented by advocates of drug liberalisation as having universal relevance, they in fact have occurred only in a handful of countries, mainly Mexico, Brazil, and Colombia. That of course does not make the human rights issues any less serious, but, as with the other law enforcement related arguments cited above, it does put the issue in perspective.

The points related to militarisation are often expanded to include forced eradication efforts targeting illicit crops. Simple eradication without the provision of alternative livelihoods can, of course, have a disastrous

[219] See eg Count the Costs (n 142) at 8.

impact on the farming communities concerned.[220] For example, Count the Costs states that:

> On average, 10,000-20,000 indigenous people have been displaced each year in Colombia due to crop eradication … Due to crop eradication, some farmers in [Afghanistan] have resorted to selling their underage daughters for marriage, underlining the centrality of poverty as a driver of involvement in drug production.'[221]

Some eradication efforts have involved aerial spraying of pesticides that have been shown to cause health and environmental problems.[222]

There are clear human rights issues involved, and an argument can surely be sustained against blanket eradication, in particular through aerial spraying (which often borders on the indiscriminate). Once again, however, this applies only to a few countries globally, mainly Colombia and Afghanistan. Both UNODC and INCB have stressed the need for providing alternative sources of livelihood for farmers engaged in illicit crop production,[223] and UNODC engages in programmes to this effect, though they are often of limited effectiveness.

In any case, there is no question that the militarisation of anti-drug efforts can be extremely problematic, as is the militarisation of any law enforcement task. As is well known, militaries are generally not trained to engage in law enforcement, and asking them to perform such roles generally leads to negative results, including human rights abuses. It is, therefore, right to call attention to this issue, and to advocate against it. Nevertheless, as is the case with arguments related to other human rights issues, close scrutiny of the statements of advocates of drug liberalisation show that facts are often presented in a somewhat misleading manner, in an attempt to show that drug control is the sole driving force behind the situation.

Indicative, for example, is a paper submitted to OHCHR by the Mexican Commission for the Defence and Promotion of Human Rights (MCDPHR). Stating that '[t]he results of the war on drugs … have left over 70,000 people killed, more than 25,000 people disappeared, over 8,000 people arbitrary detained … more than 4,000 instances of torture, at least

[220] See eg Nigel Inkster and Virignia Comolli, *Drugs, Insecurity, and Failed States* (London, International Institute for Strategic Studies, 2012); Count the Costs, 'The War on Drugs: Causing Deforestation and Pollution' (London, 2013); Ginette Léa Gautreau, 'To Rid the World of the Drug Scourge: A Human Security Perspective on the War on Drugs in Colombia and Mexico' (2012) 12 *Paterson Review of International Affairs* 61.

[221] See eg Count the Costs (n 142) 11.

[222] See eg Inkster and Comolli, *Drugs, Insecurity and Failed States* (n 220); Count the Costs (n 220).

[223] INCB dedicated a chapter to the subject in its Annual Report 2005: INCB, *Annual Report 2005* (Vienna, 2006). As for UNODC, see eg UNODC, 'Alternative Development: Our Work' at www.unodc.org/unodc/en/alternative-development/our-work.html.

280,000 internally displaced people and over 60 human rights defenders killed in the country',[224] the organisation conflates rights abuses conducted by the military and other law enforcement agencies with crimes committed by drug cartels, which is clearly problematic.

The organisation argues that the involvement of the military exacerbates violence, causing the situation to spiral out of control, stating that:

> The policy of open confrontation against drug cartels and the use of joint operatives between the army, navy, federal and local police within the framework of the war on drugs, together with the emergence of disputes for land distribution routes between the cartels, increased the criminal activity and therefore the levels of insecurity increased as well.[225]

There is surely merit to this argument, but it is difficult to see why it sustains the (somewhat general) recommendations of MCDPHR that states should be encouraged to '[e]nsure that the harm reduction approach includes the social and human rights implications of drug policies around the world'[226] and also be '[discouraged from] the application of drug policies founded on the use of the criminal justice system'.[227]

In any case, as noted above, the examples of the above sort of phenomenon are very few, amounting to a handful of countries at best. It is not universal, and there appear to be no grounds to argue that such militarisation is an inevitable result of drug law enforcement, and that consequently drug laws should be abandoned. Most human rights advocates agree that the militarisation of counter-terrorism is undesirable and leads to human rights violations, and that terrorism should be dealt with as a law enforcement issue. However, this does not automatically translate into the notion that counter-terrorism efforts are themselves by definition wrong, and should be discontinued altogether. There is ample room for countries to deal with both terrorism and drug trafficking and abuse as law enforcement issues, in accordance with human rights law—unless, of course, we accept the underlying premise of advocates of drug liberalisation, namely that attempting to ban drugs is itself wrong and should be abandoned.

Organised Crime

A related argument, though not one necessarily tied directly to human rights, is that legalisation of drugs would deprive international criminal

[224] MCDPHR, 'Human Rights and the War on Drugs in Mexico' (Mexico City, May 2015) 10.
[225] MCDPHR, 'Human Rights and the War on Drugs in Mexico' (n 224) 8.
[226] MCDPHR (n 224) 12.
[227] Ibid.

organisations of their revenue base, thereby putting them out of business (and, as a result, eradicating the violence, corruption, and general lawlessness that has been connected with the rise in influence of such organisations). HRW, for example, states that:

> the current heavy emphasis on criminalization, rather than stopping that flow of resources, seems to be only making the business more profitable … This dynamic is a significant factor contributing to human rights abuses in many countries in which [HRW] works. In Colombia, for example, while both left-wing guerrillas and right-wing paramilitary groups existed before the explosion of the drug trade in the 1980s, both sets of groups were dramatically strengthened by the enormous profits they earned once they became involved in it. The paramilitaries, in particular, over time became Colombia's biggest drug lords, involved in all stages of the trade—from production through processing to distribution. The profits from the drug trade became not only a tool to fund them, but also an objective—partly fuelling the campaign of massacres, killings, and forced displacement of hundreds of thousands …[228]

Collins makes the argument in the technocratic language of economics:

> This pattern can help explain the escalation of drug war violence over the past five decades. Market interventions by states disturb the political economy of the trade, cultivating more violent actors, in turn driving more aggressive state interventions which in turn drive more violent outcomes.[229]

The common thread running through both this notion and the arguments surrounding the militarisation of drug control efforts is that it is the illegality of drugs that is fuelling criminal organisations. If only drugs were to be legalised and controlled by the government, so this argument goes, then the criminal organisations would lose their main source of funding and be weakened considerably, or perhaps even die out altogether. An oft cited example of this by drug liberalisation advocates is the prohibition of alcohol in the US. The prohibitory policies lead to the massing of power by criminal organisations involved in the widespread trafficking of alcohol, but once prohibition was repealed, these organisations lost their might.

The above argument advanced by advocates of drug liberalisation, as well as the account of the history of prohibition in the US used to support it, is simplistic in many ways.[230] Most obviously, the notion that legalising the illicit drug trade would lead to major criminal organisations simply disappearing lacks credibility. This did not happen in the US after

[228] HRW (n 35) 4.

[229] John Collins, 'The Economics of a New Global Strategy', in LSE Expert Group on the Economics of Drug Policy (ed), *Ending the Drug Wars* (London, London School of Economics, 2014) 10.

[230] MacCoun and Reuter in Robert J MacCoun and Peter Reuter, *Drug War Heresies; Learning from Other Vices, Times, and Places* (New York, Cambridge University Press, 2001) Kindle edition at 1933, 1951/5996 note: 'Prohibition failed because it was never seriously attempted.

prohibition was repealed, and it is difficult to think it would happen in Mexico, Colombia, or anywhere else.

Though the illicit nature of the activity naturally makes accurate assessments difficult, large organised crime enterprises generally have a wide and diverse range of activities besides just drug trafficking. Though UNODC estimates that drug trafficking remains by far the largest source of income for organised crime globally,[231] this varies considerably from organisation to organisation. For example, the best estimates for the Revolutionary Armed Forces of Colombia (FARC), the main armed opposition group in Colombia and one of the oft cited examples of an organisation that relies heavily on the illicit drug trade for its income, are that it relies on the drug trade for approximately 50 per cent of its income, with the rest coming mainly from extortion of oil and other large companies operating in the region.[232] Losing income from the drug trade would no doubt be a significant blow, but arguably not one which the organisation could not recover from.[233]

In addition, legalising and regulating a commodity does not automatically exclude a criminal element from its distribution. There remains a significant illicit trade in cigarettes and alcohol in many countries where these are regulated and highly taxed (as many advocates of drug liberalisation argue should be the case with drugs). The danger of this may be reduced somewhat by lowering the taxes collected—but this would in turn bring into question one of the key arguments of advocates of drug liberalisation, namely that taxes collected on legalised drugs would be enough to fund the strengthened treatment and prevention programmes made necessary by increased consumption. The illicit trade in licit pharmaceuticals also remains a serious problem in many countries.

The loopholes in the basic law, the lack of political willingness to close them … along with a failure to commit resources for enforcement or to respond effectively to the corruption … all point to what has been characterized as a symbolic crusade rather than a public policy reform effort … In part, this was because alcohol was not regarded by much of the population as evil in itself. There was too much respectable … imbibing throughout Western society … This contrasts sharply with current attitudes towards the use of cocaine or heroin, which are generally regarded as dangerous and addictive.'

[231] See UNODC, 'Transnational Organised Crime—The Globalised Illegal Economy' (Vienna, 2012) 1, where the organisation estimates global revenue from drug trafficking at USD 320 billion. This is 10 times the value of the next most lucrative activity, human trafficking.

[232] Vanda Felbab-Brown, *Shooting Up: Counterinsurgency and the War on Drugs* (Washington, Brookings Institution, 2010) Kindle version at 1036/3499.

[233] On the other hand, FARC and other armed groups have '[derived] much more than large financial profits from their sponsorship of illicit economies. They also obtain freedom of action and, crucially, legitimacy and support from the local population … By supporting the illicit economy, belligerents both increase their military capability and build political support, whereas belligerents who attempt to destroy the illicit economy suffer on both accounts.' See Felbab-Brown, *Shooting Up* (n 232) 124/3499.

Felbab-Brown states the matter succinctly:

> … licensing and related policies such as legalization and laissez-faire are not always the appropriate response to illicit economies. Nor are suppression policies always the wrong choice. There are, after all, good reasons why some economies and activities remain illegal, even if bans can have undesirable consequences. The fact that murder is illegal creates demand for killers and establishes a highly lucrative market for professional hit men. Belligerent groups who provide such services can reap large financial profits; however, the solution is not to legalize murder … Legalization of the consumption of drugs is likely to lead to increased consumption—a serious and important reason to eschew such a policy … Finally, even when licensing is feasible, the existence of a licit economy does not translate into the elimination of the related illicit economy. The legal market for cars in the United States has not prevented the existence of an illicit market for cheaper stolen cars.[234]

Attempting to weaken criminal organisations is of course an important endeavour, and reducing their stream of revenue may be one way. However, at least in the case of the illicit drug trade, the notion that simply legalising what are now criminal activities would somehow be sufficient in doing this is naïve. Inskster and Comoli point out that:

> … caution is needed on the part of advocates of [legalisation], particularly in terms of claims about the extent to which criminality and global instability might be reduced by a legalization regime. Removing from the equation one of the most profitable and most easily trafficked sources of revenue for criminal groups is likely to have a beneficial impact over time, but this should not be equated with eliminating criminality.[235]

There are some activities for which legalisation may be a plausible answer. For example, if there were adequate opportunities for migration, in particular from developing to developed countries, the opportunities for criminal organisations to engage in human trafficking would probably be limited. However, this would appear to be an attractive policy option only because migration, it is believed, is in general a good thing, or at least not a bad one. This is not a given in the case of the drug trade, and the argument of the advocates of drug liberalisation can only be supported if we accept their underlying premise, that drugs should not be illicit to begin with.

Pain Relief and Legalisation of Opium Poppy Cultivation in Afghanistan

The above arguments, regarding militarisation and the eradication of criminal organisations, is in some ways an extension of an earlier proposal

[234] Felbab-Brown (n 232) 2239-2247/3499.
[235] Inkster and Comolli (n 220) 2569/2795.

of advocates of drug liberalisation, that focused solely on Afghanistan. Starting in the late 1990s, a number of those advocates, most prominently an organisation known as the Senlis Council (SC), attempted to argue for legalising opium poppy cultivation in Afghanistan. Noting the difficulties the international community was having in combating the illicit cultivation phenomenon, the idea was that opium poppy would be strictly controlled, with farmers given a fair wage for cultivation and the poppy released on the international market, to ensure an adequate supply of opiate medications for developing countries.

In September 2005, SC published the 'Feasibility Study on Opium Licensing in Afghanistan for the Production of Morphine and Other Essential Medicines', arguing that as the current drug trade is illegal, it is built on 'informal, untaxed opium revenues and thrives on the weak security environment and the lack of a well developed system of rule of law. This deprives the public sector of income that could be used to build much needed infrastructure.'[236] SC argued for a licensing system allowing licensed opium poppy farmers to engage in licit cultivation. Since social structures for opium poppy cultivation have existed in Afghanistan for centuries, the central government could in turn use these structures to extend its control to the provinces, exclude criminal organisations, and ensure a lasting source of revenue for the government.

It is worth noting that SC avoided the 'legalisation' terminology, preferring rather to argue for a licensing system that would increase the tax revenue of the Afghan government. Nevertheless, SC was an organisation dedicated to the legalisation of drugs,[237] and the inclination of the proposal is of course obvious. SC engaged in concentrated lobbying at the European level for its proposal, resulting in a European Parliament resolution in 2006 that stated the Parliament's concern at 'the extremely high costs and serious flaws in terms of effectiveness of a counter-narcotics strategy based only on eradication and alternative livelihood' and stated that the international community should 'take into consideration the proposal of licensed production of opium for medical purposes, as already granted to a number of countries'.[238] On the other hand, the position of the Afghan

[236] Senlis Council, 'Feasibility Study on Opium Licensing in Afghanistan for the Production of Morphine and Other Essential Medicines' (London, 2005) 1.

[237] SC's website at the time states that the organisation is an 'international policy think tank' based in London and that it focuses on 'foreign policy, security, development and counter-narcotics policies.' See eg Robert I Rotberg, 'Reviewing the Afghan State' in Robert I Rotberg (ed), *Building a New Afghanistan* (Cambridge, World Peace Foundation and Brookings Institution, 2007) note 30. In fact, however, a review of the organisation's statements and publications shows that it focused solely on critiques of international drug policy since its inception in 2002. In 2012, The Senlis Council was renamed the International Council on Security and Development. See www.icosgroup.net.

[238] European Parliament, 'European Parliament resolution on Afghanistan' (Brussels, resolution number B6-0030/2006, 11 January 2006).

government was one of strong opposition. In January 2006, the Minister of Counter Narcotics of the country sent a letter to SC, stating that 'eradication is and will remain an essential element of the Counter Narcotic Strategy of the Government of Afghanistan. Organisations and individuals who advocate activities or policies opposed to eradication may find that they are in breach of the law of Afghanistan and of the constitution.'[239] In October 2006, the Government announced that it had instructed SC to leave the country.[240]

Even taking aside the legalisation slant of the SC proposal, the proposal was so unfounded in reality that, it is submitted, it is somewhat amazing that anyone found it worthy of serious consideration. Licit cultivation requires various layers of strict administrative and legal controls to prevent diversion into the illicit market—this is not only a legal requirement under various provisions of the 1961 Convention,[241] but simple common sense. On the other hand, the security situation in Afghanistan is grave, with fierce fighting in numerous provinces where opium cultivation takes place, and the government is not in control of vast swathes of the country. It is clear that the kind of strict government controls required are simply not feasible, either now or in the foreseeable future. The notion put forward by the SC that the government would be able to strengthen its presence in the provinces through a licensing system is laughable, and betrays a fundamental ignorance of the situation in the country. Indeed, there is no serious examination in the Sustainability Study of the security situation in the country, with the one brief chapter dedicated to 'law enforcement' concluding that 'it is evident that the creation of an opium control system will also contribute to strengthening the law and order efforts in Afghanistan.'[242] One could be forgiven for wondering if the country being examined was Switzerland or Sweden, not Afghanistan.

A separate report of the SC is equally astounding in its assertion that the situation of Turkey in the late 1960s (when the government extended control over illicit opium cultivation) is 'analogous to the current situation in Afghanistan'.[243] As noted by this author in a previous paper,[244] Turkey in the 1960s was already an established centralised state with

[239] Letter from Minister of Counter Narcotics to Executive Director of Senlis Council (Kabul, 26 January 2006).

[240] 'Afghanistan Bans Senlis Council', *Pajhwok Afghan News*, 15 October 2006.

[241] See eg 1961 Convention Articles 23, 25, 30, 31, and 34.

[242] Senlis Council (n 236) 642.

[243] Senlis Council, 'The Political History of Turkey's Opium Licensing System for the Production of Medicines: Lessons for Afghanistan' (London, 2006) 1.

[244] Saul Takahashi, 'Peacebuilding Tool or Putting the Cart Before the Horse? Licensing of Opium Poppy Cultivation in Afghanistan' (Tokyo, Discussion Paper for Peace-Building Studies 11, 2007).

strong administrative institutions and relative respect for the rule of law. Afghanistan, in contrast, remains incapable of enforcing the will of the central government outside of the capital city. To compare the two is clearly neither convincing nor meaningful.

In a subsequent paper, SC attempts a rebuttal against its critics, arguing that:

> … the rhetoric against the proposal … has largely failed to recognise the capacity of Afghan communities to take charge of and influence their futures. The inclusion of community level social structures in the control of such a system would effectively acknowledge these competencies and in doing so, empower rural communities. Further, the linking of formal and informal social structures for the licensing of poppy cultivation will have important consequences for the long term stability of the country, and will generate the control necessary for wider economic development.[245]

While this may be true in theory, it is clear that far more needs to be done to ensure security and a functioning rule of law in Afghanistan before any discussion on opium poppy licensing could take place.

Yet another issue with the SC proposal is that, were opium poppy cultivation licensed without adequate centralised control, the criminal organisations that currently control cultivation may simply become the 'official' suppliers of the drug. Far from noting this as a drawback, SC's proposal appears to encourage this, arguing that there is a need for a wide ranging amnesty covering all persons engaged in the illicit opium trade, including the large number of corrupt provincial officials that are involved.[246] While large scale prosecution of poppy farmers would be neither feasible nor desirable, this once again exhibits a surprising amount of naiveté on the part of the SC.

Pain Relief Globally

Though the many flaws with the SC proposal meant that it quickly disappeared from the limelight of international policy fora, the proposal does touch on one issue that continues to be included in the arguments of some advocates of drug liberalisation, namely that of the need to ensure an adequate drug supply for global pain relief.

As noted above, one of the main purposes of the international drug control regime is to ensure an adequate global supply of licit medicine.

[245] Senlis Council, 'Integrated Social Control in Afghanistan: Implications for the Licensed Cultivation of Poppy for the Production of Medicines' (London, 2006) 31.

[246] Senlis Council (n 236) 679–80.

The global estimates system managed by INCB is geared towards this goal, with countries providing estimates of licit medication they will require over the forthcoming year, and INCB attempting to ensure that the country does not import sums over these approved estimates.

This pillar of international drug control—ensuring that there is no diversion from the licit international market to the illicit one—has been remarkably successful. The other pillar, ensuring adequate medication for countries, has seen less success. Data from INCB itself shows that a disproportionately large percentage of global opiate based medication (eg morphine), used for example for pain relief for terminally ill patients, is consumed by the developed world, with developing countries receiving an woefully inadequate amount. INCB noted in March 2015 that approximately:

> … 5.5 billion people still have limited or no access to medicines containing narcotic drugs such as codeine or morphine, leaving 75 per cent of the world population without access to proper pain relief treatment … around 92 per cent of morphine used worldwide is consumed by only 17 per cent of the world population, primarily living in the United States, Canada, Western Europe, Australia and New Zealand.[247]

This has led some advocates of drug liberalisation to argue that there is a 'global shortage' of pain relief medications, with the international drug control regime to blame. The argument is that the 'prohibitive', 'restrictive' controls laid out by the international drug control conventions discourage or even prevent developing countries from receiving necessary medications—yet another reason that the regime must be discarded. HRW, for example, states that:

> Restrictive drug policies impede medical and scientific use of controlled substances in numerous countries, condemning millions to needless suffering from pain and other symptoms … Human Rights Watch has documented the egregious impact on patients of these regulatory restrictions … The failure to provide access to palliative pain relief in those circumstances interferes with the right to the highest attainable standard of health and in some circumstances can amount to a violation of the prohibition on cruel, inhuman, and degrading treatment.[248]

SC also made similar arguments, stating that 'a system of licensed opium in Afghanistan for the production of essential medicines such as morphine and codeine could provide an effective response to this unmet global need.'[249]

[247] INCB, 'Three quarters of the world has limited or no access to pain relief medications, says INCB Report' (Vienna, 3 March 2015).

[248] See eg HRW (n 35) 8.

[249] SC (n 236) 2.

In fact, these conclusions are somewhat simplistic. What SC and other advocates of drug liberalisation describe as 'demand' is a forecast of need, assessed by international agencies such as WHO and INCB on the basis of factors such as national population and various health-related indices, including the number of sufferers of cancer (who are assumed as requiring a certain amount of pain relief medication). This is not the amount that countries report to INCB under the estimate system, nor the amount that they actually consume—both of which are generally far lower.[250] In other words, assuming the forecast of international agencies is by and large accurate, there is significant under-utilisation, in particular under-prescribing of opium based medications in the vast majority of countries.

In other words, the issue is not a lack of supply, or of INCB refusing to approve the estimates of countries—rather, there is a dearth of capacity on the part of the public health systems in many developing countries, preventing them from providing adequate estimates and from distributing medication in an effective manner. This has been pointed out by INCB on many occasions. For example, in a special report on this topic in 2010, INCB noted that it discusses this issue with governments as a matter of course when it conducts country missions, and recommends improvements to remedy any issues.[251]

INCB has identified several factors behind the problem, including 'over restrictive regulations, difficult administrative procedures, concerns about diversion and the consequences of unintentional errors; concerns about unintended addiction and inadequate or insufficient training of health personnel'.[252] Therefore, a fear of drug dependency is a factor behind the reluctance of public health officials in some countries to use opiate pain relief medication, and, one could argue, this stems in some part from a generally prohibitive attitude towards drugs (which is in turn encouraged by a restrictive interpretation of the international drug control conventions). Nevertheless, this is an issue that can and should be addressed through the strengthening of public health systems—it can hardly be characterised as a fundamental flaw with the international drug control regime. To suggest this as a reason to discard drug control altogether is unconvincing.

As noted above, INCB regularly encourages governments to ensure adequate amounts of pain relief medication, though some advocates of drug liberalisation criticise even those efforts of INCB. For example, the International Drug Policy Consortium accuses INCB of 'shifting the blame' on

[250] See eg INCB, *Availability of Internationally Controlled Drugs: Ensuring Adequate Access for Medical and Scientific Purposes* (Vienna, 2011) paras 14–15.

[251] See eg INCB, *Availability of Internationally Controlled Drugs* (n 248) para 16.

[252] INCB, 'UN Drug Control Body Concerned over Inadequate Medical Supply of Narcotic Drugs to Relieve Pain and Suffering' (Vienna, 23 February 2006).

the developing world when 'its focus is overwhelmingly on the prevention of what it insists on calling "drug abuse"'[253] Nevertheless, even some advocates of drug liberalisation admit that the true problem does not lie with INCB—including, it would appear, HRW, which published a report in 2011 stating that '[m]any countries have adopted regulations that go well beyond the requirements of the Single Convention … Drug control regulations that have a disproportionately negative effect on availability and accessibility of controlled medications will violate both drug conventions and human rights treaties.'[254]

Inkster and Comoli, though generally sympathetic towards legalisation, assess correctly that:

> … the reality that demand for opiates is determined not just by objective medical considerations, but also by a host of political and cultural factors. Many countries in the developing world are reluctant to countenance the widespread use of opiate-based medicines because of ill-founded fears of large-scale addiction or diversion, or simply because the health services in the countries concerned lack the capacity either to provide an estimate of demand or the mechanisms and resources to implement effective pain-management regimes … The INCB's argument, in effect, is that there is no point, and much risk, in accumulating substantial additional supplies unless and until better mechanisms can be devised both to estimate and meet potential global demand. For this reason, well-intentioned but ill-thought-out initiatives, such as the suggestion of buying Afghanistan's entire opium harvest for medicinal use, quite apart from the impracticalities of undertaking such an enterprise in what is still a war zone, have little relevance to the debate.[255]

On this point as well, therefore, the argument of advocates of drug liberalisation that the current, undesirable situation is a result of fundamental problems with drug control appears unfounded. The fact is that in their haste to criticise INCB, and the international drug control regime, many advocates of drug liberalisation have misrepresented the reality in this area.

[253] International Drug Policy Consortium, 'Shifting the blame: INCB and the global pain medication shortage' (London, 16 January 2015).

[254] HRW, 'Global State of Pain Treatment: Access to Medicines and Palliative Care' (New York, 2 June 2011).

[255] Inkster and Comolli (n 220) at 2411/2795.

5

Mandated Treatment and Drug Courts

AS NOTED ABOVE, advocates of drug liberalisation have reported on human rights violations taking place in drug detention centres in several countries, mainly in East and Southeast Asia. Persons are confined to these closed centres in an arbitrary manner, without due process, and are subject to a litany of abuses while in the centres, including ill-treatment and forced labour. The abuses outlined in these reports are serious violations of human rights law, and are rightly condemned. Nevertheless, at least outside of China, they are not necessarily directed only to persons who abuse drugs, and the centres are hardly an integral part of the international drug control regime.

Above and beyond the violations that take place in many of these drug detention centres, however, there is the broader question as to whether it is in principle legitimate to force persons to undergo treatment for drug dependence treatment. Does the state have the right to mandate, to force a person abusing drugs to undergo treatment for that abuse?

Unsurprisingly, advocates of drug liberalisation argue that mandated treatment is in and of itself a human rights violation. This follows, of course, inevitably from their logic that all persons have the right to abuse drugs (or any substance they may wish). The notion is closely connected with the idea that drug abuse is first and foremost a public health issue, not a law enforcement one, and should be treated as such. This reframing of drug control as a health matter suggests that measures against drug abuse should be of a health care nature, ie they should centre on the provision of treatment for the person abusing drugs, not on punishment for their infraction of (what opponents argue are anyway unjust) drug control laws.

It is worth noting that the arguments of advocates of drug liberalisation in this area receive some support by reference to international human rights standards. General Comment 14(2000) on the right to the highest attainable standard of health, states clearly that '[t]he right to health contains both freedoms and entitlements. The freedoms include … the right to be free from interference, such as the right to be free from torture, non-consensual medical treatment and experimentation.'[1] There is little

[1] Committee on Economic, Social, and Cultural Rights, 'CESCR General Comment No. 14: The Right to the Highest Attainable Standard of Health (Art. 12)' (Geneva, UN index E/C.12/2000/4, 11 August 2000) para 8.

elaboration on the right to be free from non-consensual treatment, and it may have been simply that the concept was seen to have been so obvious as not to require further explanation. Historically, involuntary 'treatment' has been the background of human rights abuses in the world, such as incarceration for 'mental illness' in the Soviet Union[2] to forced sterilisation of mentally ill people in Sweden.[3]

UNODC and WHO, in a joint position paper, follow on this principle, and state that:

> Drug dependence treatment services should comply with human rights obligations and recognize the inherent dignity of all individuals. This includes responding to the right to enjoy the highest attainable standard of health and well-being, and ensuring non-discrimination …[4]

UNODC/WHO then enumerate the very limited conditions that treatment may legitimately be imposed on an individual, which are, as one would expect, strictly confined. They state:

> As any other medical procedure, in general conditions drug dependence treatment, be it psychosocial or pharmacological, should not be forced on patients. Only in exceptional crisis situations of high risk to self or others, compulsory treatment should be mandated for specific conditions and periods of time as specified by the law.[5]

Therefore, putting aside the question of whether drug abuse should be legalised, there is some justification for the argument that people should not be forced to subject themselves to treatment for drug abuse.

HRW draws on these standards in arguing that mandatory treatment;

> … may … violate human rights standards [if] a person [is] committed to treatment without his or her consent[6] … Human Rights Watch considers that no one should be subject to detention for compulsory drug treatment except in strictly circumscribed conditions.[7]

OSF is far stronger on this topic, characterising any mandated treatment as not only a violation of the right to health, but as the more serious (or at least more serious sounding) violation of torture. After going through

[2] See eg Robin Munro, 'The Soviet Case: Prelude to a Global Consensus on Psychiatry and Human Rights' (2000) 14 *Columbia Journal of Asian Law*, republished at www.hrw.org/reports/2002/china02/china0802-02.htm.

[3] See eg Adolf Ratzka, 'Eradication of "deviants": the dark side of the Swedish Model', Independent Living Institute, October 1997.

[4] UNODC and WHO, 'Principles of drug dependence treatment' (Vienna, 2008) 10.

[5] Ibid.

[6] HRW, 'Skin on the Cable: the illegal arrest, arbitrary detention, and torture of people who use drugs in Cambodia' (New York, 2010) 22.

[7] HRW, 'Skin on the Cable' (n 6) 23.

the four elements of torture in the definition included in CAT, OSF puts forward a somewhat convoluted argument, asserting:

> In the context of administering what is ostensibly drug dependence 'treatment,' it is satisfying the ... requirement to show some improper purpose or discrimination—that may be thought to pose more of a challenge, given that it will likely be claimed that the treatment is intended to benefit the 'patient' ... However, in many instances, methods of drug dependence treatment are imposed with an explicit or implicit punitive objective, or with the objective of intimidating the person into avoiding future drug use, even if these objectives sit alongside an ostensibly therapeutic one. So in at least some instances where drug dependence treatment is abusive, the requisite improper purpose may be established in order to satisfy the definition of torture. Such approaches to drug dependence treatment, which seek to punish or intimidate drug users, are more likely in settings where government policy and/or professional directives or attitudes conflate, sometimes explicitly, the medical condition of addiction with criminality, sin or 'social evil'—as drug use is even more likely be seen as morally blameworthy conduct requiring punishment per se as well as deterrence through such intimidation ... Statements by political or government leaders, or those administering 'treatment' in drug detention settings, as well as policy documents or legislation articulating the government's objectives or governing the operations of such centers, are just some examples of evidence that could be used for a finding that abusive practices amount to 'torture' because the treatment is imposed for the improper purposes of punishing or intimidating.[8]

OSF essentially appears to be arguing that government statements against drug abuse and trafficking should be taken as evidence that mandated treatment should be characterised in a blanket manner as torture—an extremely bold statement to say the least.

Unsurprisingly, the torture characterisation is controversial, even (or perhaps particularly) amongst medical professionals. In 2013, the American Psychiatric Association (APA) and World Psychiatric Association (WPA) published a rebuttal to Mendez's 2013 report as Special Rapporteur on Torture. These bodies objected to Mendez's analysis of involuntary treatment for persons with psychiatric disorders, and his characterisation of this as 'forms of torture and ill-treatment'.[9] The APA/WPA note that though involuntary treatment may amount to torture when it 'is used to inflict severe pain and suffering, rather than for the patient's benefit', they state:

> It should be recognized that involuntary treatment, when used appropriately, is not a form of torture or ill-treatment ... [F]or the minority of persons who are

[8] OSF, 'Treatment or Torture? Applying international human rights standards to drug detention centres' (New York, 2011) 12.

[9] Juan Mendez, 'Report of the Special Rapporteur on torture and other cruel, inhuman or degrading treatment or punishment' (Geneva, UN index A/HRC/22/53, 1 February 2013) para 64.

> sufficiently disabled by their disorders to be unable to protect their own interests and/or who endanger themselves or others, the existence of involuntary interventions may be life-saving and may hold the prospect of restoring them to a fully functional, independent life … [T]he characterization of involuntary interventions for people with psychiatric disorders in the report is inaccurate and … the related recommendations are harmful.[10]

Mendez issued a response to the APA/WPA, stating:

> I regret that some inartful wording has given rise to misunderstanding of some statements included in it … I did not mean to propose an absolute ban on non-consensual interventions (including institutionalization and restraints) under any and all circumstances. I meant to restrict my condemnation to non-consensual treatment based exclusively on discrimination against persons with disabilities. In other words, the fact that a person is diagnosed as having a psychosocial disability should not by itself be enough to justify non-consensual treatment.[11]

Though not directly regarding persons who abuse drugs, the issues raised by the debate are similar, and the implication that forced treatment of persons who abuse drugs amount to torture is hardly universally accepted.

In any case, the principle that measures for persons who abuse drugs (to be distinguished from those who engage in the trafficking of drugs) should centre on the provision of treatment and rehabilitation, as opposed to punitive measures, is, it is submitted, relatively uncontroversial. The question, rather, is the use of coercion in this provision of treatment, and how to judge if the coercion is legitimate.

Many jurisdictions operate what are commonly called 'drug courts'. Though there are differences in the actual workings of such institutions, the general model is that persons found guilty of simple possession (as opposed to drug trafficking) of illicit drugs are given a choice between a criminal penalty (often including incarceration) and the completion of treatment. Specialised drug courts monitor the progress of the individual through treatment, during which period the criminal penalty is suspended, and should the individual complete the treatment programme successfully, the criminal charge is removed from their record. On the other hand, should the individual fail to complete treatment, or should they test positively for drug abuse during a specified period after the completion of treatment, the drug court normally has the prerogative to impose the initial criminal sanction, or perhaps a different sanction.

[10] APA, WPA, 'Joint statement in response to the report of Special Rapporteur on Torture', Attachment 2 (Arlington, 9 December 2013) 3.

[11] Juan Mendez, 'Letter to Dr Jeffrey Lieberman, President American Psychiatric Association; Dr Pedro Ruiz, President World Psychiatric Association; and Dr Saul Levin, CEO/Medical Director American Psychiatric Association' (Geneva, 22 January 2014) 1.

Drug courts naturally result in more people undergoing, and completing, treatment, and some studies have shown that such regimes have contributed to reducing crime in particular communities. The US National Association of Drug Court Professionals, for example, states:

> … the effectiveness of adult Drug Courts is not a matter of conjecture. It is the product of more than two decades of exhaustive scientific research … More research has been published on the effects of adult Drug Courts than virtually all other criminal justice programs combined. By 2006, the scientific community had concluded beyond a reasonable doubt from advanced statistical procedures that Drug Courts reduce criminal recidivism, typically measured by fewer re-arrests for new offenses and technical violations.[12]

The US Department of Justice of the United States stated in 2008 that drug courts:

> … quickly identify substance abusing offenders and place them under ongoing judicial monitoring and community supervision, coupled with effective, long-term treatment services … [D]rug courts increase the probability of participants' success by providing a wide array of ancillary services such as mental health treatment, trauma and family therapy, job skills training, and many other life-skill enhancement services. Research verifies that no other justice intervention can rival the results produced by drug courts. … According to over a decade of research, drug courts significantly improve substance abuse treatment outcomes, substantially reduce crime, and produce greater cost benefits than any other justice strategy.[13]

The fact that the approach has spread rapidly attests to the fact that the jurisdictions in which drug courts operate have found them to be useful tools. The approach started in the United States, in 1989,[14] and has quickly become mainstream, with drug courts currently operating in every US state and territory.[15] It has now spread to several other countries. According to OSF, in June 2015:

> Drug courts are also found in Australia, Austria, Belgium, Canada, Ireland, New Zealand, Norway, and the United Kingdom. With encouragement from the Organization of American States, a number of Latin American countries have adopted or are in the process of adopting drug courts or related problem-solving courts. These include Barbados, Bermuda, Chile, Costa Rica, Dominican

[12] Douglas B Marlowe, 'Research Update on Adult Drug Courts' (Alexandria, National Association of Drug Court Professionals, December 2010) 1.

[13] US Department of Justice, 'Painting the current picture; a national report card on drug courts and other problem solving court programs in the United States' (Washington DC, May 2008) 2.

[14] National Association of Drug Court Professionals, 'Justice Professionals Pursue a Vision', www.nadcp.org/learn/what-are-drug-courts/drug-court-history.

[15] Ibid.

Republic, Jamaica, Mexico, Suriname, and Trinidad and Tobago. The Organization of American States contracted the U.S. National Association of Drug Court Professionals, a body that sets standards for U.S. drug courts, to assist in drug court implementation in Latin America.[16]

Taking into account the aforementioned prohibition in international human rights law on forced medical treatment, from the strictly human rights perspective, there are undoubtedly some question marks surrounding the drug court approach. Though proponents present the approach as offering a choice to the offender, the reality is that it is hardly a meaningful one. It is difficult to imagine any person choosing criminal penalties, perhaps incarceration, over undergoing treatment. In this regard, there is clearly a degree of coercion involved, and to present this as a meaningful choice is somewhat akin to calling the return of failed asylum seekers in detention as 'voluntary'.

Nevertheless, both UNODC and INCB accept drug courts as both legally legitimate and practically effective. INCB has stated somewhat generally that it 'notes, for example, the positive impact of "drug treatment courts", as specialist courts for drug offenders'.[17] UNODC has elaborated on its position in greater detail, characterising the 'choice' offered as an appropriate one:

> When the use and possession of drugs results in state imposed penal sanctions, the offer of treatment as an alternative to imprisonment or other penal sanction presents a choice to the patient/offender, and although it entails a degree of coercion to treatment, the patient is entitled to reject treatment and choose the penal sanction instead.[18]

This position of UNODC is elaborated in greater detail in a 2009 paper titled, somewhat aptly, 'From coercion to cohesion: Treating drug dependence through health care, not punishment'.[19] UNODC states clearly:

> Some degree of pressure is often used to encourage drug dependent individuals to initiate drug dependence treatment and to increase their retention in treatment [including] formal legal pressure to engage in treatment as an alternative to incarceration or other legal sanctions. Depending on the way in which it is applied, treatment as an alternative to criminal justice sanctions does not violate the patient's right to accept or refuse treatment … Treatment as an alternative to criminal justice sanctions is specifically encouraged in the international drug control conventions and it has been found to be more effective … It can

[16] OSF, 'Drug Courts: equivocal evidence on a popular intervention' (New York, June 2015) 2, 3.

[17] INCB, *Annual Report 2004* (Vienna, 2005) para 55.

[18] UNODC, WHO (n 4) 10.

[19] UNODC, 'From Coercion to Cohesion: Treating drug dependence through health care, not punishment' (Vienna, 2009) ii.

> be provided in ways that do not violate the rights of the patients, provided that the decision to refuse treatment remains in the hands of the drug user and the patient's autonomy and human rights are respected.[20]

Though UNODC presents the above model as a 'health based approach', the general message is clearly favourable to the practice of drug courts:

> Treatment as an alternative to criminal justice sanctions represents an opportunity offered by the community to drug users and drug dependent individuals to accept some form of assistance. It usually allows some choice of education, health care, treatment and rehabilitation and does not force patients into treatment without their consent. This type of pressure is significantly different from compulsory treatment that does not allow the individual to decline treatment or choose the type that they receive … These alternatives to criminal justice sanctions can be offered without violating the rights of drug users and drug dependent individuals to refuse treatment, thus achieving a balance between the desire of the community to reduce drug related offences and the rights of the individual to receive treatment for drug use disorders.[21]

UNODC continues:

> Evidence suggests that legally mandated education, treatment and care can be an effective alternative to the imprisonment or compulsory residential detention of drug dependent individuals. This can be offered as an alternative to criminal justice sanctions for offences which are not specified as drug related crime by the drug control conventions but for which drug use or dependence has been a contributing factor, such as property crime to fund drug use. Such treatment needs to be provided in ways that do not violate the rights of drug users who should be allowed to decide whether they want to be involved in treatment and to choose the form of treatment that they receive … Legal pressure may encourage engagement in treatment, but the decision whether or not to enter treatment should remain with the individual … In this situation: Drug users or drug dependent individuals facing criminal justice sanctions for a drug related crime consent to treatment and are free to leave treatment at any time (although then subject to criminal justice sanctions for the original drug related crime if they do so).[22]

A line is, therefore, drawn by UNODC (and INCB) between 'compulsory treatment' and the drug court model. In the same paper, UNODC includes a section on 'long term treatment without consent', and while this term is not clearly defined, the organisation appears to envision 'compulsory treatment' as the sort of approach taken in China and several Southeast Asian countries:

> Many countries provide long term residential treatment for drug dependence without the consent of the patient that is in reality a type of low security

[20] UNODC, 'From Coercion to Cohesion' (n 19) 9.
[21] UNODC (n 19) 2.
[22] UNODC (n 19) 5, 6.

> imprisonment. Evidence of the therapeutic effect of this approach is lacking, either compared to traditional imprisonment or to community-based voluntary drug treatment. It is expensive, not cost-effective, and neither benefits the individual nor the community. It does not constitute an alternative to incarceration because it is a form of incarceration. In some cases, the facilities become labor camps with unpaid, forced labor, humiliating and punitive treatment methods that constitute a form of extrajudicial punishment. It is argued that the use of any long term treatment for drug use disorders without the consent of the patient is in breach of international human rights agreements and ethical medical standards ... With sufficient voluntary treatment resources, appropriate referral for treatment from the criminal justice system, and community mobilisation, the residual need to use this form of compulsory/involuntary treatment should decrease until it is not used anymore at all.[23]

Drug courts, on the other hand, do offer a choice to the individual, and UNODC notes that they are effective:

> The most rigorous and conservative scientific estimates from five 'meta-analyses' have all concluded that drug courts significantly reduce crime by as much as 35 percent compared to imprisonment. In addition, drug courts produce \$2.21–\$3.36 in avoided Criminal Justice benefits for every \$1 spent on them. Up to \$12.00 (per \$1.00 invested) are saved by the community on reduced emergency room visits and other medical care, foster care and victimization costs such as property loss.[24]

Nevertheless, the assertion that undergoing treatment under the drug court model is a free choice is clearly somewhat problematic. Though there may be some individuals who would prefer criminal punishment and incarceration to submitting to treatment, it is obvious that would be an extremely minuscule minority, and the characterisation of the drug court model as based on free choice appears somewhat self-serving. This is not necessarily to argue against the drug court model, but merely to state the obvious: it is not truly voluntary in any meaningful definition of the word.

Given the apparent conflict with human rights norms, one would think that advocates of drug liberalisation would have a heyday criticising drug courts. Surprisingly, though, until recently, those advocates have been relatively silent on the issue. HIV/AIDS Law Canada argued in 2007 that 'there are a number of human rights concerns that have yet to be fully evaluated in the context of drug treatment courts',[25] but fail to elaborate

[23] UNODC (n 19) 8.

[24] UNODC (n 19) 8, 9.

[25] HIV/AIDS Law Canada, 'Dependent on Rights: Assessing Treatment of Drug Dependence from a Human Rights Perspective' (Toronto, July 2007) 30. Ghodse also states that there are 'important implications for civil rights' with drug courts, but does not have objections in principle to the approach; rather, he states 'it is essential that confidentiality is guaranteed and that effective and ethical treatment is provided when individuals may have little choice but to co-operate.' See Hamid Ghodse, *Drugs and Addictive Behaviour: a Guide to Treatment*, third edition (Cambridge, Cambridge University Press, 2002) 238.

in detail. A small number of papers have been issued, though they tend to be very focused predominantly on examining drug courts in the US, and are generally very technical in nature, for example pointing to deficiencies in official evaluations. They argue that the data is skewed, in that in most jurisdictions many persons are unable to enter treatment under the drug court system because of non-drug related reasons, eg prior convictions. The result of this is that the persons with the most minor issues in terms of drug abuse and general lifestyle tend to be the ones entering the drug court system, with those the most likely to 'fail' being screened out. In other words, the persons undergoing treatment by order of a drug court are the ones most likely to succeed and are, therefore, neither representative of the persons arrested for drug offences as a whole, nor an appropriate target group for drug courts to begin with.[26] Advocates of drug liberalisation also argue that evaluations of drug courts are rarely independent. They are often conducted by the institution responsible for implementing the courts, meaning there is a strong incentive to show success.[27]

The Global Commission on Drug Policy (GCDP) raises other, more fundamental concerns:

> Compared to more punitive responses, drug courts appear—at least superficially—to be a move in the right direction. Yet the devil is in the detail of how such programs are administered. Most sentences issued by drug courts demand abstinence, with opioid substitution treatment often arbitrarily denied ... Abstinence is typically enforced with regular drug testing and the threat of incarceration for those who register positive results. This in effect means that people are punished for relapse—an acknowledged reality in drug dependence ... Individuals are required to waive constitutional trial rights to participate in drug court programs: failure to successfully complete the program results in an automatic criminal conviction.[28]

The above arguments have merit, but it is not clear that they pose fundamental questions to the drug court approach. In general, advocates of drug liberalisation appear to have difficulty in mounting a comprehensive criticism of drug courts—perhaps because of their ideological devotion to the idea that persons should not be punished in any way for drug abuse, and should not be mandated to undergo drug treatment in any but the most extreme circumstances. In other words, since they oppose the involvement of criminal justice or any form of official coercion on principled grounds, they seem unable to oppose drug courts in a truly convincing manner.[29]

[26] See eg Drug Policy Alliance, 'Drug Courts are Not the Answer: Towards a Health Centered Approach to Drug Use' (New York, 2011).

[27] See eg OSF (n 16).

[28] GCDP, 'Taking Control: Pathways to Drug Policies that Work' (Rio de Janeiro, 2014) 22.

[29] OSF, for example, argues only that '[o]ther alternatives to incarceration should be considered, including those that remove incarceration for minor infractions from the penal code

The somewhat general arguments of the GCDP are indicative:

> The Commission finds that, on their own, drug courts are conceptually flawed and insufficient. They represent an attempt to retrospectively impose a health-based approach within a failed criminal justice paradigm. What is required is a more fundamental realignment towards a public health centered paradigm, one that both reduces the likelihood of people who use drugs coming into contact with the criminal justice system in the first place, and that also makes prevention, harm reduction and treatment services available according to need.[30]

The GCDP offers little justification for this argument, and it appears that it can be essentially reduced to the idea that courts should not be involved, persons should not be sanctioned for drug abuse, and, as the GCDP argues, drugs should not be illegal in the first place, fullstop.

Drug courts are of course not a panacea, and concerns have been raised by researchers not necessarily affiliated with the advocates of drug liberalisation cited in this book. Perhaps the most serious concern is that drug courts increasingly examine details of the individual's life that go far beyond the initial drug offence, making unrelated aspects requirements for graduation. For example, Tiger notes:

> The extremely broad criteria used by some drug courts to determine a defendant's readiness to 'graduate' reflect both encompassing theories of addiction recovery and greatly enhanced goals for the court. These theories and goals reflect moral considerations that extend far beyond the clinical 'facts' of addiction or the legal 'facts' of the case that brought the defendant under the criminal justice systems' jurisdiction in the first place. … Overall, drug court advocates are less concerned that people are sick and far more concerned with how their sickness manifests itself, namely in 'antisocial', not just criminal, behavior. It is at the level of treatment that drug courts actually make their intervention, and they make judicially enforced coercion the key feature of that intervention.[31]

Tiger shows how drug court judges increasingly tend to expand their oversight, citing one proponent of the approach as stating:

> 'We've got to make sure they can work, that they're educated, that they can get a job, that they can keep a job, that they have skills, that they … learn how to get up in the morning and go to work. That they learn that when their boss pisses them off they don't slug them. That they learn behavior they've never learned before. How do you get a job, how do you raise kids? … If you don't have a holistic view of this person's recovery, you're setting these people up for failure.'

and measures that do not confer authority for essential health services to the criminal justice system.' See OSF (n 16) 16.

[30] GCDP (n 28) 22.

[31] Rebecca Tiger, *Judging Addicts: Drug Courts and Coercion in the Justice System* (New York, New York University Press, 2012) 89, 91.

> … The court, then, becomes concerned with behaviors that aren't necessarily illegal but over which courts stake their claim in the name of recovery.[32]

Some drug courts, for example, require that participants obtain a secondary school certificate and a job for 'graduation' from the programme.[33]

In a somewhat indicative statement hinging on the meaningfulness of the individual's 'choice', the chief judge of one jurisdiction tells Tiger:

> 'I see less of a need to establish limits on the court's authority when participation is voluntary. In our court, defendants have a choice: you can go into the regular court system and be prosecuted, or you can go into [the] drug court. Having signed a contract for the drug court, you have sold your soul to me for the natural jurisdiction of our court—five years for a felony, three for a misdemeanor. You have to comply with the program or I'll impose sanctions, including jail.'[34]

Another judge argues that drug courts should examine the defendant's relationship with family members and ask:

> 'Is this person developing new, healthy relationships?' And follow-up measures of success should examine the participant's 'pro-social participation in the community. How do they give back?' … 'I've heard drug court judges talk to participants about who they're having sex with, how are they eating, where are they living, get an education, get a job. And it's very, very intrusive…'[35]

There is the danger, therefore, that drug courts can become essentially paternalistic methods of social control—a danger which Tiger argues is reminiscent of similarly well intended institutions of an earlier era.[36] The judge imposes intrusive, even arbitrary, requirements on the individual. If the individual fails to comply, they can be expelled from the drug court system, resulting in them serving the initial prison sentence. This results in the somewhat ironic situation whereby their supervision by the court, and the prison sentence for having failed the drug court 'treatment', can total a period much longer than if they had accepted incarceration at the outset (especially since that may have resulted in a suspended sentence). Tiger notes that '[t]ying into the idea that addicts are like children, the judge assumes a parental role in the defendant's life.'[37] This transformation from judge to father figure is presumably well intentioned, but raises questions regarding the extent to which drug courts can assert authority over an individual's life—in particular aspects which are not directly

[32] Tiger, *Judging Addicts* (n 31) 103, 104.
[33] Tiger (n 31) 104.
[34] Tiger (n 31) 104.
[35] Tiger (n 31) 105, 106.
[36] Tiger (n 31) 9.
[37] Tiger (n 31) 98.

connected with the initial offence—without being justifiably criticised as having acted in an arbitrary manner.

The above notwithstanding, however, it is not entirely clear that these aspects are inherent to the drug court model. Tiger argues that they are, and unsurprisingly, and though they lack the methodological rigour and level of analysis that Tiger has, advocates of drug liberalisation do as well. OSF argues:

> Drug courts are depicted by some as a 'third way' solution between harsh prohibition and extreme liberalization of drug laws, and drug court evaluations include moving testimonials from judges about how court supervision transforms people's lives and brings them hope of a new life in mainstream society. But in spite of good intentions, these courts do not represent reform if they undermine health and human rights, if they put health decisions in the hands of judges and prosecutors who reject clinically indicated treatment, or if they impose punishment for relapses that are a normal part of drug dependence.[38]

Certainly, the model, as it operates in many jurisdictions in the US, bestows wide-ranging, even sweeping powers on the judge, leaving open the potential for abuse. Nevertheless, it is submitted that with proper oversight and greater involvement of health professionals, it should be able to operate drug courts in a different manner. This is recognised by even some advocates of drug liberalisation. For example, in an attempt to criticise drug courts in the United States, the Drug Policy Alliance notes that '[d]rug court adaptations in Canada, Australia and the United Kingdom have expanded measures of success to include decreased drug use and crime, while broadly allowing opioid-maintenance therapy (such as methadone) and, in some circumstances, tolerating cannabis use',[39] indicating that the model can indeed be implemented in a different manner that is more respectful of the situation of drug dependent persons.

As noted above, from the strictly human rights viewpoint, questions remain regarding the drug court approach. Submission to treatment can hardly be called voluntary when the alternative is a prison sentence and/or a criminal record. At the same time, the righteousness of the notion that any element of coercion is illegitimate except in the most extreme of circumstances is not necessarily self-evident. Society has a definite interest in ensuring that persons refrain from abusing drugs, and in ensuring that drug-dependent persons undergo treatment to stop their abuse. As things stand now, drug courts do appear to be an effective tool towards this end, and the limitations on persons' rights that they entail appear to

[38] OSF (n 16) 16.
[39] Drug Policy Alliance (n 26) 16.

be within boundaries that are acceptable. As stated by this author in a previous paper, 'blanket statements that any kind of mandated treatment is violative of the addict's human rights are neither helpful nor practical, and, at the end of the day, are not grounded in the reality of drug addiction.'[40]

Advocates of drug liberalisation are, of course, against this as a matter of principle, at least in part because of their dedication to harm reduction. The Canadian Centre on Substance Abuse states its position succinctly:

> Harm reduction is founded on the notion of offering participants choices and options for their treatment, while recognizing that many individuals with substance abuse problems may not be willing or able to stop using drugs. In such cases, it is important to 'meet them where they are' in order to gradually reduce high-risk and harmful behaviors … Forcing individuals to undergo treatment for substance abuse may be seen as violating their civil liberties.[41]

Advocates of drug liberalisation, therefore, argue against any penalty for drug abuse, preferring information campaigns to convince persons who abuse drugs to stop, and to undergo treatment willingly. As a practical matter, there is little question that treatment is generally more successful when the individual undertakes it voluntarily, but the notion that this is always a viable option is mere fantasy, and is not based on the reality of drug abuse. As Ghodse notes:

> … motivation for abstinence is very important and may be crucial to the long-term success of detoxification. For some patients, motivation is triggered by the legal, social, or medical consequences of their drug abuse and dependence … [However,] [f]or others, any latent motivation that they may have to become abstinent is counteracted by the profound psychological dependence induced by opiates, by their intense craving and need for drugs, which becomes more severe the longer they take opiates (illicit or prescribed). Thus, lack of motivation can be seen as a symptom and as an indication of the severity of dependence, and waiting for motivation to 'happen' may be a confortable collusion with the patient that nothing can or should be done to interrupt their drug-dependent condition.[42]

Not exercising any coercion can be, in essence, tantamount to simply standing by and watching the drug dependent person waste away.

Herein lies the truly problematic nature of the 'harm reduction trumps all' paradigm that advocates of drug liberalisation promote. These

[40] Saul Takahashi, 'Drug Control, Human Rights, and the Right to the Highest Attainable Standard of Health; By No Means Straightforward Issues' (2009) 31 *Human Rights Quarterly* 776.

[41] Canadian Centre on Substance Abuse, 'Fact Sheet on Mandatory and Coerced Treatment' (Ottawa, January 2006) 2.

[42] Ghodse, *Drugs and Addictive Behaviour* (n 25) 261.

advocates argue that states should abandon the criminalisation of drugs, focus only on the provision of harm reduction, and refrain from imposing treatment on individuals with problematic drug abuse. This is presented as a compassionate, rights-respecting approach, one that is concerned with the human rights of the person abusing drugs. Certainly, the harm reduction approach is better than simply locking persons up in prison for abusing drugs. However, the inevitable result of removing any possibility of coercion on the part of the state will be that even more persons who abuse drugs, even to a problematic extent, will not undergo treatment. At least, under the drug court model, the state has the possibility of ensuring that persons who come into contact with law enforcement are treated. Without that power, it is not difficult to foresee that far fewer persons with problematic abuse problems will access treatment, with worsening health as a result. This is mere abandonment—not a 'compassionate', 'rights-respecting' approach. It is also hardly an effective way of ensuring the right to the highest attainable standard of health of the individual concerned (or of society in general), despite what advocates of drug liberalisation may argue.

I. PORTUGAL

The system established in 2001 in Portugal to deal with drug abuse has some similarities (as well as some important differences) with the drug court model. Possession of illicit drugs (without distinction regarding the substance, eg cannabis is in theory treated in the same manner as heroin or cocaine) remains an offence in the country, but an administrative one, not a criminal one. Persons apprehended for possession of illicit drugs receive a summons to appear before a local Dissuasion Commission, bodies that are made up of legal professionals and persons with medical, psychological or pharmacological experience. These commissions review the case and the situation of the individual in a non-adversarial manner, assess whether they are dependent on drugs, and, if so, generally refer them to treatment. If the individual does not appear as summoned, they may be subject to an administrative penalty, such as a fine or revocation of a driving licence.[43]

The Cato Institute (CATO) notes:

> … [the] overriding goal of [the] process is to avoid the stigma that arises from criminal proceedings. Each step of the process is structured so as to de-emphasize

[43] See eg Artur Domosławski, 'Drug Policy in Portugal: the Benefits of Decriminalizing Drug Use' (New York, Open Society Foundation, 2011) 25.

> or even eliminate any notion of 'guilt' from drug usage and instead to emphasize the health and treatment aspects of the process. The alleged offender, for instance, can request that notice of the proceedings not be sent to his home in order to preserve privacy. Commission members deliberately avoid all trappings of judges, and the hearing is intentionally structured so as to avoid the appearance of a court. Members dress informally. The alleged offender sits on the same level as the commission members, rather than having the members sit on an elevated platform. Commission members are legally bound to maintain the complete confidentiality of all proceedings. At all times, respect for the alleged offender is emphasized.[44]

The power of Dissuasion Commissions to impose sanctions on the offender is very limited. Portuguese law states that offenders may be subject to a somewhat cursory fine of up to EUR 25, though 'such fines are expressly declared to be a last resort. Indeed, in the absence of evidence of addiction or repeated violations, the imposition of a fine is to be suspended.'[45] The commissions typically make undergoing treatment a condition of suspending sanctions, though as noted by the CATO Institute, 'in practice, there are very few ways to enforce the condition, since violations of a commission's rulings are not, themselves, infractions of any law.'[46]

As can be noted, there are similarities between the Portuguese system and the drug court model. Drug possession remains an offence, and persons who abuse drugs are not simply given a slap on the wrist, but are subject to official encouragement—one might even term it coercion—to undergo treatment. The main difference is that the Dissuasion Commissions in Portugal operate outside of the criminal justice system, and do not have the sweeping powers to impose intrusive mechanisms or harsh penalties that drug courts do, at least in the US. Whether this constitutes a fundamental difference is arguable—one could term the Portuguese system as a 'soft' version of drug courts (though the drug court model was not necessarily the inspiration for the Portuguese system).

The same advocates of drug liberalisation who express concern about the drug court model tend to have praise for the Portuguese system. After all, the Dissuasion Commissions are not part of the criminal justice framework, and the fact that the new procedure has not resulted in skyrocketing

[44] Cato Institute, 'Drug Decriminalization in Portugal: Lessons for Creating Fair and Successful Drug Policies' (Washington, 2009) 6.
[45] Cato Institute, 'Drug Decriminalization in Portugal' (n 44) 3.
[46] Ibid.

drug abuse would appear to buttress the argument for decriminalisation. The GCDP argues that Portugal is evidence that:

> … the removal of criminal penalties, combined with the use of alternative therapeutic responses to people struggling with drug dependence [reduces] the burden of drug law enforcement on the criminal justice system and the overall level of problematic drug use … [Governments should] [r]eplace the criminalization and punishment of people who use drugs with the offer of health and treatment services to those who need them.[47]

OSF states:

> Governments worldwide can learn a lot from Portugal's experience … Perhaps the greatest lesson of the Portuguese decriminalization policy is that it demonstrates that there are ways to overcome the lack of will among political elites and societies made afraid by the fear-mongering propaganda of the 'war on drugs' and, in doing so, to constructively build rational and humanitarian drug policies.[48]

Nevertheless, the praise of those advocates for Portugal is somewhat general, if not even arguably tepid, and it is submitted that it is not difficult to see why. As much as advocates of drug liberalisation like to present the Portuguese approach as one of harm reduction, the framework is still based on the tenet that drug abuse should be stopped, and on the principle that the state has a strong role in coercing persons towards that direction. The level of compulsion that the state can and should exercise in performing this task is rightly a subject of debate, and it is indicative that Portuguese Dissuasion Commissions are able to function effectively with powers that pale in comparison with drug courts in the US. Nevertheless, they do have some measure of powers. There is no intention to merely look the other way in cases of drug abuse.

The picture of drug abuse in the country since the new system was introduced is somewhat mixed. Naturally, advocates of drug liberalisation would like to present a positive picture, and while recognising that different surveys have produced different pictures of the effect on drug abuse in Portugal of these policies, Transform, for example, states that '[o]verall [the evidence] suggests that removing criminal penalties for personal drug possession did not cause an increase in levels of drug use.'[49] OSF stated in 2011 that 'one of the greatest achievements of the policy is in fact the decrease in consumption among the most at-risk age group

47 GCDP, 'War on Drugs' (Rio de Janeiro, 2011) 10.

48 Domosławski, 'Drug Policy in Portugal' (n 43) 46.

49 Transform, 'Drug decriminalisation in Portugal: setting the record straight' (London, July 2014) 2.

of 15- to 19-year-olds.'[50] On the other hand, the European Monitoring Centre for Drugs and Drug Addiction (EMCDDA) stated more recently that although 'the latest study indicates that the use of illicit substances in Portugal since 2007 might be on the decline',[51] recent studies show an increase in drug abuse amongst Portuguese students since 2006. 'This trend is observed among both male and female students.'[52] There are naturally a multitude of social and other factors involved in any increase or decrease of drug abuse, but what does appear clear is that, overall, there has not been a dramatic increase in drug abuse in Portugal since 2001. The Cato Institute is correct in noting that 'none of the nightmare scenarios touted by pre-enactment decriminalization opponents—from rampant increases in drug usage among the young to the transformation of Lisbon into a haven for "drug tourists"—has occurred.'[53]

INCB did appear to express some measure of concern regarding the new system in Portugal in its Annual Report 2001, where it 'reminds' state parties of their obligations under Article 3 of the 1988 Convention to criminalise drug possession.[54] Subsequent to a mission to Portugal in 2004, however, INCB appears to have retreated from this position somewhat. In its subsequent Annual Report, it notes:

> ... the acquisition, possession and abuse of drugs ... remained prohibited [in Portugal] ... [T]he practice of exempting small quantities of drugs from criminal prosecution is consistent with the international drug control treaties ... The Board calls on the Government of Portugal to examine ways in which the commissions for the dissuasion of drug abuse can contribute towards preventing drug abuse.[55]

Given that the Dissuasion Commissions have the stated aim of ensuring persons who abuse drugs undergo treatment, the last sentence of INCB's statement would seem to be somewhat redundant, and contrary to, for example, the question of injection rooms, INCB has made no subsequent statement expressing concern or displeasure regarding the Portuguese practice. This would seem to suggest that INCB has accepted the framework as within the limits stipulated by the international drug control conventions.

[50] Domoslawski (n 43) 45.

[51] EMCDDA, 'Portugal Country Overview: Prevalence' in *European Drug Report 2015*, at www.emcdda.europa.eu/countries/portugal.

[52] Ibid.

[53] Cato Institute (n 44) 1. However, see also Transform, 'Drug decriminalisation in Portugal' (n 49) 1: '... such improvements are not solely the result of the decriminalisation policy; Portugal's shift towards a more health-centred approach to drugs, as well as wider health and social policy changes, are equally, if not more, responsible for the positive changes observed.'

[54] INCB, *Annual Report 2001* (Vienna, 2002) para 501.

[55] INCB (n 17) para 583.

Any apparent success, or at least lack of failure, of the Portuguese system may serve as evidence against the notion that the decriminalisation approach inevitably results in widespread abuse—though, naturally, there may be social and cultural factors specific to the Portuguese situation that prevent ready extrapolation to other countries.[56] However, the Portuguese system is simply not one aiming at legalisation of drugs and, therefore, its utility for advocates of drug liberalisation in arguing for legalisation—which, as shown repeatedly throughout this study, is their ultimate goal—is somewhat limited.

[56] For example, CATO notes that offenders can request that official correspondence from the Dissuasion Commissions not be sent to their home, 'in order to preserve privacy.' CATO Institute (n 44) 6. This suggests a relatively closely knit community where social pressure not to abuse drugs may remain strong. Whether transposing such an approach to other societies, where such social ties are arguably weaker, would be effective is an open question. It is submitted that more anthropological research needs to be conducted on this issue, and what factors have contributed to the relative success, or at least lack of disastrous failure, in Portugal.

6

The 'Right to Abuse Drugs'

THROUGHOUT THIS STUDY, this author has highlighted the misleading and, at times, disingenuous nature of the human rights arguments of advocates of drug liberalisation. Though statements based on human rights often have instant appeal, when one unpacks their logic, it is clear that the views of those advocates are predicated on the notion that individuals have (or should be recognised as having) a right to abuse drugs.

Nevertheless, advocates of drug liberalisation have in general been hesitant to argue openly for a 'right to abuse drugs', perhaps because of a recognition that the notion remains too politically controversial to be as readily or widely accepted as the 'human rights based approach'. As Flacks points out:

> The right to use drugs is frequently associated with harm reduction, though the former is also often erroneously regarded as one of the foundational principles of the latter. An explicit aim of the harm reduction movement has been to distance itself from value or moral judgments concerning drug use, and that includes advocating for decriminalization of drug use or a right to use drugs.[1]

Nevertheless, Flacks continues, 'the proposed existence of such a right is sometimes the "elephant in the room" during discussions of drug control: it is, for example, difficult to justify the decriminalization of drug use without also asserting a right to use drugs.'[2]

Flacks makes the somewhat sweeping statement that 'such a right already falls within the purview of international legal provisions on the right to privacy, including the ICCPR and European Convention on Human Rights',[3] though he offers no grounds for this assertion. Nowak also states elsewhere that the right to abuse drugs is included in the right to privacy, arguing that:

> … privacy covers that area of individual autonomy in which human beings strive to achieve self-realisation by way of actions that do not interfere with the

[1] Simon Flacks, 'Drug Control, Human Rights, and the Right to the Highest Attainable Standard of Health: A Reply to Saul Takahashi' (2011) 33 *Human Rights Quarterly* 874.

[2] Flacks, 'Drug Control, Human Rights, and the Right to the Highest Attainable Standard of Health' (n 1) 874.

[3] Flacks (n 1) 875.

> liberty of others ... Examples of ... interference range from ... more or less rigid prohibitions of alcohol, nicotine and addictive drugs to the duty to wear protective helmets or use seat belts.[4]

Again, Nowak offers little justification for this statement, and appears to simply think that it is self-evident.

Perhaps along the lines of Nowak's above notion of 'self-realisation', Van Ree proposes a new article for the UDHR, to read: 'Everyone has the right to use psychotropic substances of one's own choice.'[5] Arguing from the point of view of 'liberal thinking, which provides space for individual freedom as well as for established custom and tradition',[6] he argues in a paper published in the *International Journal of Drug Policy*:

> Human rights concern forms of behaviour which we regard as positive and enriching for our lives to such a degree, that we experience it as a violation of our personal dignity when we are forced to give them up. Drug use belongs in that category. Instead of being included in the category of murder and rape, drugs should be appreciated as a cultural asset, similar to religion and art. Despite the possibility of abuse, drugs provide its users with access to a unique inner field of experience, that would remain closed for ever without them.[7]

This author finds this entire argument questionable at best.

As does van Ree, Neil Hunt (no relation to Paul Hunt, former Special Rapporteur on the Right to Health) cites at length John Stuart Mill as grounds for his support of what he terms a 'strong rights'[8] approach, one which:

> ... embodies these principles of sovereignty over the body and limits the means by which we may promote health to those approaches that are essentially persuasive. In accordance with [John Stuart] Mill, compulsion is not permitted other than when, by exercising one's rights, they 'produce evil to someone else'. This strong rights version is therefore rights-based: rights over the body are prioritised.[9]

Hunt seems to have no care for the increase in public health issues that would result from the logic of his position:

> Within the strong rights formulation of harm reduction the role of the public health-driven harm reductionist would then be to assist people to reduce the harms that arise within the legitimate exercising of this right ... In other words,

[4] Manfred Nowak, *UN Covenant on Civil and Political Rights; CCPR Commentary*, 2nd revised edition (Kehl, NP Engel, 2005) 388, 389.

[5] Erik van Ree, 'Drugs as a Human Right' (1999) 10 *International Journal of Drug Policy* 89.

[6] Van Ree, 'Drugs as a Human Right' (n 5) 89.

[7] Van Ree (n 5) 89.

[8] Neil Hunt, 'Public health or human rights: what comes first?' (2004) 15 *International Journal of Drug Policy* 232.

[9] Hunt, 'Public health or human rights' (n 8) 232.

> the right to use drugs—so long as it is exercised without offending the rights of others—overrides health considerations. If recognising this right were to result in a net increase in both drug use and drug-related harm this would be regarded as an undesirable but necessary price to pay by harm reductionists who cherish individual sovereignty over the body.[10]

Not only does Hunt not seem to have any solution for this, he appears to believe that there is no need for any solution, save to say in vague terms that 'the recognition of a right is entirely different from encouraging people to exercise it'[11] and that the community can continue to use 'persuasion and social marketing'[12] in convincing persons to abstain from drug abuse, while at the same time ensuring—through harm reduction measures—that the harm from drug abuse is mitigated. While it is not necessarily the responsibility of the researcher (or the advocate) to propose solutions for every problem, blind ignorance of the implications of the argument seem questionable at best.

A recurring concept in the argument of advocates of drug liberalisation for a right to abuse drugs is that of 'personal autonomy'. As noted above, for example, HRW argues:

> Criminalizing personal drug use per se is itself problematic in terms of human rights, as it tramples on the person's right to privacy and basic concepts of autonomy underpinning all rights, and undermines the right to health. The decision to use drugs is a matter of personal choice protected by the right to privacy, a cornerstone of respect for personal autonomy and human dignity. Limitations on autonomy and the right to privacy are justified only if they meet the criteria of legitimate purpose, proportionality, necessity, and non-discrimination. Human Rights Watch believes these criteria can rarely if ever be met for the criminalization of personal drug use or possession of drugs for personal use.[13]

However, the view of 'personal autonomy' as a trump card to justify human rights arguments against drug control is deeply problematic. 'Personal autonomy' does not appear in any international human rights text, and there is no definition of the concept in international law. Any attempt to come to a common international understanding of the term would clearly be fraught with difficulty, given the widely differing views on what exactly it should constitute.

In addition, even supposing that some kind of common international understanding of 'personal autonomy' could be reached, it is unclear why it would necessarily indicate an inalienable right to abuse drugs.

[10] Hunt (n 8) 234.
[11] Hunt (n 8) 234.
[12] Hunt (n 8) 235.
[13] HRW, 'Re: Call for Submissions on the Issue of Drugs and Human Rights (the implementation of Resolution A/HRC/28/L.22)' (New York, 15 May 2015) 10.

Advocates of drug liberalisation appear to use this term as a way of justifying the claim that every individual has a right to do to his body what he may wish, insofar as he does not cause harm to others. For many proponents of human rights, this notion seems intuitively attractive, and, at first glance, the assertion that this traditional liberal philosophy is at the core of modern human rights thinking seems correct. Nevertheless, the reality in the modern state is somewhat more complex, and the arguments of advocates of drug liberalisation have implications that, it is submitted, are less desirable.

Drug abuse, at least drug dependency, brings with it immense health care costs for the state. For example, the US National Institute on Drug Abuse estimates that health care for drug abuse costs the country USD 11 billion a year, with total costs, including 'crime, lost work productivity and health care' amounting to USD 193 billion.[14] UNODC and WHO note that the total costs to society of drug abuse:

> … are difficult to estimate. In addition to the health care costs and other costs associated with the consequences of drug use, drug dependence involves also social costs in the form of loss of productivity and family income, violence, security problems, traffic and workplace accidents, and links with corruption. These result in overwhelming economic costs and an unacceptable waste of human resources.[15]

The assertions of advocates of drug liberalisation notwithstanding, these costs are not all connected with the fact that drugs are illicit, ie legalising drugs would not make these costs disappear or necessarily alleviate them. For example, according to the US National Institute on Drug Abuse, the costs to society of tobacco and alcohol (both of which are licit goods) are much higher than those of drug abuse, with alcohol at USD 224 billion and tobacco at a staggering USD 295 billion.[16]

Much of these costs are born by all citizens and residents, who, in most advanced industrialised economies, pay for the public health care system through taxes. The argument that drug abuse has no implications for other members of the community is, therefore, false as a matter of fact—the rest of the community does suffer, in terms of a higher tax burden to maintain public health care. This is not to assert that purely economic, utilitarian arguments should carry the day, in either this field or in any field of public policy. It is only to point to the obvious fact: even speaking only in monetary terms, the assertion that other members of the community

[14] National Institute on Drug Abuse, 'Trends and Statistics: Costs of Substance Abuse', at www.drugabuse.gov/related-topics/trends-statistics#costs.

[15] UNODC/WHO, 'Principles of Drug Dependence Treatment', Vienna, March 2008 2.

[16] National Institute on Drug Abuse, https://www.drugabuse.gov/related-topics/trends-statistics#costs.

do not suffer from an individual's drug abuse is simply not true. And though advocates of drug liberalisation might argue that the vast majority of persons who abuse drugs do not advance into the level of dependency that would require a public health intervention, small or large, there will always be a proportion of person requiring such interventions, and the abuse of drugs always carries an element of risk.

Therefore, as a matter of logic, the notion that advocates of drug liberalisation propagate that a person 'can abuse drugs, or otherwise do with his body whatever he so wishes, since such actions do not harm others' is only truly sustainable if other members of the community had no responsibility for that individual's care. The picture painted here is of a state where there is no public health system, and the state accepts no responsibility for the right to health of its citizens. All persons are left to fend for themselves, either through their own financial means or membership in voluntary, private insurance schemes. It is difficult to imagine any proponent of international human rights arguing for a model of this nature, and in any case that model arguably falls foul of international human rights obligations. Amongst advanced industrial economies, the US is arguably closest to that picture, though even in that country the state ensures the provision of certain areas of health care, and the scope of state intervention has been increasing significantly over recent years.

The reliance of the above advocates of drug liberalisation on John Stuart Mill is indicative, for one of the somewhat uncomfortable truths for those advocates is that a traditionally prominent proponent of drug liberalisation, at least in the US, has been the libertarian movement. The Libertarian Party, the political party that is at the centre of this movement, states that it 'seeks a world of liberty; a world in which all individuals are sovereign over their own lives and no one is forced to sacrifice his or her values for the benefit of others'.[17] Minimising government intervention in all areas of society is the key tenet of liberalism, with laissez-faire economics being at the core of the philosophy. The Party states that:

> ... [t]he only proper role of government in the economic realm is to protect property rights, adjudicate disputes, and provide a legal framework in which voluntary trade is protected. All efforts by government to redistribute wealth, or to control or manage trade, are improper in a free society.[18]

The protection of what the Libertarian Party calls 'civil liberties' is also one of the principles of libertarianism, and the Libertarian Party calls for a complete dismantling of all drug control laws. The Party states that: 'We must immediately end the failed War on Drugs, dismantle and abolish the

[17] Libertarian Party, 'Libertarian Party Platform' (Columbus, 2014) at preamble para 1.
[18] Libertarian Party, 'Libertarian Party Platform' (n 17) para 2.0.

federal Drug Enforcement Agency, release every nonviolent drug offender from prison, and cut taxes accordingly', arguing somewhat implausibly that this will '[send] the right message to kids: Be personally responsible. Be just, be reasonable, and honor individual rights.'[19]

In its statement titled 'Solution to America's Epidemic of Violent Crime', the Party states that 'drug prohibition has increasingly led to the violation of constitutional rights. Virtually no part of the Bill of Rights has been immune. The innocent suffer along with the guilty. The Libertarian Party has consistently called for an end to drug prohibition for more than 20 years.'[20] In the same statement, the Libertarian Party calls for restrictions on parole for criminal offenders, for minors to be held 'fully accountable'[21] for crimes they commit, for restrictions on welfare benefits for single mothers as out-of-wedlock births are a 'root cause of crime',[22] and stronger protection of the 'right to self defence'.[23]

Though their material includes various justifications for this policy, including the mass incarceration of non-violent drug offenders in the US, abolition of drug control is connected with the fundamental tenets of libertarian philosophy, namely that the individual should be free to do with his body what he wishes. The Party argues that '[i]t's time to re-legalize drugs and let people take responsibility for themselves … Drugs should be legal. Individuals have the right to decide for themselves what to put in their bodies, so long as they take responsibility for their actions.'[24]

Libertarians also have the same position as advocates of drug liberalisation on 'personal autonomy' as a justification for the dismantling of drug control. They state:

> … changing one's physical and mental state is among the most personal of decisions. Some legal analysts contend that drug use should be viewed as part of the 'zone of privacy' or 'personal autonomy' that most Americans have come to expect … Just as people have a moral right to make other lifestyle choices, despite the potential negative impacts, they have a moral right to consume drugs, despite potentially harmful effects. For this reason, drugs should be legalized, not just decriminalized. Even some advocates of prohibition prefer to direct criminal penalties at producers and sellers rather than users. However, if

[19] Libertarian Party, 'The case for ending the failed war on drugs', at www.lp.org/lp-candidate-pledge-end-the-war-on-drugs.

[20] Libertarian Party, 'The Libertarian Party's Solution to America's Epidemic of Violent Crime', at www.lp.org/the-libertarian-partys-solution-to-americas-epidemic-of-violent-crime.

[21] Ibid.

[22] Ibid.

[23] Ibid.

[24] Libertarian Party, 'Should we Re-legalize Drugs?', in Samuel Walker, *Civil Liberties in America: a Reference Book* (Santa Barbara, ABC-CLIO, 2004) 194.

consumption does not warrant jail, why should those who make it possible for people to consume face jail?[25]

Unsurprisingly, libertarians are also keen on John Stuart Mill in making their arguments against drug control:

> … human beings, as the basic moral agents in any society, should be generally free to act so long as they accept the consequences of their actions. One of the freedoms that should be treated as a legal right is drug use. Making this argument is not to encourage drug use. Rather, it is to hold that government may not properly criminalize drug use. The basic moral case was famously articulated by John Stuart Mill.[26]

The advocates of drug liberalisation that are the focus of this book tend to distance themselves from the Libertarian movement, and there is no evidence of operational co-operation or common platforms. Nevertheless, the fact remains that the two groups share common philosophies, as well as logical conclusions—a somewhat awkward truth for advocates of drug liberalisation, who wish to present their cause as thoroughly modern, advanced, and caring examples of human rights principles. And though those advocates may avoid using the work of libertarians (besides John Stuart Mill) in their advocacy, the opposite does not hold true—libertarians draw freely from the work of advocates of drug liberalisation in their statements, using the reports of, for example, the GCDP and the Transnational Institute to bolster their arguments.[27]

As noted above, it is worthy to reiterate that there is no internationally agreed definition of 'personal autonomy', and the notion that it necessarily includes the right of the individual to do with his body what he wishes is hardly universal. In many cultures, familial and community bonds are a strong factor in convincing persons not to abuse drugs (or other abusive substances). Indeed, in some countries, that remains a key message in drug prevention programmes. Some advocates of drug liberalisation coming from a bourgeois, Western culture may find these messages questionable, even oppressive, but these messages may be effective in those societies, and there appears to be no justification for stating that the particular version of 'personal autonomy' that advocates of drug liberalisation subscribe to should be adopted elsewhere. The somewhat casual, undefined use of the term betrays a lack of understanding amongst advocates of drug liberalisation that their assumptions do not automatically translate to cultures outside of their own.

[25] Doug Bandow, 'From Fighting the Drug War to Protecting the Right to Use Drugs: Recognizing a Forgotten Liberty', in Fred McMahon (ed), *Towards a Worldwide Index of Human Freedom* (Vancouver, Fraser Institute, 2012) 264.

[26] Bandow, 'From Fighting the Drug War to Protecting the Right to Use Drugs' (n 25) 254.

[27] See eg Bandow (n 25) 254.

This sort of cultural bias is not uncommon amongst advocates of drug liberalisation. An indicative example is the GCDP, which, the name notwithstanding, can hardly be said to be globally representative. Of its 25 members ('commissioners'), 21 come from Europe, North America, or Latin America. Of the remaining four, two are from South Asia (Anand Grover, from India, and Asma Jahangir, former UN Special Rapporteur on extra-judicial executions, from Pakistan), and two from Africa (Kofi Annan, former UN Secretary General, from Ghana; and Olusegun Obasanjo, former President of Nigeria).[28] Representation is not a panacea, and the fact that the GCDP is not representative of the world's population makeup does not necessarily mean their arguments are flawed. Nevertheless, the lopsided nature of the membership is worth noting because it is precisely those regions (Western Europe, North America, and Latin America) where the drug liberalisation movement has made the most inroads. The movement remains marginal outside of those regions.

This regional bias is apparent in the reports of the GCDP. The examples they cite in their 2011 report of 'good practice' are all from Western European countries or Australia. Advocates of drug liberalisation may argue that this is merely because those governments are more advanced in their understanding of the drug issue and in their approaches. Of course, the human rights movement in general was initially a European creation, and only later on spread to other regions (though some would argue that it is still a distinctly European movement at its core).[29] A general discussion of accusations of cultural imperialism is out of the scope of this book, but it is worth recalling that drug liberalisation is not a universal movement in the same way that the human rights movement in general has developed into being.

In another example, in mentioning the need for strengthening prevention efforts in their 2011 report, the GCDP argues that states should '[e]schew simplistic "just say no" messages and "zero tolerance" policies in favor of educational efforts grounded in credible information and prevention programs that focus on social skills and peer influences.'[30] This simplistic statement ignores the fact that, as noted above, 'just say no' messages actually have worked in some countries, in particular in Asia.[31] Whether such messages will remain effective is an open question, but of all activities aimed at reducing drug abuse, prevention is generally recognised

[28] See GCDP, 'Commissioners', at www.globalcommissionondrugs.org/bios/.

[29] See eg Stephen Hopgood, *The Endtimes of Human Rights* (Ithaca, Cornell University Press, 2013).

[30] GCDP, 'War on Drugs' (Rio de Janeiro, 2011) 3.

[31] See eg Ministry of Health, Welfare, and Labour, 'Current situation of drug abuse and measures', 2014, at www.mhlw.go.jp/bunya/iyakuhin/yakubuturanyou/dl/pamphlet_04.pdf (in Japanese).

as the most culture-specific, barring the kind of sweeping generalisations cited here. Other advocates of drug liberalisation have advanced similarly questionable arguments regarding prevention messages: for example, Barrett and Veerman criticise a Russian prevention campaign for sending messages that could 'serve to stigmatise children or to degrade them'.[32] Certainly the example they give of this campaign would suggest that it is extreme, but there is no indication as to why they feel qualified to judge what prevention measures might be effective in the Russian context.

The issue of cultural bias is also apparent in the argument of advocates of drug liberalisation that drug control is based on moral judgments regarding drug abuse (and regarding persons who engage in such activities). The notion that the 'war on drugs' is a 'moral crusade', inevitably leading to disaster, features prominently in the arguments of advocates of drug liberalisation, as noted before. For example, HRW states:

> Different purposes have been advanced to justify the criminalization of drug use. One of those purposes is that of morality; drug use is seen by many as morally dubious or reprehensible, regardless of whether someone is harmed by it. Human rights principles, however, support each individual's autonomy and right to privacy, which encompasses engaging in conduct that the majority may eschew as immoral or indicative of a weak character.[33]

These arguments contain two assumptions, both of which are assumed to be self-evident by advocates of drug liberalisation, namely that: (1) countries criminalise drugs through a misguided obsession regarding the immorality of drugs; and (2) any sort of moral judgments on the part of the state are by definition illegitimate.

Regarding the first assumption, such accusations are generally made in a casual manner by advocates of drug liberalisation, without citing any specific examples. In fact, it would be extremely rare, at least in international fora, for a country to justify efforts against illicit drugs on the basis of morality, and it is not clear why it can be assumed that morality is a significant undercurrent of drug policy.

As noted in previous chapters, the international drug control regime is based on the understanding that drug abuse is harmful to society in general and to public health in particular. It is true that terms such as 'evil' are used somewhat regularly in the description of drug abuse: for example, the preamble of the 1961 Convention states that 'addiction to narcotic drugs constitutes a serious evil for the individual and is fraught with social

[32] Damon Barrett and Philip E Veerman, *A Commentary on the United Nations Convention on the Rights of the Child: Article 33: Protection from Narcotic Drugs and Psychotropic Substances* (Leiden, Martinus Nijhoff, 2012) 51, 52. According to Barrett and Veerman, the anti-drug campaign in question includes depictions of 'children and adolescents ... eating human faeces, being raped, and looking at photographs of mutilated bodies.'

[33] HRW (n 13) 6.

and economic danger to mankind'.[34] However, the insinuations of the advocates of drug liberalisation notwithstanding, to note that drug abuse can be extremely harmful (which is what the use of the 'evil' language in this case seems to imply) is not the same as 'moralising' about drug abuse, and it certainly does not automatically mean that states' efforts are based on the notion that persons who abuse drugs have moral failings. There may have been moral angles to the messages that are used in some countries to convince persons not to abuse drugs, but the overarching concern is one for public health, not a moral one.[35]

Perhaps more importantly, the notion that the state has no role in protecting public morality is, obviously, simplistic. The definition of 'morality', and the role of the state in protecting it (at least in public spaces), is an issue of wide debate in many countries. This is not to argue for cultural relativism in opposition to universal human rights standards, but merely to note that what constitutes moral conduct, and the extent to which the state has a role in regulating such conduct, naturally differs between cultures. HRW, for example, outlines the background of government anti-drug policies in Vietnam thus:

> Beginning in the mid-1990s, the intensification of a broad campaign against 'social evils' triggered frantic legislative activity. The government adopted detailed regulations in an effort to control an array of activities, ranging from sex work to vagrancy to the influence of foreign culture, going so far as to ensure karaoke rooms had transparent glass doors …[36]

It is unclear why this is relevant to a report on anti-drug policy, and it is submitted that there appears to be a general (though unsaid) message of disdain towards government efforts to ensure any sort of morality in society. That karaoke bars have glass doors in Vietnam might seem somewhat silly to middle class Western sensibilities,[37] and whether it is worthy of government intervention is debatable. Nevertheless, it is hardly connected with any human rights violation, unless HRW intends to argue that the right to privacy includes the right to sing karaoke behind closed doors.

Indeed, as with their analogies between drug abuse and sexual orientation, some of the arguments of advocates of drug liberalisation against

[34] 1961 Convention preamble para 3.

[35] Of course, some religious figures do condemn drug abuse as morally wrong. See eg the statements of the Catholic Pope on the subject in 'Pope Francis condemns the "evil" of drug abuse', *The Catholic Herald*, 20 June 2014. It appears that the Pope is also against substitution therapy, calling it: 'not an adequate therapy but rather a veiled means of surrendering to the problem'.

[36] HRW, 'The Rehab Archipelago: forced labour and other abuses in drug detention centers in southern Vietnam' (New York, 2011) 14.

[37] Karaoke rooms also tend to have glass doors in Japan, though this is not due to any government regulation.

'moralising' on drug issues, could have negative effects for other groups of persons, or even for human rights globally. Indicative, for example, is this evaluation by HRW of persons who abuse drugs in Cambodia, at the outset of their 2010 report:

> Cambodians who use drugs confound the notion that drug dependence is a self-inflicted condition that results from a character disorder or moral failing. When Human Rights Watch talked with these people, they were invariably softly spoken and polite. They talked openly and honestly about difficult childhoods (in many cases still underway) living on the streets, or growing up in refugee camps in Thailand. [They are] [o]ften young and poorly educated ... Despite many hardships in their lives, their voices rarely became bitter except when describing their arrest and detention in government drug detention centers.[38]

While human rights organisations may be justified in raising concerns about the labelling of certain categories of persons as 'immoral', it is also important to recall that all individuals have human rights, even if they do happen to commit immoral acts, or are not personally likeable as the persons interviewed by HRW appear to have been. This is not to argue that persons who abuse drugs are or are not engaging in immoral acts, but rather to make the point that, in this case, morality is irrelevant. The notion propagated by HRW in the above text (and throughout the reports and statements of advocates of drug liberalisation), that persons who abuse drugs are not necessarily immoral, and, so it would seem, *therefore* they do in fact have rights, is dangerous—persons have rights, regardless of whether they are moral or not. Connecting the two, in any way or form, is in essence agreeing with the notion that persons not abiding to a set code of morality somehow forfeit their human rights, which of course is not the case. Facile calls for pity may be effective marketing tools, but they cheapen the entire concept of human rights.

In sum, there is no foundation for any so-called 'right to abuse drugs'. There is nothing in international human rights law that points to such a right, and the only justifications that advocates of drug liberalisation are able to muster on this point consist of classical liberal philosophy from the 19th century, and concepts specific to bourgeois Western culture. Such justifications ring somewhat hollow in the ears of most people in the world, and are extremely weak grounds on which to stand for organisations or individuals promoting modern international human rights standards.

[38] HRW, 'Skin on the Cable: the illegal arrest, arbitrary detention, and torture of people who use drugs in Cambodia' (New York, 2010) 1.

Afterword: Views of the Author

THIS STUDY HAS analysed, from the point of view of human rights law, the arguments of advocates of drug liberalisation in advancing a 'human rights based approach to drug control'. I believe that it has demonstrated throughout that these arguments are by and large lacking, and do not stand up to serious scrutiny. There is very little substance to the term 'human rights based approach to drug control', and, it is submitted, it is being used essentially as a marketing strategy to promote the legalisation of drugs.

This conclusion is often met with gasps of horror within the human rights circles this author tends to frequent. Surely, my colleagues argue, the human rights 'prism' is important in viewing any field of public policy, and the 'human rights based approach' to anything is by definition the correct one. There is, I fear, an intellectual myopia that grasps many human rights experts, to the extent that many of them believe that human rights is a panacea—it is the answer to all social ills. Of course, this is hardly unique to experts in the human rights field: this myopia afflicts experts in nearly, perhaps all fields of policy debate.[1]

The truth of the matter is that drug control is, at its heart, simply not a human rights issue. The human rights framework is obviously necessary in looking at criminal justice as a whole, and we must roundly condemn violations of human rights, such as arbitrary detention and excessive use of force by police officers, that take place in drug law enforcement (and any law enforcement). However, when it comes to issues of drug abuse itself, and whether societies should legalise what are now illicit substances, the human rights 'prism' is simply not all that relevant—it is not the sole, or even the most important one to use.

Human rights specialists need to accept that human rights are not all-encompassing. They are an important, even vital part of the picture, but they are not the entire picture, and pretending that human rights can provide the comprehensive answer to all problems is naïve and dangerous (if not even arrogant). Without a clear view of the limitations of human rights, there will always be the danger of them being abused by persons who have other goals. This is prominent in the debate regarding human trafficking,[2] and is prominent with drug control, as has been shown in

[1] See eg this author's introductory chapter in Saul Takahashi (ed), *Human Rights, Human Security, and State Security: the Intersection* (Santa Barbara, ABC-CLIO, 2014).
[2] Ibid.

this study. The notion that human rights requires the legalisation of drugs cheapens human rights, making it a tool for something that is not within its remit. In sum, I am against the so-called 'human rights based approach to drug control' not because I am against human rights, but precisely because I believe in human rights, and wish to preserve the concept's true value.

I am, therefore, against the use (or abuse) of human rights in the debate on drug legalisation. It will come as no surprise after having read this study that I am also against the legalisation of drugs in a general sense. I say this because, having worked in the drug control field for some years (which is much more than can be said for most of the human rights advocates who have advanced the aforementioned arguments), I am mindful of the serious damage that drug abuse can cause to communities, and believe that states have a legitimate interest in preventing the spread of drugs. The portrayal by advocates of drug liberalisation of the debate as being one between a 'criminal justice' approach and a 'public health' one is simplistic—I am against drugs precisely for public health reasons, and also believe that criminal justice has a part to play.

Though some advocates for drug liberalisation argue that legalisation would not result in an increase of consumption of drugs, simple common sense makes it difficult to take this seriously. Serious researchers point to the deterrent effect that legal prohibition has, and estimate sizeable increases in consumption in the case of legalisation—though just how sizeable this would be, and how problematic the consumption would be (ie how much of it would lead to lasting addiction), is impossible to forecast with any accuracy.[3] What is obvious is that drugs would be much more easy to obtain, especially for children. One does not need to examine CRC Article 33 to come to the conclusion that this would be problematic.

As noted above, advocates of drug liberalisation have recently introduced the term 'regulation' into the debate, in a somewhat transparent attempt at dodging the negative connotations that the legalisation terminology has in the minds of many in the general public. This is merely a slight of hand, and has no effect on the core of their argument, namely that drugs should be licit substances, available, in principle, freely. The obvious parallels are alcohol and tobacco, and advocates of drug liberalisation cite those examples often. Their argument is often that the funds raised through legalisation (and taxation) would be used for aggressive public information campaigns against drug use, somehow negating any negative consequences that might arise. This argument is based on over-optimism at best, and fantasy at worst—there is no assurance that tax revenue would

[3] See eg Robert J MacCoun and Peter Reuter (ed), *Drug War Heresies: Learning from Other Vices, Times, and Places* (New York, Cambridge University Press, 2001).

be used for that purpose, and no assurance that any such prevention campaigns would be any more successful than the ones now.

It is also worthy to note that the mere fact that alcohol is cited as a 'good' example shows the ignorance (or disingenuousness) of the entire argument. Alcohol abuse is the cause of monumental societal damage in nearly every country in the world. If alcohol were discovered today, states might move to ban it, and this author might agree. Many middle class Americans (a social class that produces more than its share of well-meaning human rights activists) state approvingly that excessive drinking has become taboo in their circles, and claim that, over time, the same could be done with what are now illicit drugs. However, the number of adults in the US who 'suffer from alcohol abuse or dependence' is estimated at an astounding 17.6 million.[4] Whether tobacco is a success story is debatable—it might turn out to be—but it is worthy to note that it has taken many decades, indeed centuries, to reach the point we are at now. It also needs to be stressed that strict regulation of tobacco, and generally widespread understanding of its ill effects, is still limited to a handful of industrialised, mostly Western countries. As with alcohol, the notion that tobacco is a success story is based on ignorance of the situation in most of 'the rest of' the world.

Of course, if society is to have a debate regarding drug legalisation, so be it—this author sees no inherent reason why the topic should be off limits. What this author strongly objects to is the use of human rights jargon in what is essentially not a human rights matter.

Being against the so-called 'human rights based approach' and against legalisation of drugs in general has resulted in this author being portrayed as a wild eyed, extremist drug warrior, complete with a rifle and camouflage gear, ready to jump out of helicopters armed and ready. Such simplistic pictures are obviously useful to advocates of drug liberalisation in painting their opponents in a negative light, but naturally they have little value in a serious discussion.

Indeed, as has been suggested in many places in this study, this author is in agreement with advocates of drug liberalisation on not a few points. It is clear that imprisoning persons for mere drug abuse (or possession) is misguided, not necessarily because it is a human rights violation as such, but because it is disproportionate, and because it accomplishes little in terms of addressing the problem of drug abuse. In this regard, this author would welcome a legal regime under which drug abuse (not drug production or trafficking) is decriminalised. Drug abuse would perhaps be subject to only administrative penalties, and official encouragement to

[4] National Council on Alcoholism and Drug Dependence, 'Learn about Alcohol, FAQs', at ncadd.org/learn-about-alcohol/faqsfacts.

address any addiction issues, perhaps similar to the system that exists in Portugal. Removing drug abuse from the criminal justice system altogether does raise issues of treaty compliance, in particular with the 1988 Convention; nevertheless, many countries have done this de facto, and in any case INCB appears to accept the approach in Portugal. In addition—and here too I agree with advocates of drug liberalisation—treaty compliance is not necessarily an end upon itself.

The question would be whether to remove completely the 'stick' of criminal sanctions that exists in the drug court model. To this I believe there is no clear-cut answer: it is clear that a measure of coercion can be useful in ensuring that persons who abuse drugs undergo treatment, and to pretend otherwise (as many advocates of drug liberalisation attempt to do) is simple delusion. Nevertheless, whether criminal justice is the best tool to ensure this may be something that each community has to decide for itself. This author has no principled objections to the drug court model, but the intrusive manner in which their control over the individual has expanded, at least in the US, is a legitimate source of concern, and surely measures must be taken to address this.

There is one other issue on which I agree, at least partially, with advocates of drug liberalisation, and that is the controversial question of cannabis. Having written that I am against the legalisation of drugs, I would qualify that in stating my belief that the legalisation of cannabis, while certainly not overwhelmingly desirable, may have a relatively small impact on society as a whole, assuming heavy regulation and measures to ensure that children and others could not access the drug. All evidence shows that the health and societal risks posed by cannabis abuse are so clearly less than drugs such as heroin or cocaine that subjecting these substances to the same control measures seems to be clearly mistaken. This is not to say that there are no health risks from cannabis—there clearly are, and depending on an individual's physical and psychological situation, they can be serious. However, elevating these risks to the same level as those posed by so-called 'hard' drugs puts the entire system into disrepute—a fact that has been exploited by advocates of drug liberalisation.

Many, perhaps most, persons with principled objections to drug liberalisation have a knee-jerk reaction to cannabis legalisation, because they believe it is merely a first step towards a wholesale abandonment of drug control. Many advocates of drug liberalisation, for their part, agree: though not always stated clearly (and sometimes it is), they see cannabis as a stepping stone to bringing down the entire drug control regime. This dynamic has led to both sides becoming increasingly rigid on their positions, making reasoned debate difficult. Developments in Uruguay and several states in the United States might bring about change in this situation, which, this author believes, would be welcome, if only so that rational debate could take place. On the other hand, it would be very unfortunate if any success—or at least lack of disastrous failure—in those jurisdictions leads to an increased impetus for the legalisation of all drugs.

The above rigidity is also apparent in the debate surrounding harm reduction, and on this point as well this author agrees partially with advocates of drug liberalisation—in general, public health measures to mitigate the harm caused by drug abuse should be strengthened, and care should be taken to ensure that persons who abuse drugs are able to access those services. Of all the related issues, this one fits most readily with a human rights analysis—states need to ensure that all persons, including persons who abuse drugs, can access public health services. However, giving harm reduction legitimacy through human rights is problematic in the absence of any clear definition of the term. Practically anything could be included as harm reduction—and since, as with cannabis, many advocates of drug liberalisation view harm reduction as a means to weaken and eventually bring down drug control as a whole, it is natural that opponents of drug liberalisation are wary. In this regard, the guidance of INCB regarding specific harm reduction measures is important, though arguably it is not gospel, and states can legitimately disagree with the body.

In any case, as stressed throughout this study, it should always be recognised that harm reduction does not aim at reducing drug abuse—that is not what it is for. This being the case, harm reduction can never be more than one element in a country's drug strategy, at least if society is going to—and it should—maintain the principle that drug abuse is an undesirable phenomenon that should be eradicated.

It is worth noting that there are extremely powerful interests at play in the drug control debate, and not just on one side. Advocates of drug liberalisation often point to the role of the military industrial complex, including law enforcement agencies, in arguing for a retention (and expansion) of the 'war on drugs', and I believe they are correct—government and corporate actors in many countries fuel international drug law enforcement (as the enforcement of many other laws).

At the same time, the image those advocates like to give of the legalisation movement of consisting solely of well-meaning, wholesome human rights activists is equally false. My experience in the drug control field showed me that there are powerful players behind the legalisation movement, including billionaire currency speculators and tobacco companies that are looking to cash in on cannabis legalisation. This fact alone does not mean that legalisation is wrong, but it should be recognised. Things are not always what they seem.

On numerous occasions, advocates of drug liberalisation shocked that I do not share their views on the 'human rights based approach' have suggested in a sarcastic fashion that perhaps I believe that 'drugs are wrong.' Of course, drugs are inanimate objects and, therefore, cannot have moral qualities in and of themselves: they can only be 'right' or 'wrong' in how they are used. What advocates of drug liberalisation really want to ask is if I believe that taking drugs is 'wrong'. From their end, this is of course a loaded question: the suggestion is that, since I am against the 'human rights based approach', clearly I take a moralistic stance on the abuse of drugs, and think that persons who abuse drugs are immoral wrongdoers who should be punished for their sins. The implication is that I am a missionary on a moral crusade, hell bent on imposing my views on the rest of society. Since I am against drugs, in their eyes I clearly must also be against homosexuality, women's rights, religious freedoms, and generally anything that contributes towards social justice.

If the question is whether I believe taking drugs is wrong, then I would answer in the affirmative: it is wrong because it can be very harmful to that individual and his community, so it should be avoided. Saying that the action of taking drugs is 'wrong' is a wholly different matter from saying that the person taking that action is immoral, or that he should be punished: normally moral people do immoral things all the time. However, to say that for a person to take drugs is 'not wrong' is to argue that others—mainly the state, but also the individual's family and his community—have no business in trying to prevent him from taking that action. Here is where this author has a fundamental disagreement with advocates of drug liberalisation: the state has a definite interest, perhaps even a duty, to do its utmost to prevent drug abuse from spreading. How this is done in the most effective manner is a question open to debate, but, in my mind, the principle is not.

Advocates of drug liberalisation are fond of quoting classical liberal philosophers in an attempt at arguing that the state should not attempt at preaching morality to its citizens. Laws should be restricted to prohibiting conduct that harms other persons, so the argument goes, and drug abuse does not all into that category. I have already dealt with this argument in this study: mainly, the assertion that drug abuse does not affect the rest of the community is incorrect as a matter of fact. The enormous public health costs caused by drug abuse are themselves a good argument for government intervention. Reliance on liberal philosophers from the nineteenth century is a very weak grounding for human rights activists in the modern day.

Likewise, those advocates' use of ill-defined concepts such as 'personal autonomy' to justify their arguments is extremely weak and unconvincing. As has been noted earlier, advocates of drug liberalisation have used this term in a somewhat casual manner, without any recognition of the fact that their understanding of the term is specific to their (overwhelmingly

Western) culture. Throwaway statements to the extent that 'personal autonomy necessarily requires that the individual can abuse drugs' are met with blank stares, if not outright hostility, in many non-Western societies, where the notion of duty to one's family and community arguably remain stronger. As an example, the message that 'abusing drugs will cause grief to your family' would be sneered at in most countries in the West, but has been used with considerable effect in many East Asian societies. This is not to enter into a debate regarding the transferability of human rights to 'other', non-Western cultures: there is no need to enter into this debate here, since (the arguments of advocates of drug liberalisation notwithstanding) once we enter the realm of 'personal autonomy', the discussion goes beyond anything that could possibly be construed as related to the international legal framework of human rights. Human rights, a regime outlining minimum standards of conduct for governments, is in no way synonymous with 'personal autonomy', and it is a dark day for the human rights movement when prominent organisations such as HRW attempt to justify their arguments with such vague, culturally specific notions (citing John Stuart Mill in the process).

Regarding the argument that law should not be about personal morality, I would simply state the obvious, namely that to some extent nearly all law is based on morality. The human rights framework says that some conduct, regardless of whether the majority of the community believes it is immoral, should not be prohibited—not necessarily because the conduct does not affect others, but because it is a legitimate exercise of a human right. Religious beliefs and political opinion fall into the category, and it is belatedly becoming widely recognised that sexual conduct between consenting adults of whatever sex does as well. Despite the efforts of advocates of drug liberalisation, the abuse of drugs is not, as of yet, recognised as a right.

Of course, it is not inconceivable that this may change in the future, since concepts of morality, and the extent to which individual conduct can and should be regulated by the state, do change. However, the implications of drug legalisation for society could be disastrous, in the ways of a significant, perhaps dramatic increase in abuse. For the sake of the children of the world, this author hopes that the abuse of drugs remains prohibited. Whether he is on the winning side of history or on the losing side remains to be seen.

As noted throughout this study, one argument that is repeated again and again by advocates of drug liberalisation is that the 'war on drugs' has not only failed, but was ill-conceived from the start. The notion that persons should not abuse drugs, so this argument goes, is based on empty morality, not hard facts related to human nature, and is unrealistic. Many of those advocates state openly that we must accept drug abuse as inevitable, and, instead of attempting to eradicate the problem, we must shift gears towards managing it. The Transnational Institute states that:

> ... a world without drugs will never exist. The ideology of 'zero tolerance' needs to be replaced by the principle of harm reduction, which offers a more pragmatic approach that favours policies capable of reducing drug related harms as far as possible, for the consumer and for society in general.[5]

Couched in more technocratic and seemingly reasonable language, yet with the same message, McAllister proposes a policy framework based entirely on harm reduction:

> ... how might one define success in the complicated world of drug policy? One option worth considering is to set realistic use and abuse targets and then adjust policy to maintain them ... This scenario assumes that there is a irreducible minimum use/abuse rate for any given drug in any given society, eschewing the 'zero tolerance' standard, not because it is not laudable, but because it is unrealistic by all standards of human behaviour.[6]

Whether it is factually correct to assert that there has never been a society without substance abuse is debatable. Nevertheless, one could easily make the same assertion regarding human rights, or poverty. At least since the advent of agriculture, there has (probably) never been a society without human rights abuses, without oppression, without haves and have-nots. This does not serve as an argument to stop international efforts against such social ills. We do not say 'we will never be able to reduce human rights violations to zero, so let us abandon the goal entirely and try to manage the problem', or 'eliminating extreme poverty completely will never happen, so let us be pragmatic and simply accept it'. There are some phenomena that we can all agree are undesirable in any quantity, and our goal must be complete eradication. How realistic attaining this goal may be within a specified period of time is a legitimate topic of debate, but the overarching goal cannot be anything but complete—otherwise the effort would be de facto abandoned altogether.

Of course, as shown throughout this study, that is exactly what advocates of drug liberalisation are arguing for—a dismantling of the international drug control regime and an abandonment of efforts against drugs. In this regard, their statements must be viewed with caution, if not downright skepticism. The underlying premise of advocates of drug liberalisation is that drug abuse is, at its core, legitimate and should be legal. To them, human rights is not a guiding principle, but a marketing tool to bring about legalisation of drugs through the back door.

[5] Transnational Institute, 'Rewriting history; a Response to the 2008 World Drug Report' (Amsterdam, June 2008) 3.

[6] William B McAllister, 'Reflections on a Century of International Drug Control', in *Governing the Global Drug Wars*, LSE Ideas (London, London School of Economics, 2012) at Kindle version 456/2572.

Index

www.ingramcontent.com/pod-product-compliance
Ingram Content Group UK Ltd.
Pitfield, Milton Keynes, MK11 3LW, UK
UKHW020143290926
15471UKWH00004B/662

9 781509 926435